baby . . .
. . names

baby . . .
. . names

*Thousands of Names
and Their Meanings*

Nick HARRISON & Steve MILLER

WHITAKER
HOUSE

BABY NAMES:
Thousands of Names and Their Meanings

ISBN: 978-1-60374-504-8
Printed in the United States of America
© 2007, 2012 by Nick Harrison and Steve Miller

Contact for Steve Miller: srmbooks@comcast.net
Contact for Nick Harrison: www.nickharrisonbooks.com

Whitaker House
1030 Hunt Valley Circle
New Kensington, PA 15068
www.whitakerhouse.com

Library of Congress Cataloging-in-Publication Data (Pending):

1 2 3 4 5 6 7 8 9 10 11 12 **ᵾ** 20 19 18 17 16 15 14 13 12

Dedication

To the people in our lives whose names mean the most to us:

● ● ●

Henry, Patricia, Raymond, Joan, Beverly (of course!),
Rachel, Rebecca, Bethany, Winston, Michael, Sean, Joshua,
Matthew, Emma, and Abbi

—Nick Harrison

My wife, Becky; our three sons, Keith, Nathan, and Ryan;
my mother, Betty; and my in-laws, Marty and Pat

—Steve Miller

Acknowledgments

Thanks to my family, as always.   —Nick Harrison

With special appreciation to Priscilla Cameron of the Eugene Bible College library. Thank you for your help with the resources needed to research the information given in this book.

                                                —Steve Miller

Contents

● ● ●

Before You Begin

One of the first important duties parents face is choosing a name for their baby. Not only does the child usually carry his or her given name throughout life, but, also, studies show that names can have an effect on the child's personality and how others perceive him or her.

For Christians, the selection of a name has yet another dimension. In the Bible, we find that God places a high priority on names. There are, for example, many men and women whose names were actually chosen by God, and the meanings of those names carried special significance.

In the very first pages of the Bible, we meet Adam ("made from the earth") and Eve ("life-giver"), both of whose names were significant. In Adam's case, his name tells us of his origin; in Eve's case, we learn about her role in history as the mother of all humankind.

Consider, also, the best-known patriarch of the Bible: Abraham. At first his name was Abram, which means "the father is exalted." But God later entered into a covenant (an agreement) with Abram, part of which included a name change consistent with his future. God gave him the name Abraham, which means "the father of a multitude"—a reflection of God's destiny for this great man of faith. The covenant also included a name change for Sarai, Abraham's wife, who now became Sarah, "a princess."

Another great patriarch of the Bible, Jacob, was born just after his fraternal twin, Esau. Jacob's name means "one who supplants another." This name expresses what happened as Jacob followed Esau out of the womb and as they grew up. Later in his life, after Jacob wrestled with an angel in an effort to receive a blessing, his name became Israel, which means "he shall become a prince of God." Again, God's plan for the man was evident in the name given to him.

In the New Testament, the disciple known as Simon was given the new name Peter by Christ, because Peter means "rock," and Peter's role in history was to be a solid support for the new Christian faith.

In addition to being intentional about the names of many characters in the Bible, God was careful concerning the revelation of His own name. When God commanded Moses to lead the people of Israel out of Egypt, do you remember His answer to Moses' question?

> Moses said to God, "Suppose I go to the Israelites and say to them, 'The God of your fathers has sent me to you,' and they ask me, 'What is his name?' Then what shall I tell them?" God said to Moses, "I AM WHO I AM. This is what you are to say to the Israelites: 'I AM has sent me to you.'" God also said to Moses, "Say to the Israelites, 'The LORD, the God of your fathers—the God of Abraham, the God of Isaac and the God of Jacob—has sent me to you.' This is my name forever, the name by which I am to be remembered from generation to generation." (Exodus 3:13–15)

God was very protective of His name. He revealed in other places in the Old Testament that He was to be known as Jehovah-Jireh ("the Lord will provide"), Jehovah-Nissi ("the Lord our banner"), Jehovah-Shalom ("the Lord is peace"), Jehovah-Shammah ("the Lord who is present"), and Jehovah-Tsidkenu ("the Lord our righteousness").

Consider, also, the importance God put on the name of His Son, Jesus Christ. Before Jesus was born, His name was prophesied to be *"Wonderful Counselor, Mighty God, Everlasting Father, Prince of Peace"* (Isaiah 9:6).

In the New Testament, it was revealed to the apostle Paul that God had given Jesus Christ *"the name that is above every name,"* and that *"at the name of Jesus every knee should bow, in heaven and on earth and under the earth"* (Philippians 2:9–10).

Further, consider the power that God invested in the name of Jesus Christ. We're told by Jesus, *"I will do whatever you ask in my **name**, so that the Son may bring glory to the Father"* (John 14:13, emphasis added). We're also told that the purpose for John's gospel was that *"by believing you may have life* *in his **name***" (John 20:31, emphasis added).

When Peter and John met the lame man at the Gate Beautiful, they prayed for him in the name of Christ, and he was healed. When Paul delivered a slave girl from a demon in Acts 16:18, he did so in the name of the Lord Jesus.

We're told that there's no other name under heaven than that of Jesus Christ by which men can be saved. (See Acts 4:12.) And Jesus said that those of us who are believers should rejoice because our names are written in heaven. (See Luke 10:20.)

Finally, in Revelation, the last book of the Bible, we're told that, one day, we shall all receive a new name—a name that God Himself chooses for each of us. (See Revelation 3:12.) That's pretty special, isn't it?

As you read through the following pages, we think you'll enjoy discovering the meanings of the many names offered. If you're awaiting the birth of a new baby or a phone call telling you that you've been chosen to adopt—congratulations! May the many blessings that babies bring to parents be yours in abundance. And may God direct you in this important decision of naming your child!

Practical Suggestions for Choosing Your Baby's Name

When you choose a name for your new baby, there are a number of things you'll want to consider:

Prayer. First, as a Christian, you have the advantage of prayer in selecting a name. Be sure to submit this important choice to God, as well, as you pray for your baby's health, delivery, and similar concerns.

Heritage. Consider honoring your family's heritage by selecting a grandparent or other ancestor's name. A good choice for a middle name, or sometimes even a first name, is often the mother's maiden name. Some parents have created an interesting name for their baby that is taken from their own names. For instance, a father named Ray and a mother named Jean gave their daughter the created name RaeJean.

Character. If you choose a name with a meaning you hope is eventually evidenced in the child's character, be sure to occasionally remind the growing child of the significance of the name and that it was chosen with great love and care. Don't force your child, however, to assume an attribute or identity that's not truly his or hers. God will mold a child's character His way. Guide, but don't force.

Role Models. Many of the names in this book include references to noted Christians with the same name. Consider honoring the memory of a great Christian man or woman—and, at the same time, providing your child with an excellent role model—by selecting that person's name for your child. For instance, a boy might be named Wesley after John Wesley, or a girl might be named Florence after the noted Christian nurse Florence Nightingale.

As your children grow, they can be told the stories of their namesakes.

They can even be given books with the stories of the heros or heroines after which they are named. A boy named David might be told not only of King David in the Bible, but also such exemplary Christians as David Brainerd, David Livingston, and David Wilkerson. To call your attention to these possibilities, we've noted some well-known Christian leaders in special sidebars throughout the book.

Dishonorable Names. We suggest you don't choose a name that is honoring to false gods or evil men and women from past generations. For example, the name Judas is discouraged, as are names from pagan religions, such as Malini, which, although melodic, is also the name of the Hindu god of the earth. We have not included such names in this guide, except when they are also biblical names. We have, however, made a special effort to select names that *do* have special meaning to Christian believers.

Difficult Spellings. Beware of choosing names with unusual spellings. Such names can be creative and unique, but realize that, for many years, the child will be correcting teachers, friends, and even relatives who may inadvertently spell the name the more traditional way.

Finding Balance. Remember that your child will carry the name you choose throughout his or her life. Sometimes, parents who want to mark their children as different do so by picking names that eventually become troublesome or embarrassing. Think carefully before you give your child an awkward or cumbersome name.

An unattractive name—one that may be considered "weird"—can become a source of stigma or ridicule. On the other hand, having a name that's abundantly popular may cause a child to feel less special than his or her peers who have more distinctive and attractive names. Try to find the balance between popularity and uniqueness when choosing a name.

Initials. Keep your child's initials in mind as you consider various names. A child is liable to experience teasing when it's discovered that his or her initials are ICK, DOG, or some other undesirable acronym.

Sound. After you've narrowed your choices to a few favorites, say the first, middle, and last names together out loud several times and listen to how they sound. Do the first and middle names fit with your last name? If not, is there a similar name that will work better? Several years ago, a friend of mine mentioned that she had always dreamed of having a son named

Nick, but when she married a man with the last name of Knack, she knew she had to forever abandon that dream.

"Prayer verse." Once you've chosen a name, you might want to consider searching the Bible for a relevant "prayer verse" based on a Bible passage that corresponds to the name's meaning. For example, the name Melinda means "gentle one." An appropriate prayer verse might be Philippians 4:5, which says, *"Let your gentleness be evident to all. The Lord is near."*

Tips for Creating a Unique Name

One increasingly popular trend among parents today is that of creating a name especially suited for their child. A name is the first gift—and one of the most important gifts—you give to your child. You may want to gift your newborn with a name that sets him or her apart as a unique individual, one that provides a special sense of identity. The following are a number of ways to create a new name.

Alter the Spelling of an Existing Name

The vast majority of names today already have a wide range of spelling variations, so this method doesn't guarantee your child will end up with a truly one-of-a-kind name. However, some spelling variations are used so rarely that your son or daughter will still possess an unusual or distinct name if you choose this option. For example...

- Instead of Danielle, you can use a name such as Ranielle by changing the first letter to another letter that works well with the rest of the name.

- Instead of Susan, you can use Suzahn by altering the spelling according to sounds or phonetic elements within the name.

- You can also shorten the syllables of a name, as Deborah has been altered to create Debra, or lengthen the syllables of a name, such as adding to Rosa to create Rohsah.

Combine Two Existing Names to Make a New One

As we mentioned earlier, we know of a father and mother named Ray and Jean who combined their names and called their daughter RaeJean. Another possibility is to take two names that don't usually appear in combined form and put them together, such as Ray and Anne to create Rayanne. Or, you could use Ron and Ellen to create Ronel or Ronelle.

Use a Proper Noun (or a Variation of It) as a Name

The abbreviated form of Texas, which is Tex, is often used as a name or nickname. Boys have been named Tennessee, and girls Montana. Willow (a tree) and Dahlia (a flower) have also been used. What can you come up with?

Turn a Common Noun into a Name

For example, the English word *ocean* has become the girls' name Oceana, and the Spanish word *niña*, which means "girl," has become the name Nina, Ninetta, or Ninette.

● ● ●

Of course, as we've already pointed out, before you finalize your child's name, you'll want to ensure that it won't make him or her vulnerable to ridicule. Ask yourself: Does this name lend itself to inadvertent negative associations? Does it look or sound too similar to other names or words that might subject my child to teasing? And, do the initials say or spell something that is potentially embarrassing?

How to Use This Book

In creating *Baby Names*, our goal was not to list every conceivable name in existence. Rather, we wanted to equip you, the new parent, with the resources we believe will help you choose the ideal name for your baby.

For that reason, we have deliberately selected what we think are the "cream of the crop" names, with their most popular and reasonable variations and diminutives. Thus, you will find a wide selection of the best names, without some of the more outlandish spellings and variations of those names. And for those who are less traditionally inclined, we have included suggestions for creating your own unique name in the "Tips for Creating a Unique Name" segment in the previous section.

Also, in our research, we discovered that different sources often give varying meanings and origins for the same name. So, in our effort to create the best possible baby name resource, we've sifted through the many options for these disputable points and have offered what we believe to be the most commonly agreed-upon origins and meanings.

Reading the Entries

Each entry in the book begins with a name that appears in boldface text. This main entry is then followed by the origin and meaning of the name, as well as its variations and diminutives. Below is a sample entry, with the various elements of the entry explained:

ASTERISK INDICATES A BIBLICAL NAME

ENTRY   ORIGIN   MEANING

*Ruth: Hebrew, "friend, companion"
Ruthe, Ruthelle, Ruthi, Ruthie,   ◄———————— DIMINUTIVES AND
Ruthina, Ruthine   VARIATIONS

Ruth was a loyal daughter-in-law   ◄———————— BIBLE CHARACTER
who moved to Israel with her moth-
er-in-law, Naomi. Eventually, she
became the wife of Boaz and the
great-grandmother of David. Their
story is told in the book of Ruth.

RUTH BELL GRAHAM   ◄———————— NOTABLE
(1920–2007)   CHRISTIAN WHO
BEARS THIS NAME
was born in Quinjiang, China, the
daughter of medical missionaries.
She was the wife of evangelist
Billy Graham and the mother
of five children.

Variations

For simplicity's sake, we use the word *variation* to mean an alternate spelling, a common tweaking, or a foreign version of a name. For example, the name Katherine has *variations* that include Kathryn, Catherine, and even Caitlin. It also has *diminutives* such as Kathy, Kate, and Kay. Some names also have variations for the opposite gender. For instance, Charles has variations that include Charlton, Carlos (Spanish), and the feminine name Charlene. The diminutives for Charles are such names as Charlie, Chuck, Chip, and Chaz.

If the main entry name has any diminutives or variations (or other forms), those will appear on subsequent lines. As previously stated, we have not attempted to list every possible spelling variation. Rather, we have focused on what are, in general, the more common spellings. With this information, you can go the extra step, if you wish, to create a more unusual form of a name.

Cross-Referencing the Entries

If you see an entry that reads like the following:

Patty: *diminutive of Patricia*

you will want to go to the main entry Patricia in order to find out the origin, meaning, and various forms of the name Patty.

If you don't find a name you're looking for, consider that it might be a variation or diminutive of another name. Thus, you may find it listed with the name from which it originated.

Finding Bible Names

Another feature we've included in the book is a significant number of the best names found in Scripture. In most instances, we also point you to the references in the Bible where those names are found.

All the Bible names are preceded by an asterisk. In some cases, you will also find, at the end of a Bible name entry, details about the individual who bore that name.

We did not include every name found in the Bible. Many of these names are simply too unusual; or, they have histories or meanings connected to them that may make them less desirable as names for your baby. If, however, you wish to look up every Bible name, there are several resources at your disposal. See "Selected Sources for Bible Names" at the end of this book for some ideas.

Noted Christians

We've also added some short biographical sketches of Christians who bore certain names. Many parents like to honor the memory of a noted Christian by naming their child after that hero of the faith.

Finally, throughout the book, we've provided what we believe are some entertaining insights regarding names.

So, go ahead and start your search for the perfect name for your baby...and have fun!

The Twenty Most Popular Boys' and Girls' Names

These lists are from the United States Social Security Administration. Its "baby name" site is extremely interesting. The popularity of names is accessible by year, by decade, or even by state. Check it out at http://www.socialsecurity.gov/OACT/babynames/.

Top Twenty Boys' and Girls' Names in the 2000s

Rank	Boys' names	Girls' names
1	Jacob	Emily
2	Michael	Madison
3	Joshua	Emma
4	Matthew	Olivia
5	Daniel	Hannah
6	Christopher	Abigail
7	Andrew	Isabella
8	Ethan	Samantha
9	Joseph	Elizabeth
10	William	Ashley

Rank	Boys' names	Girls' names
11	Anthony	Alexis
12	David	Sarah
13	Alexander	Sophia
14	Nicholas	Alyssa
15	Ryan	Grace
16	Tyler	Ava
17	James	Taylor
18	John	Brianna
19	Jonathan	Lauren
20	Noah	Chloe

Girls' Names
A-Z

A

Abella: A feminine variation of Abel, "breath of life"

Abela, Abelia, Abelle

*Abia: Hebrew, "God is my father"

Ahi, Abby, Abiah, Bia

An ancestor of the Lord Jesus Christ.
(See 1 Chronicles 2:24.)

*Abigail: Hebrew, "source of the father's joy"

Abbe, Abbie, Abby, Abbygaile, Abbygale, Abbygayle, Gail, Gale, Galia, Galya, Gayle.

In the Bible, Abigail gained favor in King David's sight while imploring the king to spare her family after her husband Nabal's foolishness. Later, after Nabal's death, Abigail, described as "an intelligent and beautiful woman," became one of David's wives.
(See 1 Samuel 25.)

*Abihail: Hebrew, "source of strength"

Abby, Abi

Can be both masculine and feminine. Queen Esther's father was named Abihail, as were three women in the Bible.

*Abijah: Hebrew, "God is my father"

Abby, Abi

Abijah is mentioned in 2 Kings 18:2 and 2 Chronicles 29:1.

Abra: Hebrew, "mother of a multitude"—a feminine variation of Abraham

Abi, Abby, Abrah

Abriana: Italian, feminine variation of Abraham, "father of a multitude"

Abby, Abrianna, Abrielle, Ana, Anna, Bree

Acacia: Greek, "honored one"

Cacia, Cacie, Casey, Cass, Cassia, Cassie, Cayce

Wood from the acacia tree was used in the construction of the ark of the covenant and the tabernacle in the wilderness.

*Achsah: Hebrew, "breaking the veil"

Achsah was the daughter of the Old Testament hero Caleb. (See Joshua 15:16–17; Judges 1:12–13; 1 Chronicles 4:15.)

Ada: Old English, "prosperous"— in some cases, a diminutive of Adelaide

Adda, Addiah, Addie, Addy, Adi

*Adah: Hebrew, "adorned by God"

Adda, Addy, Adiah

Two Adahs are mentioned in the Bible. (See Genesis 4:19–23; 36:2, 4, 10, 12, 16.)

Adail: German, "she who is noble"

Ada, Adale, Adalia, Addy, Dale

Adair: Greek, "she who is beautiful"

Adara, Adare

Adama: Hebrew, "made of the earth"—a feminine variation of Adam

Ada, Adamma, Addy

Adelaide: Old German, "she who is noble"

Addie, Addy, Adela, Adele, Adella, Adelle, Adelina, Adeline, Addey, Adellia, Della

Adelpha: Greek, "sisterly"

Addie, Adelle, Adelphia, Dell, Della

Adia: Swahili, "she is a gift from God"

Addiah, Addie, Addy, Adiah, Ady

Adina: Hebrew, "she who is delicate"

Addy, Adeana, Adeena, Adene, Adina, Adine, Deana, Dena, Dina

Adna: Hebrew, "she who is delightful"

Addie, Addy, Ady

Adnah: Hebrew, "eternal rest"

Addie, Addy, Ady

Adora: Latin, "she who is adored"

Addie, Addy, Adoria, Ady, Dora, Dorrie, Dory

Adrian: Greek, "she who is rich"

Addy, Adria, Adriah, Adriana, Adrienne, Anna, Dree

Afra: Hebrew, "doe-like"

Affra, Affrey, Aphra

Afton: Old English, from the town of Afton, England

Aftyn

Agate: Old English, "precious stone"

Aggie, Aggy

Agatha: Greek, "she who is kind"

Agace, Agacia, Agathe, Aggie, Aggy

Agnes: Greek, "she who is pure"

Aggie, Aggy, Agna, Agnella, Agnelle, Agness

Ahava: Hebrew, "essence"

Ahiva, Ahuda

*Ahlai: Hebrew, "she who beseeches"

(See 1 Chronicles 2:31, 34; 1 Chronicles 11:41.)

Ahn: Asian/Vietnamese, "she who is peaceful"

Aida: Latin, "she who helps"

Aidan (also Gaelic, "fiery one")

Aileen: Scottish/Irish variation of the name Helen, "light"

Ailene, Alena, Alene, Alina, Aline, Ally, Alyna, Lena, Lina

Aimee: See Amy

Ainsley: Scottish, "meadow"

Ainslee, Ainsleigh, Ansley

Alana: Irish, "fair one"—also a feminine variation of Alan

Alaina, Alaine, Alainna, Alena, Ally, Laine, Lana, Laney, Lena

Alarice: Old German, "ruler"—a feminine variation of Alaric

Alaricia, Alarise, Alerica, Ally

Alba: Latin, from the Italian city of the same name

Albina, Albine, Alva

Alberta: Old German, "she who is brilliant"—also a feminine form of Albert

Albertina, Albertine, Ally, Berta, Bertie; also Elberta, Elbertina, Elbertine

Alcina: Greek, "strength of mind"

Alceena, Alcine, Alcy, Ally, Alsina, Alsine, Alsyna

Alda: Old German, "she who is prosperous"

Aldea, Aldina, Aldis, Aldona, Aldys

Aldora: Old German, "gift"

Aldara, Ally, Dora, Dorrie; also Eldora, thus Ella, Ellie

Alea: Arabic, "exalted one"

Aleah, Alia, Ally, Leah, Lia

Aleda: Latin, "winged one"

Alida, Alleda, Ally, Leda

Alena: A Russian variation of Helen, "light"

Aleen, Aleena, Alina, Aline

Aleta: Greek, "she who is true"

Aletha, Alethea, Aletta, Leta,
Letha, Letta, Lettie, Thea

Alexandra: Greek, a feminine
variation of Alexander, "he
who defends"

Alandra, Alex, Alexa,
Alexandria, Alexia, Alexina,
Alexine, Alexis, Ally, Landra,
Lanny, Lex, Lexa, Lexandra,
Lexie, Xandra—many
additional variations and
diminutives can be created
from the name Alexandra

Alfreda: Old English, "she who is
wise"—a feminine variation of
Alfred

Alfie, Ally, Elfreda, Freda

Alice: Greek, "she who tells the
truth"—also considered by
many to be a variation of
Adelaide

Alecia, Alicia, Alisa, Alisha,
Alison, Allison, Ally, Allysa,
Alycia, Alysa, Alyssa, Lecia,
Lysa—many additional
variations and diminutives
can be created from the name
Alice

Aliya: Hebrew, "one who ascends"

Aleeya, Aliah, Ally

Allegra: Latin, "she who is full of
cheer"

Alegra, Alegria, Allegria, Allie,
Legra

Allison: A variation of Alice, "she
who tells the truth"

Alcy, Alison, Alli, Ally, Allyson

Alma: Latin, "soul"

Almah

Almeta: Latin, "she who reaches
for the goal"

Almeda, Elmeda, Elmeta,
Meta

Almira: Arabic, "royal one," or a
variation of Elmira

Almera, Almyra, Mira, Mirra,
Mirrah

Aloysia: Old German, "heroine
of war"—also a feminine
variation of Aloysius

Ally, Aloys, Aloyse

Alta: Spanish, "high"

Althea: Greek, "healer"

Ally, Altheda, Altheya, Althia,
Thea

Alva: Spanish, "she who is a fair
one"

Albeena, Albena, Albina

Alvina: Old English, "she who is friendly"

Ally, Alveena, Alvine, Alvinia, Vina

Amalia: Hebrew, "the work of God"

Mahlia, Malia, Malie

AMANDA SMITH
(1837–1915)

was born into slavery and, after her conversion as a young woman, became a noted evangelist.

Amanda: Latin, "easy to love"

Amandah, Manda, Mandi, Mandy

Amara: Greek, "she who is beautiful"

Amaris: Hebrew, "promised of God"

Amariah, Maris

Amber: French, from the color amber

Amberlee, Amberleigh, Amberly, Amberlyn, Ambi, Ambur

Amelia: Latin, "she who is ambitious"

Amalia, Amelie, Amylia—this name easily lends itself to many creative variations. Emma and Emily are both considered variants of Amelia.

Amina: Arabic, "she who is worthy of trust"

Amy, Mina

Amity: Latin, "she who is friendly"

Amy: Latin, "she who is beloved"—from the same root as the word *amor*

Aimee, Ami, Ammie, Ammy

AMY CARMICHAEL
(1867–1951)

was a determined missionary to the poor of India, with a focus on temple prostitutes. In 1926, she began her Dohnavur Fellowship. She was the author of many popular books, including the classic *If*.

An: Chinese, "she who is peaceful"

Anabel: Latin, "she who is lovable"

Anabella, Annabell, Annabella, Annabelle

*Anah: Hebrew, "she who sings" (See Genesis 36:2, 18, 25.)

*Anah: Hebrew, "God has answered" (See Genesis 36:2, 18, 25.)

Anastasia: Greek, "resurrection" Ana, Anastacia, Anastasha, Stacey, Stacia, Stacie, Stasha

Andrea: Greek, "she who is full of courage"—also a feminine variation of Andrew Andee, Andi, Andra, Andrah, Andrana, Andreanna, Andri, Andriah, Andriana, Andrina

Angela: Old English, "heavenly being"—literally "angel" Angel, Angelica, Angelina, Angeline, Angelique (French), Angelita, Angella, Angie

Ani: Hawaiian, "she who is beautiful"

Anika: Slovak form of Ann, "she who is full of grace" Anaka, Annika, Anouska

Anita: Spanish, "she who is full of grace"—a variation of Ann Aneeta, Anitra, Nita

Ann: English, "she who is full of grace," from Hannah

Ana, Anele, Anna, Anne, Annelle, Annette (French), Annora, Anora. Many variations and name combinations can be created using the name Ann. It works well in combination with other proper names (Mary Ann, Bobbi Ann, Sue Ann, Ann Marie, etc.).

ANN JUDSON (1789–1826)

was the first female American missionary to the Far East. She and her husband, Adoniram, translated the Bible into Burmese, undergoing much suffering and trial along the way.

*Anna: A variation of Ann, "she who is full of grace," from Hannah

Ana, Annah, Annette (French), Anya (Russian). Many variations of this name occur in combination with other popular names. Examples include Annabelle, Annalisa, Annalysa.

Anna (the New Testament form of Hannah) was a widow,

a prayer warrior, and one of the first messengers of the good news of the Savior's birth. (See Luke 2:36–38.)

Anthea: Greek, "flower"

Anthia, Thea, Thia

Antoinette: French, "she who is praiseworthy"—a feminine variation of Anthony

Antonia (Italian), Antonietta, Netta, Netty, Toni, Tonia

April: Latin, "open"—from the month of April, the seasonal "opening" to spring

Aprila, Aprilette, Aprilina, Avril

Ara: Latin, "altar"

Arah, Ari, Aria, Ariah

Arabella: Arabic, "ornate altar"

Arabelle, Arbelina, Arbeline, Arbella, Arbelle, Bella, Belle

Ardelle: Latin, "enthusiastic"

Arda, Ardeen, Ardella, Ardina, Ardine, Dell, Della

Ardis: Latin, "she who is eager"

Arda, Ardah, Ardie, Ardra, Ardrah, Ardy

Ardith: Hebrew, "field of flowers"—also a feminine

variation of Arden

Ardath, Ardys, Ardyth, Aridatha

Areta: Greek, "she who is virtuous"

Aretha, Retha

Ariadne: Greek, "divine"

Aria, Ariadna

Ariana: Welsh, "as valuable as fine silver"

Ariane, Arianna, Arianne

Ariel: Hebrew, "lion of God"— can also be a male name

Ari, Ariella, Arielle, Ella

Arlene: Celtic, "promise"

Arla, Arlana, Arleen, Arlie, Arlinda, Lana

Arva: Latin, "pasture"

Arvilla

Ashira: Hebrew, "rich"

Ashyra

Ashley: Old English, "from the ash tree"

Ashlee, Ashleigh, Ashly

Astra: Greek, "star"

Astrid: Old German, "she who has strength from God"

Athalia: Hebrew, "our God is exalted"
Athalie, Thalia, Thalie

Athena: Greek, "she who is wise"
Athene, Thena

Aubrey: Old German, "she who is noble"
Aubree, Bree

Audrey: Old German, "she who is noble"—a variation of Etheldreda
Audie, Audra, Audree, Audreena, Audrina, Audrine

Augusta: Latin, "full of majesty"—a feminine variation of Augustus
Augie, Augustina, Austina, Austine, Gussie

Aurea: Latin, "golden"
Aura, Aurel, Aurelia, Auria, Aurie, Oralia, Oralie

Aurora: Latin, "dawn"
Aurore, Rora, Rori, Rory

Austa: Latin, a feminine variation of Austin, "majestic"
Austina, Austine

Autumn: Latin, from the season

Ava: Latin, "bird"
Avis, Aya, Ayla

Aviva: Hebrew, "youth"
Avi, Viv, Viva

Ayanna: Swahili, "she who is as beautiful as a flower's blossom"

Azaria: Hebrew, "she who hears the Lord"—usually a male name
Azariah, Azzie

Aziza: Arabic/Swahili, "she who is beloved"
Azzie, Azziza, Azzy

B

Babette: French, "she who is foreign"—generally accepted as one of many diminutives for Barbara
Babbie, Babbs, Babe, Babetta, Etta

Bailey: Old English, "bailiff"
Baily, Bay, Bayley

Bambi: from the Disney film of the same name; or possibly from the Italian word for small child, *bambino*
Bambee, Bambie, Bamby

Barbara: Greek, "she who is foreign"—from the same root as the word *barbarian*

Babbie, Babbs, Babbsie, Babs, Barb, Barbie, Barbra, Bebe, Bobbie—many additional variations and diminutives can be created from the name Barbara

Barri: Irish, "excellent spearsman"—also a feminine variation of Barry

Bari, Barrie

Basilea: Greek, "royal"—a feminine variation of Basil

Basilia

*Bathsheba: Hebrew, "daughter of promise"

Read Bathsheba's sad story of adultery with King David in 2 Samuel 11:2–3; 12:24; 1 Kings 1:11–31; 2:13–19.

Beatrice: Latin, "bearer of blessings"

Bea, Beah, Beatrix, Bebe, Bee, Trix, Trixie, Trixy

Becky: See Rebecca

Belicia: Spanish, "she who is devoted to God"

Belice, Belisha

Belinda: Spanish, "attractive serpent"

Bella: Latin, "she who is beautiful"

Belle, Belina, Bellina, Belline

Belva: Latin, "beautiful vista"

Berdine: Old German, "attractive young woman"

Berdie, Berdina, Dina

Bernadette: French, "strong as a bear"—also a feminine variation of Bernard

Bern, Bernadine, Bernetta, Bernette, Bernie, Bernita, Bern

*Bernice: Greek, "she who brings victory"

Berenice, Berniece, Beri, Bern, Bernie, Berri

(See Acts 25:13, 23; 26:30.)

Bertha: Old German, "she who is radiant"

Berta, Bertie, Bertina

Beryl: Greek, from the jewel of the same name

Ber, Berri, Berrie, Berry, Beryle

Bess: Hebrew—a diminutive of Elizabeth, "consecrated to God"

Bessie

Beth: Hebrew—a diminutive of Elizabeth, "consecrated to

God," or Bethany, "house of
God"

Bethann, Bethanne

Bethany: Hebrew, "house of God"

Beth, Bethanee, Bethel,
Betheny

Bethesda: Hebrew, "house of
mercy"

Beth

Betsy: Hebrew—a diminutive of
Elizabeth

Betsey, Betsie

Bettina: Hebrew—a diminutive
of Elizabeth

Betina, Bettine, Tina

Betty: Hebrew—a diminutive of
Elizabeth

Bette, Bettie

*Beulah: Hebrew, "betrothed," a
name for the nation of Israel

(See Isaiah 62:4.)

Beverly: Old English, "meadow of
the beaver"

Bev, Beverlee, Beverlie, Bevy

Bevin: Irish, "young woman"

Bev, Bevan, Bevina, Bevinn

Bian: Asian/Vietnamese, "she who
will not reveal a secret"

Bianca: Latin, "white, fair"

Blanca

Bibi: Latin, "she who is full of life"

Bebe, Bebee

Billie: Old English, "she who
is determined"—usually a
diminutive for Wilhemina,
Willa, etc.

Often used in combination
with other names: Billie Ann,
Billie Jean, Billie Jo, Billie Sue,
etc.

Bindi: East Indian, "a tiny drop"

Bindee, Bindie, Bindy

Bird: English, literally "bird"

Birdie, Birdy

*Bithia: Hebrew, "daughter of
God"

Bithiah, Thea, Thia

(See 1 Chronicles 4:18.)

Blaine: Irish, "she who is slender"

Blane, Blayne

Blair: Celtic, "field of battle"

Blaire

Blake: Old English, "dark one"

Blakelee, Blakely

Blanche: Latin, "she who is fair"

Belanche, Blanca, Blanch, Blanka

Blenda: Old German, "glorious"

Bliss: Old English, "joyful one"
Blisse, Blyss

Blossom: English, literally, a flower blossom

Blythe: Old English, "she who is cheerful"
Blithe, Blyth

Bo: Chinese, "dear one"

Bobbi: Usually a diminutive for Barbara or Roberta
Often used in combination with other names, e.g., Bobbi Ann, Bobbi Jo, Bobbi Lynn, Bobbi Sue, etc.
Bobbette, Bobbie, Bobbina

Bonita: Spanish, "she who is pretty"
Bonnie, Nita

Bonnie: Scottish/English, "pretty, attractive, good"
Bonnee, Bonny, Bunny

Bopha: Asian/Cambodian, "she who is like unto a flower"

Brandi: Dutch, from the strong

drink, brandy
Brandee, Brandie, Brandilyn, Brandy

Breanna: Irish, "she who is strong"—also a feminine variation of Brian (Irish, "powerful one")
Breanne, Bree, Breena, Briana, Brianna, Brianne, Brinna, Bryana, Brynna

Breck: Irish, "freckled one"

Brenda: Irish, "raven"—also a feminine variation of Brendan
Bren, Brenn, Brenna, Bryn, Brynn

Brett: Latin, "she who is from Britain"
Bretta, Britt

Briana: See Breanna

Bridget: Celtic, "she who is strong"
Birget, Birgette, Birgit, Bridgett, Brigetta, Brigette, Brigitte

Brittany: Irish, "she who is strong"
Britt, Britney, Brittin, Brittney

Bronwyn: Welsh, "she who is full-figured"
Bronny, Bronwynn

Brooke: Old English, literally, a brook of running water

Brook, Brooks

Brunhilde: Old German, "she who is a warrior"

Brunhilda, Hilda, Hilde, Hildy

Bryn: Gaelic, "she who is honorable"

Brynn, Brynna, Brynne

Buffy: English, nickname—possibly derived from the American buffalo

Bunny: English, a synonym for rabbit—also a variation of Bonnie. Often a nickname that begins as an endearment in early childhood.

Bunni, Bunnie

C

Note: Many "C" names may also be spelled with "K" or sometimes "S" (Catherine/Katherine, Cheryl/ Sheryl). You may wish to experiment and see what creative variations you can come up with.

Cadence: Latin, "to fall," as used in music terminology—the "cadence" of the melody

Cadda, Caddie, Cadena,

Kadena, Kadence

Cailyn: A variation of Catherine, "untainted, pure"

Cailin, Caylin, Kay, Kaylee, Kaylyn

Caitlin: Irish variation of Catherine, "untainted, pure"

Cate, Catelin, Catelynn, Kaitlin, Katelin, Katelynn

Calandra: Greek, "lark"

Cal, Callia, Callie, Cally

Calantha: Greek, "flower"

Cal, Callie, Cally

Calista: Greek, "astonishingly attractive, most beautiful"

Cala, Calesta, Calla, Callie, Callista, Cally, Lista

Callie: A variation of Calandra, Calantha, and Callista, but occasionally a proper name in its own right

Calvina: A feminine variation of Calvin, "bald one"

Cal, Callie, Cally, Vina

Camilla: Latin, "religious attendant"

Cam, Camille, Cammie, Cammy

*Candace: Latin, "bright white"
Candee, Candice, Candis,
Candiss, Candy
(See Acts 8:27.)

Candida: Latin, "white, without
blemish"
Candi, Candide, Candy

Caprice: Italian, "she who is
impulsive, capricious"

Cara: Italian, "she who is dear"
Carah, Carra, Kara

Carilla: Feminine form of Carillo,
a Spanish variation of Charles,
"masculine, manly, virile"
Carrie, Corilla

Carissa: Greek, "she who is dear"
Carisa, Charisa, Charissa

Carita: Latin, "charity"
Karita

Carla: A feminine variation of
Charles, "masculine, manly,
virile"
Carlie, Karla, Karlie

Carlene: A feminine variation of
Charles, "masculine, manly,
virile"
Car, Carleen, Carlina, Carline,
Carlita

Carlotta: Italian, feminine
variation of Charles,
"masculine, manly, virile"
Car, Carrie, Lotta, Lottie

Carly: Usually a diminutive for
any of several names, including
Carlene, Caroline, Carolyn,
Charlotte, and others; often
used as a proper name on its
own
Carlie, Karlee, Karli, Karlie

Carmel: Hebrew, "garden"
Carm, Carmela, Carmelina,
Carmie

Carmen: Latin, "song"
Carm, Carma, Carmie

Carol: French, "song"
Carola, Carole, Carroll

Caroline: A feminine variation
of Charles, "masculine, manly,
virile"
Carolina, Carrie, Lina

Carolyn: A feminine variation of
Charles, "masculine, manly,
virile"
Many additional variations
and diminutives can be created
from the name Carolyn. Some
may prefer to use "K" as the
first initial in creating many of
these names.

Caralyn, Carolin, Carrie, Lyn

Carrie: Often a diminutive for Carol, Caroline, Carolyn

Cari, Cary, Kari, Karrie, Kary

Caryn: A variation of Karen, from Katherine, "pure one"

Carina (Danish), Carine (Swedish)

Casey: Irish, "she who is full of courage"

Casie, K.C., Kaycee

Cassandra: Greek, "temptress"

Cass, Cassaundra, Cassie, Kassandra, Sandra, Sandy

Cassia: Greek, from a seasoning akin to cinnamon

Cassidy: Irish, "she who is clever"

Cass, Cassie, Kassidy

Casta: Latin, "she who is modest"

Cass, Cassie

Catalina: Spanish variation of Catherine, "untainted, pure"

Cat, Cata, Cataline, Lina

Catherine: Greek, "untainted, pure"

Many variations and diminutives are possible for Catherine, including many alternate spellings beginning with the letter "K." Some of the more popular variations include Cath, Catharine, Cate (Italian), Caterina, Cathleen, Cathrine, Cathryn, Cathy, Katharine, Katherine, Kathrine, etc.

> **CATHERINE BOOTH**
> **(1829–1890)**
>
> was, along with her husband, William, a founder of the Salvation Army, one of the most effective ministries in modern times.

> **CATHERINE MARSHALL**
> **(1915–1983)**
>
> was one of the most popular Christian authors of the last half of the twentieth century. Her best-known book is the novel *Christy*, based on the life of her mother, Leonora Wood.

Cathleen: An Irish variation of Catherine, "untained, pure"

Cathy, Kathleen, Kathy

Catia: Japanese, "she who is

precious"
Cat, Tia

Cecile: Latin, a feminine variation of Cecil, "blind one"
Cec, Cecilia, Cecily, Ceil, Celia, Cicel, Cicely, Cilla

Celeste: Greek, "of the heavens"
Celesta, Celestina, Celestine

Celine: Latin, "heavenly"
Celina, Celinda, Celindra, Selina, Selindra, Seline

Chantel: French, "song"
Chantele, Chantelle, Shantel, Shantele, Shantelle

Charity: Greek, "grace"
From root "charis" (meaning "gift"), the same root from which we get "charismatic" or "charisma," referring to the "gift" or charisma. In many Christian circles, charity also refers to love, as manifested by good deeds toward others. In the King James Version of the Bible, 1 Corinthians 13 uses the word *"charity"* where more modern versions use the word *"love."*
Char, Charis

Charlotte: A feminine variation of Charles, "masculine, manly, virile"

Char, Charleen, Charlene, Lottie, Lena

Charmain: Greek, "she who is joyful"
Char, Charmaine, Charmian

Chastity: Latin, "pure, undiluted"
Chas, Chaz

Chelsea: Old English, from a seaport in Britain
Chelsey, Chelsie

Chenda: Asian/Cambodian, "she who is wise"

Cherise: French, "she who is cherished"
Cher, Cherry, Sherise

Cheryl: French, "she who is beloved"
Cher, Cherie, Cherilyn, Sheryl

Chita: English, "kitten"

*Chloe: Greek, "verdant"
Clo, Cloe
(See 1 Corinthians 10:11.)

Christabel: Latin, "beautiful Christian"
Bella, Belle, Chris, Christabella, Christabelle, Christy

Christiann: Greek, "anointed one"

Chris, Christiana, Christianna, Christianne, Christy, Christyann

Christine: Old English, a feminine variation of Christian, "anointed one"

Chris, Chrissie, Chrissy, Christa, Christiana, Christin, Christina, Christy, Cristina, (all of these variations may also be spelled with a "K")

CHRISTINA ROSSETTI (1830–1894)

was an English Christian and widely respected poet. Her work remains popular today.

Cindy: A diminutive for Cynthia, "luminous, moonlike"

Clara: Latin, "clear"

French variations include Clair, Claire, Clare, Claretta, Clarette, Clarita; other variations include Clarice, Clarina, Clarinda, Clarine, Clarissa, Clarita (Spanish), Clorinda

Clarise: A variation of Clare

Clarice, Clarissa

*Claudia: Latin, "she who is lame"—also a feminine variation of Claude

Claudella, Claudelle, Claudette, Claudina, and Claudine

(See 2 Timothy 4:21.)

Clementine: Latin, "full of mercy"—from the same root as the word *clemency*

Clem, Clementina, Clemmy, Tina

Cleopatra: Greek, "daughter of the reknowned one"

Cleo, Pat, Patty

Clio: Greek, "praise"

Cleo

Cloris: Greek, "floral"

Chloris, Clo

Clover: Old English, "to cling"— also from the blossom of the clover

Clo

Cody: English, "pillow"

Codee, Codi, Codie

Colby: Old English, a British regional name

Colette: French, "necklace"

Coletta

Colleen: Irish, "girl"

Coleen, Colene, Colline

Connie: Usually a diminutive for Constance

Constance: Latin, "unchanging"— from the same root as the word *constant*

Conna, Connie

Consuelo: Spanish, "consolation"

Consuela, Connie

Cora: Greek, "young woman"

Coralee, Coralie, Coralina, Coraline, Coretta, Corette, Corey, Corrie, Cory

Coral: A name derived from the sea coral

Coralie, Koral, Koralie

Cordelia: Latin, "tenderhearted"

Corrie, Cory, Delia, Della

Corine: Greek, "maiden"

Coreen, Corina, Corinna

Corinthia: A place name, from Corinth in ancient Greece

Paul's two letters to the Corinthian church are part of the New Testament.

Cornelia: Latin, a feminine variation of Cornelius, "war crier"

Cora, Corrie, Cory

Corona: Spanish, "crown"

> ### CORRIE TEN BOOM
> ### (1892–1983)
>
> was a Dutch woman who worked in her family business and was rounded up by the Nazis and taken to the Ravensbruck death camp with her sister Betsie. Their crime was being part of a Christian family who hid Jews in their attic, rather than see them exterminated by the Nazis. Betsie died in the camp, but Corrie was eventually released and began a worldwide ministry, telling her dramatic story to whoever would listen. Her best-selling book, *The Hiding Place*, was made into a successful movie.

Cosette: French, "the people's victory"

Cosetta

Courtney: Old English, "court"

Court, Cortney, Kourtney

Crystal: Latin, "clarity, clearness,

purity"

Christal, Chrystal, Krystal

Cybil: See Sybil

Cybele, Cybelle

Cynthia: Greek, "luminous one, moonlike"

Cinda, Cindee, Cindi, Cindie, Cindy, Cynda, Cyndra, Cynthea

D

Dacey: Usually a diminutive of Candace

Dacie, Dacy

Dacia: Latin, an Italian regional name

Dada: Yoruba (Nigeria), "she with the hair of curls"

Dagmar: Danish, "the Dane's joy"

Dar

Dahlia: From the flower of the same name, after the Swedish botanist Andrew Dahl

Dalia, Dally

Daisy: Old English, "day's eye"

Daisey, Daisie

Dakota: A Native American tribal name

Dale: Old English, "valley"

Daile, Dayle

DALE EVANS (1912–2001)

was the stage name of the woman born Frances Octavia Smith. She changed her name to Dale Evans when she embarked on a successful singing career. She later married cowboy star Roy Rogers. Her best-selling books include *The Woman at the Well* and *Angel Unaware*, the story of Robin Elizabeth, the Down syndrome daughter of Dale and Roy, who died shortly before her second birthday.

Dallas: Irish, "she who is wise"

*Damaris: Greek, "heifer"

Damara

(See Acts 17:34.)

Dana: Old English, "she who is from Denmark"

Dania, Danna, Dayna

Danica: Slavic, "dawn star"

Danika

Danielle: A feminine variation of Daniel, "God is my judge"

Danella, Danessa, Danette, Danila, Danita, Danna, Dannie, Danny

Daphne: Greek, "laurel tree"

Dafna, Dafne, Daphna

Dara: Hebrew, "she who is wise"

Daragh, Darah, Darragh

Daralis: Old English, "she who is beloved"

Daralice, Daraliss, Daralyce

Darby: Irish, "at liberty," "unfettered, free one"

Darbie

Darcy: French, "dark"

Darce, Darcee, Darcey

Daria: Greek, "prosperous"—also a feminine variation of Darius, "kingly"

Darian, Darice, Darien, Darrie

Darlene: English, "she who is beloved"

Darla, Darlah, Darleene

Davida: A feminine variation of David, "beloved"

Davena, Davene, Davina, Davita

Dawn: Old English, "daybreak"

Dawna

Deanna: Old English, "valley"— also a variation of Diana and the feminine variation of Dean

Deana, Deanne, Dee, Deena, Dina

*Deborah: Hebrew, "bee"

Deb, Debbie, Debby, Debra, Debrah, Debs

There are two Deborahs in the Bible. The first was Rebekah's nurse (see Genesis 24.59, 35.8). The second and more commonly recognized Deborah was the faithful woman who became a judge of the Hebrew people. (See Judges 4–5; Hebrews 11:32–34.)

Dee: Usually a diminutive for many names, such as Deirdre, Delores

DeeDee, Didi

Deirdre: Irish, "sorrowful one"

Dee, DeeDee, Deidra, Deidre

Delaney: Irish, "she who is born of the challenger"

Delcine: Latin, "sweet one"

Delcy, Dulcine, Dulcy

Delia: A diminutive of Cordelia

*Delilah: Hebrew, "yearning with desire"
(See Judges 16:4–21.)

Della: A diminutive of Adelle

Delma: Spanish, "from the sea"

Delores: Spanish, "lady of sorrows"
Dee, Deloris, Dolores, Lorie, Loris

Delta: Greek, "entryway"

Dena: Often a diminutive for Dinah, Diana, or Deanna
Deana, Deena, Dina

Denise: A feminine variation of Dennis, "follower of [the false god] Dionysius"
Deniece, Denys

Dep: Asian/Vietnamese, "she who is beautiful"
Depp, Deppa

Derry: Irish, "redheaded one"
Deri, Derri

Deryn: Welsh, "birdlike"

Desdemona: Greek, "she who needs the blessing of God"
Des, Desi, Mona

Desiree: French, "she who is fondly desired"
Des, Desi, Desiri

Desma: Greek, "pledge, oath"
Des, Dessie

Destiny: Old French, "future" or, literally, destiny
Des, Dessie

Diana: Latin, "divine one"
Deana, Dena, Di, Dian, Diane, Dianna, Dyana, Dyanne

Diella: Latin, "she who worships God"
Dyella

Dina: See Deana

*Dinah: Hebrew, "vindicated one"
Dyna, Dynah
Dinah was the daughter of Jacob and Leah. (See Genesis 34.)

Dionne: Greek, "source of love"
Diona, Dione, Dionna

Dixie: English, "wall"
Dixee, Dixy

Docilla: Latin, "she who is calm"—from the same root as the word *docile*
Dosilla

Dodie: Hebrew, "she who is beloved"

Dody

Dolly: Usually a diminutive for Dorothy

Doll, Dolley, Dollie

Dolores: Latin, "lady of sorrows"—see Delores

Delora, Delores, Dolora

Dominique: Latin, "she who belongs to God"—also a feminine form of Dominic

Doma, Domini, Dominica

Donata: Latin, "she who is worthy"

Donica: Latin, "gift"

Donna: Italian, "lady"

Dona, Donella, Donelle, Donetta, Donita

Dora: Greek, "gift"

Often a diminutive for Dorothea, Dorothy, Theodora, Eudora, etc.

Doralia, Doralyn

*Dorcas: Greek, "gazelle"

Dor, Dorcia, Dorrie

Dorcas was a generous New Testament believer in Christ and benefactress of the early church. (See Acts 9:36–43.)

Doreen: Greek, derived from a Celtic word meaning "sullen."

Dor, Dorena, Dorene, Dorine, Dorrie

Doris: Greek, "one from the sea"

Do, Dorea, Doria, Dorie, Dorinda

Dorit: Hebrew, "generation"

Dorita, Dorrit

Dorothy: Greek, "gift of God"

Doretta, Dorette, Doro, Dorothea, Dory, Dottie, Dotty, Thea

DOROTHY SAYERS (1893–1957)

was an influential Christian thinker, an associate of C. S. Lewis, and the author of the popular Lord Peter Wimsey mysteries, as well as several Christian works, including *The Man Born to Be King*.

Dova: English, "dove"

Dove, Dovie

*Drusilla: Latin, "watered by the dew"

Drew, Dru, Drucilla

(See Acts 24:10–27.)

Dulcie: Latin, "sweet"
Dulcia, Dulcine, Dulcy, Dulsea

Dusty: German, "she who contends"—also sometimes a diminutive for Dustin

Duyen: Asian/Vietnamese, "she who is full of grace"

E

Earlene: Irish, "oath"
Earla, Earleen, Earletta, Earlette, Earline

Eartha: English, "from the earth"
Erda, Herta, Hertha

Ebony: Greek, "dark one"
Eb, Ebonie

Edana: Celtic, "passionate"

Edeline: Old German, "she who is cheerful"—sometimes a variation of Adeline
Eddy, Edelene, Edy

Eden: Hebrew, "pleasantness"
Edena, Edin

Edina: English, "she who prospers"
Adina, Dina, Edie

Edith: English, "valuable gift"
Dita, Edie, Edita, Edithe, Edy, Edyth

EDITH SCHAEFFER
(1914–)

along with her husband, Francis, started the L'Abri Fellowship in Switzerland in 1955. The influence of L'Abri reached far and wide, affecting many young searchers who found Christ through this unique and powerful ministry.

Edna: Hebrew, "pleasant"—from the same root word as *Eden*

Edra: Hebrew, "she who is strong"

Edwina: English, "treasured friend"—also a feminine variation of Edwin
Edie, Edina, Wina

Eileen: An Irish variation of Helen, "light"
Ailene, Alene, Ayleen, Ilene

Elaine: Greek, "light"—a variation of Helen
Alain, Alaina, Alaine, Elaina, Elayne, Ellie, Lainie, Laney

Elana: Hebrew, "tree"

Elberta: Old German, "exceedingly brilliant"
Berta, Bertie, Ellie

Eleanor: A variation of Helen, "light"

Eleanora, Elinor, Elinore, Ellie, Nora

Eldora: Spanish, "as precious as gold"

Eldoria

Electra: Greek, "shining one"

Elena: An Italian variation of Helen, "light"

Elfrida: Old German, "she who is wise"—a feminine variation of Alfred

Elfreda, Ellie, Freda

Eliana: Hebrew, "God has answered my prayer"

Anna, Elianna, Ellie

*Elizabeth: Hebrew, "consecrated to God"

Beth, Betha, Bethy, Bess, Bessie, Betsy, Bette, Bettina, Betts, Betty, Elisa, Elisabeth, Elise, Elisheba (see Exodus 6:23), Elissa, Eliza, Lisette, Liz, Liza, Lizabeth, Lizzie

Read the story of Elizabeth, the mother of John the Baptist, in Luke 1:5–80.

Elke: German, "she who is noble"

Elka

ELISABETH ELLIOT (1926–)

was married to Jim Elliot, one of the five missionaries martyred in 1956 by the Huaorani (Auca) people. She wrote about his life in several of her many books, which include *Shadow of the Almighty* and *Through Gates of Splendor.*

ELIZABETH FRY (1780–1845)

was a pioneer of prison reform in nineteenth-century England.

Ella: Greek, "elf-like"—also a variation of Helen

Ellie, Elly

Ellen: A Scottish variation of Helen, "light"

Ellie, Ellyn

Elma: Greek, "she who is easy to please"—also a feminine variation of Elmo

Elmira: Arabic, "noble lady"

Ellie, Mira

Eloise: French, "great in battle"—a variation of Louise
Aloysia, Ellie, Eloisa, Elouisa

Elora: A diminutive of Eleanora and variation of Helen, "light"

Elsa: German, "noble young woman"
Elsie, Elsy

Elspeth: Hebrew, "dedicated to God"
Ellie

Elvira: Latin, "fair"
Ellie, Elva, Vira

Elysia: Greek, "fully satisfied"
Elicia, Elisha, Elysa

Elza: Hebrew, "God is the source of my joy"

Emelda: A variation of Emily, "she who is industrious"
Emeline, Emmy, Imelda

Emerald: From the gem, which is the birthstone for May

Emily: Latin, "she who is industrious"—also a variation of Amelia
Amalie, Ameline, Em, Ema, Emilyn, Emlyn, Emmalee, Emmi, Emmy, Emylee

Emma: Old German, "all-encompassing"—also can be a diminutive of Emily
Em, Emmy

Emmanuelle: Hebrew, "God with us"—a feminine variation of Emmanuel
Emmy

Emmylou: A combination of Emily, "she who is industrious," and Louise, "strong warrior"

Enid: Latin, "of the soul"

Erica: Old German, "one of great strength"—a feminine variation of Eric
Erika, Ricki

Erin: Irish, the old name for Ireland
Errin, Eryn

**ETHEL WATERS
(1900–1977)**

was a popular singer and movie star when she was converted to Christ. She worked with the Billy Graham Crusades, and her signature song was "His Eye Is on the Sparrow," which became the title of her best-selling autobiography.

Erma: A variation of Irma, "warrior"

Ernestine: Old German, "purposeful one"
Ern, Erna, Ernesta

Esme: English, "guardian"
Es, Essie

Esmeralda: Spanish, from the gemstone emerald
Es, Essie

Esperanza: Spanish, "hope"

Estelle: French, "starlike"—also a variation of Esther
Es, Essie, Estee, Estella, Estrella, Stella

*Esther: Persian, "starlike"
Es, Essie, Esta, Estra, Hester
Read the compelling story of the Bible heroine Esther in the book that bears her name.

Ethel: Old German, "she who is noble"
Ethelinda, Ethelyn, Ethlyn

Etta: Usually a diminutive for Georgetta, Henrietta, Marietta, etc., but also used as a proper name in its own right

Eudora: Greek, "pleasant gift"
Dora

Eugenia: Greek, "of noble birth"—also a feminine variation of Eugene
Eugenie, Genie, Jean, Jeanie

EUGENIA PRICE
(1916–1996)

was an extremely successful Christian writer of both nonficton and fiction.

Eula: Greek, "well-spoken"

*Eunice: Greek, "glorious victory"
The mother of Timothy. (See Acts 16:1–3; 1 Timothy 1:5; 3:14; 4:5.)

Eurydice: Greek, "large one"

Evangeline: Greek, "messenger of good news," as in "evangelist"
Eva, Evangelina, Vannie

EVANGELINE BOOTH
(1865–1950)

was the daughter of William and Catherine Booth, founders of the Salvation Army. She continued their work well into the twentieth century.

*Eve: Hebrew, "life-giver"
Eva, Evie, Evita

The mother of all living, Eve's story is found in Genesis 2 and 3.

Evelyn: English, "hazelnut"

Avelyn, Evie

F

Faith: Middle English, "she who believes"

Fanny: Usually a diminutive for Frances

Fannie

Farrah: Middle English, "attractive"

Fara, Farra

Fausta: Latin, "she who is blessed"

Faustina, Faustine

Fawn: Old French, "young deer"

Faunia, Fawna, Fawnia

Fay: Old French, "fairy" or "elf-like"—or sometimes a diminutive for Frances or Faith

Fae, Falina, Faline, Faye, Fayetta, Fayette, Faylena, Faylina, Fayline (the latter four variations may also be traced to the word *feline*, meaning "catlike")

Fedora: Russian, "gift of God"

Felice: Latin, "happy, merry, gay"—also a female variation of Felix

Felicia, Felise, Felita, Licia, Lise, Lita, Phelicia, Phylicia

Fern: Old English, derived from the fern plant

Fernanda: A feminine variation of Ferdinand, "adventurous one"

Anda, Fern, Nan, Nana, Nanda

Fifi: Usually a diminutive or nickname; very rarely used as a proper name

Fiona: Irish, "she who is a fair one"

Fionna, Fionne

Flannery: Irish, "redheaded one"

Flan, Flanna, Flannary

Flavia: Latin, "golden one"

FLORENCE NIGHTINGALE (1820–1910)

was the mother of modern nursing. She declared that "Christ is the author of our profession."

Fleur: A French variation of

Florence, "flower"
Fleurette

Florence: Latin, "flower"
Flo, Flora, Floria, Florice, Florida, Florinda, Floris, Florrie, Flory, Flossie, Flossy

Foluke: Yoruba (Nigerian), "she who is protected by God"—can be masculine or feminine

Frances: Old German, "free one"—also a female variation of Francis
Fanny, Fran, Francesca, Francine, Francisca, Francoise, Franny

---

**FRANCES "FANNY" CROSBY
(1820–1915)**

was one of Christianity's most famous and beloved hymn writers. Among her nine thousand hymns are "Blessed Assurance," "To God Be the Glory," and "Rescue the Perishing."

Frederica: A feminine variation of Frederick, "peaceful ruler"
Freda (often a diminutive for Winifred), Freddie, Freddy, Fredia, Fredrika, Frieda, Rica, Ricca

Fritzi: German, a feminine variation of Fritz, which is a diminutive for Frederick
Fritzie

**FRANCES RIDLEY
HAVERGAL
(1836–1879)**

was an English poet, author, and hymn composer. Among her most memorable hymns is "Take My Life and Let It Be."

G

Gabrielle: A feminine variation of Gabriel, "God is my strength"
Gabbi, Gabbie, Gabriella, Gaby, Gavrielle

Gail: Hebrew, usually a diminutive for Abigail
Gael, Gale, Gayla, Gayle

Galina: A Russian variation of Helen, "light"
Galeen, Galena, Galene, Gay, Gaylene, Gayline

Galyn: Hebrew, "the Lord is a redeemer"
Galia, Gaylia

Gana: Hebrew, "garden"

Garnet: Middle English, a "precious jewel," the gemstone garnet

Garnett, Garnette, Garney

Gay: Old French, "merry one"

Gaye

Gemma: Latin, "precious stone"— from the same root as "gem"

Jemma

Geneva: Old French, "juniper tree"

Gen, Genny, Gin, Ginny

Genevieve: Old French, "white wave"

Gena, Genny, Gin, Ginny, Jenny

Genna: Arabic, "little bird"

Jenn, Jenna, Jenny

Georgia: Greek, "one who farms or works with the land"

Georgette, Georgiana, Georgina, Georgine, Georgy. Many more combinations are possible.

Geraldine: German, "spear warrior"—a feminine variation of Gerald

Geralda, Geri, Gerilyn, Gerri, Jeri, Jerri

Germaine: French, "from Germany"

Germane, Jermaine

Gertrude: Old German, "spear maiden"

Gerda, Gert, Gerta, Gertie, Trudy

Gianna: Italian, "God is gracious"

Gigi: Usually a diminutive; no known independent meaning

Gila: Hebrew, "she who is joyful"

Gilana

Gilda: Old English, "gilded"

Gildy

Gillian: Latin, "she who is youthful"

Gilliana, Gilliann, Gillie, Jill, Jillian, Jilly

Gina: Usually a diminutive for Angelina, Eugenia, Regina, Virginia, etc.

Geena, Gena, Ginna

Ginger: Latin, "spice"—also a common diminutive for Virginia

Giselle: Old German, "promise"

Gisella, Gizella, Gizelle

Gladys: Irish, "princess"

Gladdis, Glady

GLADYS AYLWARD
(1902–1970)

was a very successful missionary to China. Her story is told in the Alan Burgess biography *The Small Woman*, which inspired the popular movie *The Inn of the Sixth Happiness*.

Glenna: Welsh, "valley" or "glen"—a feminine variation of Glen

Glena, Glenda, Glenice, Glennis, Glinda, Glynis

Gloria: Latin, "glory, praise, adulation"

Glorianna, Glorianne, Glory, Glorya, Gloryanna

Golda: Old English, "gold"

Goldia, Goldie, Goldy

Grace: Latin, "full of grace"

Gracia, Gracie, Gratiana

Greer: Scottish, "watchful one"

Greta: A common diminutive for Margaret, but also commonly used as a proper name

Gretchen, Grete, Gretel, Gretha

Griselda: Old German, "gray warrior"

Griesella, Grishilda, Zelda

Guadalupe: Spanish, "valley of the earth"

Lupe, Lupita

Guinevere: Welsh, "white lady"

Guinna, Gwen, Gwenna, Gwenny

Gwendolyn: Irish, "white-browed one"

Gwen, Gwenn, Gwenna, Gwenyth, Gwyn, Gwynne

H

*Hadassah: Hebrew, "myrtle tree"—the Hebrew name of Esther (Persian, "starlike") in the Bible

*Hagar: Hebrew, "one who flees"

Hagar was Sarah's handmaiden and the mother of Abraham's first son, Ishmael. Read Hagar's story in Genesis 16 and 21, and in Galatians 4:24–25.

Halcyon: Greek, "kingfisher"

This name has come to be associated with happy memories. Thus, a more meaningful definition in keeping with the current usage of the word might be "she who brings pleasant memories."

Haley: Norse, "heroine"

Hailey, Halley, Hallie, Hally, Hayley

Halle: African, "unexpected delight"

Halla

Hana: Japanese, "flower"—also a variation of Hannah

**HANNAH WHITALL SMITH
(1832–1911)**

was a noted speaker at the popular Keswick conventions in nineteenth-century England. Her classic book *The Christian's Secret of a Happy Life* is still a perennial best seller and a "must-read" for every Christian.

---

*Hannah: Hebrew, "favored one of God"

Hana, Hanna, Hanne, Hanni

Hannah was the barren wife of Elkanah. In desperation, she cried out to God and, in faith, received the blessing she sought. Samuel was the firstborn of her six children. In gratitude, and in keeping with a pledge she made to God, Hannah dedicated Samuel to God's service. Read the story of Hannah in 1 Samuel 1 and 2.

Harley: Old English, "meadow"

Harlee, Harleigh, Harlene

Harmony: Greek, "harmony" or "in accord"

Harmonia, Harmonie

Harper: Old English, "one who plays the harp"

Harriet: Old German, "mistress of the home"—also a feminine variation of Henry (from Henrietta) and Harry

Harrietta, Harriette, Hattie

**HARRIET BEECHER STOWE
(1811–1896)**

was an abolitionist whose best-selling novel, *Uncle Tom's Cabin* (1852), has been suggested as a contributing factor to the American Civil War.

Hasia: Hebrew, "she who is protected by the power of God"

Hattie: Usually a diminutive for Harriet

Haviva: Hebrew, "beloved daughter"

Hazel: Old German, "victory"
Hazell, Hazelle

Heather: Middle English, from the plant of the same name

Hedda: Old German, "warrior"
Heda, Heddi, Heddy, Hedy, Hetta

Heidi: German, "she who is cheerful"—also a diminutive of Adelaide
Heide, Heidy

Hein: Asian/Vietnamese, "she who is gentle"—can be either masculine or feminine

*Helah: Hebrew, "sickly"
(See 1 Chronicles 4:5–7.)

**HELEN ROSEVEARE
(1925–)**

is a British doctor who was a medical missionary to the Congo.

Helen: Greek, "light"
This name has many variations, including the following names and their variations and diminutives:
Aileen, Eileen, Elaina, Eleanor, Elena, Ellen, Helena, Helene, Helyn, Lenore

Helga: Old German, "godly one"

Heloise: A French variation of Louise, "strong warrior"
Eloisa, Eloise, Heloisa

**HENRIETTA MEARS
(1890–1963)**

was an educator and important figure in Christian ministry in the mid-twentieth century. In 1933, she founded Gospel Light, a successful Christian publishing house that is still producing many excellent Christian resources.

Henrietta: A feminine variation of Henry, "he who rules the home"
Etta, Ettie, Hen, Henny, Henriette, Hettie, Hetty

Hermione: Greek, "daughter of the earth"

Herma, Hermia, Herminia

Hester: A variation of Esther, "starlike"

Hess, Hestia, Hestina, Hestine

Hila: Hebrew, "worthy of praise"—also a feminine variation of Hillel

Hilary: Greek, "she who has a merry heart"

Hil, Hillarie, Hillary, Hilly

Hilda: Old German, "she who is a warrior"—can be a diminutive for Brunhilde

Hilde, Hildy

Hildegard: Old German, "one who protects"

Hildegarde, Hildy, Hilly

Hinda: Hebrew, "doe"

Hynda

Holly: Old English, from the plant of the same name

Hollie, Hollis

Honey: Old English, from bee's honey; often used as an endearment

Honora: Latin, "she who is honorable, worthy of praise"

Honorah, Honore, Honoria, Nora, Norah

Hope: Old English, "expectancy"

Hope is one of the Christian virtues.

Hortense: Latin, "gardener"— from the same root as the word *horticulture*

Hortensia

Hosanna: Greek, "Praise the Lord!"

*****Huldah:** Greek, "weasel"

Hulda

(See 2 Kings 22:14–20; 2 Chronicles 34:22–33.)

Hyacinth: Latin, from the plant of the same name

Hyacintha, Hyacinthia

I

Ianthe: Greek, "flower"

Iantha, Ianthia

Ida: Old German, "she who is joyful"

Idella, Idelle

Ilene: A variant spelling of Eileen, a variation of Helen, "light"

Ileene

Ilka: Slavic, "she who aspires"
Ilke

Ilsa: An Old German diminutive
for Elizabeth
Ilse

Imelda: Latin, "image"—also a
variation of Imogene

Imogene: Latin, "imaginative
one"—from the same root as
the English word *imagination*
Emogene, Gene, Genie,
Imogenia

Ina: Latin
Originally a diminutive for
names ending in "ine" or "ina,"
such as Albertina, Albertine,
Bernadina, Bernadine,
Clementina, Clementine.
More recently, Ina has become
a proper name in its own right.

Inez: Greek, "she who is gentle"
also a Spanish variation of
Agnes
Ines, Ynes, Ynez

Ingrid: Scandinavian, "daughter"
Inga, Inge, Inger, Ingmar

Iola: Greek, "dawn"

Iona: A Scottish place name,
from an island off the coast of
Scotland

Ione: Greek, "beautiful flower"

Irene: Greek, "peaceful one"
Erina, Ireen, Irina (Russian),
Irine

Iris: Greek, "rainbow"
Irisa, Irissa

Irma: Old German, "warrior"
Erma, Irmina, Irmine

Isabel: Hebrew, "she who is
consecrated to God"—a
variation of Elizabeth
Bella, Belle, Isabella, Isabelle,
Isobel, Izabel, Izabela, Izzy,
Ysabel, Ysabella, Ysabelle

Isadora: Greek, "gift"
Dora, Dorrie, Isadore, Izzy

Isolde: Celtic, "fair daughter"
Isolda, Isolte

Ivana: Greek, "gift of God"—also
a feminine variation of Ivan,
which is a Russian version of
John
Iva, Ivah, Ivanna, Yvanna

Ivory: English, from the desirable
substance derived from the
tusks of elephants and other
tusked animals

Ivy: Old English, from the plant
of the same name
Ivie

J

Jacinda: A Spanish variation of Hyacinth, from the flower

Jacenda, Jacenta, Jacinta, Jacinth, Jacinthia

Jacoba: A feminine variation of Jacob, "one who supplants another"

Jacobina, Jacobine

Jacqueline: An Old French variation of Jacob and one of its variations, James, meaning "one who supplants another."

Many variations, including Jacke, Jackee, Jackie, Jacklyn, Jacklynn, Jacklynne, Jaclyn

Jade: English, from the gemstone of the same name

Jada, Jayda, Jayde

*Jael: Hebrew, "one who climbs" (as a goat)

Yael

(See Judges 4:17–22; 5:6, 24–27.)

Jaime: French, "beloved one"

Jamie: Hebrew—a feminine variation of James, a variation of Jacob, "one who supplants another"

Jama, Jami, Jayme

Jamila: Arabic, "she who is lovely"—also a feminine variation of Jamil

Jamilla, Jamille

Jane: Hebrew, usually a feminine variation of John, "God's gracious gift"

Many variations, including Jan, Jana, Janae, Janella, Janelle, Janessa, Janet, Janice, Janine, Janis, Janna, Jayne, and Jeanette

> ### JAN (JANICE) KARON (1937–)
>
> is the author of the best-selling Mitford series of novels.

Jardena: Hebrew, "flowing downward"—a feminine variation of Jordan

Jasmine: Persian, from the flower of the same name

Jasmin, Jasmina, Jaz, Jazmynne

Jayleen: American, usually a combination of Jay and Lynn

Jay, Jaylene, Jaylynn

Jean: A Scottish form of Jane, "God's gracious gift"

Gean, Genie, Jeana, Jeananne,
Jeane, Jeanette (French),
Jeanice, Jeanie, Jeanine, Jeanna,
Jeanne

**MADAME JEANNE GUYON
(1648–1717)**

was a French Christian
mystic much persecuted for
her faith. Her autobiography,
Life of Madame Guyon,
is still in print and is
considered by many to be
a Christian classic. Other
books of her writings also
remain popular.

***Jedidah:** Hebrew, "beloved of
Jehovah"
Jedida
(See 2 Kings 22.)

***Jehosheba:** Hebrew, "promise of
God"
(See 2 Kings 11:2; 2
Chronicles 22:11.)

***Jemima:** Hebrew, "dove"
Jem, Jema, Jemimah, Jemma,
Jemmy
Jemima was the eldest of Job's
daughters born to Job and his
wife after the tragic loss of
their first family.
(See Job 42:14.)

Jennifer: Celtic, "white wave"
Genna, Gennie, Gennifer,
Jen, Jenn, Jenna, Jennie, Jenny,
Jinny

Jerri: American, usually a
diminutive for Geraldine
Geri, Gerri, Jera, Jeri, Jerilyn,
Jerrie, Jerry

***Jerusha:** Hebrew, "a goodly
inheritance"
Geri, Gerri, Jeri, Jerri
(See 2 Kings 15:33; 1
Chronicles 6:12;
2 Chronicles 27:1–6.)

**JESSIE PENN-LEWIS
(1861–1927)**

was a forceful presence in
Christian work during the
early part of the twentieth
century, largely associated
with the Welsh revival. She
wrote widely and was editor
of *The Overcomer*, one of the
early deeper-life magazines.

Jessamyn: A French variation of
Jasmine, from the flower
Jess, Jessie, Jessy

Jessica: Hebrew, "rich"
Jess, Jessa, Jessalyn, Jessie,
Jessika, Jessy

Jessie: Hebrew, a feminine variation of Jesse, "he who is graced by God"
Jessy

Jestine: A variation of Justine, "she who is just"
Jess, Jessie, Jesstina, Jessy

Jewel: English, literally, a precious stone
Jewelle

*Jezebel: Hebrew, "unworthy"
Read the tragic story of Jezebel in 1 Kings 16:31; 18:4–9; 21:5–25; 2 Kings 9.

Jillian: Latin, "young one"—also a variation of Julia
Gill, Gillian, Gilly, Jill, Jillianne, Jilly, Jillyanna

Joakima: Hebrew, "God is my judge"
Joachima

Joan: Hebrew, "God is gracious"—often a variation of Jane, a feminine variation of John
Joane, Joanie

*Joanna: Hebrew, "God is gracious"—a variation of Jane
Joanne, Johanna, Johna, Jone, Jonna
(See Luke 8:1–3; 23:55; 24:10.)

Jobeth: American, usually a combination of Jo and Beth
Jobie, Joby

Jobina: Hebrew, "afflicted one"—a feminine variation of Job
Jobie, Jobina, Joby

Jocelyn: Latin, "she who is joyful"
Joceline, Joseline, Joselyn

*Jochebed: Hebrew, "the glory of God"
(See Exodus 2:1–11; Hebrews 11:23.)

Jodi: American, usually a diminutive for Joan, Joanna, Jocelyn, Judith, etc.
Jodee, Jodie, Jody

Joelle: Hebrew, "Jehovah is God"—a feminine variation of Joel
Jo, Joela, Joella, Joellen, Joelyn

Joleen: Hebrew, "God, our increase"
Jo, Jolena, Jolene, Joline, Jolynn

Jolie: French, "beautiful"
Jolee, Joli, Joly

Joni: American variation of Joan, a variation of John, "God's gracious gift"

JONI EARECKSON TADA
(1949–)

is the author of many books, including her best-selling autobiography, *Joni*, which tells the dramatic story of the 1967 diving accident that left her a quadriplegic.

Jonina: Hebrew, "like a dove"—a female variation of Jonah
Jo, Nina

Jora: Hebrew, "autumn rain"
Jorah

Jordan: Hebrew, "flowing downward" (as does the Jordan River)
Jorda, Jordana, Jorden, Jordi, Jordine, Jordy, Jorie, Jorrie, Jory

Josephine: French, la feminine variation of Joseph, "God shall add"
Jo, Josefina, Josephina, Josetta, Josette, Josie

Jovana: Possibly a variation of the Italian Giovanna, a feminine variation of John, "God's gracious gift"
Jo, Jovanna, Jovannah

Joy: English, "she who is joyful"
Joi, Joye

Joyce: Latin, "she who is joyful"
Joice, Joyse

Juanita: Spanish, a variation of Jane/Joan/John, "God's gracious gift"
Juana, Wanita

*Judith: Hebrew, "praiseworthy"
Jude, Judi, Judy, Judye
(See Genesis 26:34.)

*Julia: Greek, "youthful one"
Julian, Juliana, Julianna, Julianne, Julienne, Juliet, Juliette (French)
(See Romans 16:15.)

JULIA WARD HOWE
(1819–1910)

was an American poet, author, and ardent abolitionist. Her stirring "Battle Hymn of the Republic" is still one of the most beloved of American songs.

JULIAN OF NORWICH
(1342–1413)

was an English Christian mystic whose writings remain popular today.

June: English, after the month of the same name—also "young one"

Juna, Junetta, Junette, Junia

Justine: Latin, "she who is just"—a feminine variation of Justin

Justa, Justina, Tina

K

Note: "K" names have much in common with "C" names. Many popular names beginning with either letter are simply spelling variations. Some of these names include Candace/Kandace; Carla/Karla; Carolyn/Karolyn; Casey/Kasey; Catherine/Katherine; Cathleen/ Kathleen; Cody/Kody; and so on. When you see a "K" name you like, consider that it might also be spelled with a "C."

Kai: Native American, "willow"

Kaitlin: Irish, "pure"—a spelling variation of Caitlin

Kaitlyn, Katelyn, Kathlynn

Kale: Possibly a variation of Carl/ Charles, meaning "masculine, manly, virile". Currently appropriate for either sex.

Cale, Kaley, Kalie, Kayleigh

Kalena: Hawaiian, "she who is pure"

Kalina, Kalinda

Kanya: Asian/Thai, "a young woman of grace"

Kania

Kara: Greek, a variation of Katherine, "pure one"

Cara, Karah, Karrah

Karen: Greek, a variation of Katherine, "pure one"

Caren, Carin, Caron, Caryn, Karin (Scandanavian), Karina (Russian), Karon, Karyn

Kari: A diminutive of Carolyn, but increasingly a proper name in its own right

Carey, Carrie, Karie, Karilyn, Karrie, Kerry

Karla: A German variation of Carla, which is a feminine variation of Charles, "masculine, manly, virile"

Kassia: A Polish variation of Katherine, "pure one"

Cassia, Cassie, Kasia, Kass, Kassie

Kate: Greek, a diminutive of Katherine

Cate, Kati, Katie, Katy

Katharine: Greek, "pure one"

Many variations exist for this name, including spelling variations and diminutives.

Catherine, Cathy, Kate, Katherine, Kathryn, Kathy, Katie, Kit, Kitty

> **KATHERINE VON BORA (1499–1552)**
>
> was the beloved wife of Martin Luther. As an endearment, he called her "Kitty."

Kathleen: Irish, a variation of Katherine, "pure one"

Cathleen, Kate, Kathlyn, Kathy, Katy

Kathryn: See Katharine

Cathryn

Kathy: Usually a diminutive for Katharine

Katrina: German, a variation of Katharine, "pure one"

Kate, Katrine, Katy, Trina, Trinie, Triny

Kay: Greek, "she who rejoices" — in some cases, a diminutive of Katharine

Kaye

Kayla: Hebrew, "crown of laurels"

Cayla, Kala, Kalah

Keara: Celtic, "dark one"

Kiera, Kierra

Keely: Irish variation of the masculine name Kelly, "courageous warrior"

Keena, Kina, Kyna

Kelila: Hebrew, "laurel-crowned one"

Kelly: Irish, "victorious warrior"

Kelley, Kelli, Kellie, Kellina

Kelsey: A Scandinavian variation of Chelsea, from a seaport in Britain

Kelcy, Kelsi, Kelsy

Kendall: Old English, "she who is from the bright valley"

Kenda

Kendra: Old English, "she who is learned or knowledgeable"

Kenda, Kendry

Kenna: Irish, "she who knows" — also a feminine variation of Kenneth

Kenzie: Scottish, a variation of MacKenzie, "son of the wise ruler"

Kerry: Irish, "dark one"
Carrie, Kari, Keri, Kerri,
Kerrie, Kiera

Keshia: African, "she who is favored"
Kesia

*Keturah: Hebrew, "sweet-smelling incense"
Ketura
Keturah became Abraham's wife after the death of his beloved Sarah and bore him six sons. Read her story in Genesis 25:1–6.

Kevyn: Irish, a feminine variation of Kevin, "he who is gentle"

*Kezia: Hebrew, from the sweet-smelling herb cassia
Kez, Keziah, Kezzie
Kezia was the second daughter of Job (after Jemima) following his restoration. (See Job 42:14.)

Kiana: Irish, "ancient one"
Kia, Kianna, Kianne

Kiara: Possibly a variation of the Italian Chiara, a variation of Claire, from Clara, "clear"

Kimberly: An English place name
Kim, Kimberley, Kimberli, Kimmie, Kimmy, Kym

Kirby: Old English, "she (or he) who is from the village church"
Both girls and boys are named Kirby.

Kiri: Asian/Cambodian, "she who comes from the mountains"

Kirsten: Greek, "anointed one"
Kiersten, Kierstin, Kirsta (Scandinavian), Kirstie, Kirsty

Kitty: Greek, usually a diminutive of Katherine or an endearment
Ketty, Kit

Koren: Greek, "young woman"

Kristin: Greek, "anointed one"
Kris, Krista, Kristi, Kristia, Kristie, Kristina, Kristine, Kristy

Kyle: Irish, "she who is pretty"
Kyla, Kylie, Kylyn

Kyra: Greek, a feminine variation of Cyrus, "sun"
Kira

L

Labonya: Asian, "she who is beautiful"

Lacey: Latin, "she who is happy"— often a diminutive of Larissa,

Alicia, and similar names
Lacie, Lacy

LaDonna: American, "the pretty one"
Ladonna

Lae: Laotian, "she who is dark"

Lael: Arabic, "she who was born at night"
Laela, Leila, Layla

Laine: French, often a diminutive for Elaine, "light"
Laina, Lainey, Lane

Laini: Swahili, "she who is tenderhearted"

Lan: Asian/Vietnamese, from the Vietnamese word for "flower"

Lana: Latin, "soft"—also a feminine variation of Alan or a diminutive of Alana
Lanetta, Lanette, Lanna

Lane: American—see Laine

Lani: Greek, "sent from heaven"— also a diminutive of Leilani
Lanni, Lanny

Lara: Latin, "well-known, loved"—also a diminutive of Larisa, Russian version of Larissa
Larra

LaRae: Possibly a variation of Laura, which is a variation of Laurel, from the plant, or Rae, "doe"

Larine: Latin, a name derived from a bird of the gull family
Larina

Larissa: Latin, "she who is playful"
Larisa

Lark: Middle English, from the bird of the same name

Latifah: Arabic, "she who is gentle"
Latiffah

Laura: See Laurel

Laurel: Latin, "from the laurel plant"—a crown made from which signifies victory.
Many variations and diminutives (often used as proper names), including LaRae, Larina, Larine, Laura, Laurella, Laurelle, Laureen, Lauren, Laurena, Laurene, Lauretta, Laurette, Laurie, Loraine, Loree, Loretta, Lori, Lorice, Loricia, Lorinda, Lorna, Lorraine, Lory

Laverne: Latin, "of springtime"
Lavern, Laverna

Lavinia: Latin, "she who is pure"
Lavina, Vin, Vina, Vinny

Layla: Swahili, "she who is born at night"

*Leah: Hebrew, "she who is weary"
Lea, Leia
Leah was the wife of Jacob, given to him in place of her sister, Rachel, for whom Jacob worked seven years to marry. After marrying Leah, he worked another seven years for Rachel. Read their story in Genesis 29–30.

Leandra: Latin, a feminine variation of Leander", he who is as fierce as a lion"
Andie, Leanda, Lee

Leanne: English, a combination of Lee, "meadow," and Anne, "she who is full of grace"
Leann, Leanna, Lee Ann

Lee: Irish, "meadow"
Leigh

Leila: Hebrew, "one with dark beauty"
Layla, Leilah, Lela, Lelah

Leilani: Hawaiian, "daughter from heaven"

Lemuela: Hebrew, "dedicated to God"—a feminine variation of Lemuel

Lena: Greek, "light"
Lenetta, Lenette, Lina, Lynette

Lenore: Greek, "light"
Leanore, Lenny, Lenora, Leonora, Lyn, Nora

Leona: Latin, "lioness"—also a feminine variation of Leo
Leola, Leontine, Leontyne

Leonora: Greek, "she who is from the light"—a variation of Eleanor/Eleanora
Lenora, Lenore, Leonore

Lesley: Scottish, "meadow"
Leslee, Leslie

LETTIE COWMAN
(1870–1960)

along with her husband, Charles, was a missionary but is best remembered for her work in compiling several devotional books, including the classic *Streams in the Desert.*

Leta: Latin, "she who is joyful"
Lita

Letha: Greek, "she who forgets"
Lethia

Letitia: Latin, "she who is joyful"
Leticia, Letta, Lettie, Letty,
Tish, Tisha

Levia: Hebrew, usually a feminine
variation of Levi

Lewanna: Hebrew, "moonlike"
Levana, Lewana, Lou, Lu,
Luanna

Lexine: Greek, "she who helps
others" — often a diminutive of
Alexandra
Lexia, Lexy

Liana: French, "vinelike"
Lian, Liane, Lianne

Libby: Usually a diminutive of
Elizabeth or Olivia
Libbie, Livvie

Liesl: A German diminutive of
Elizabeth

Lilith: Arabic, "she who is of the
night"

LILIAS TROTTER
(1853–1928)

was a talented artist who
set aside her natural gift
to pursue the life of a
missionary to the Muslims
of North Africa.

Lillian: Latin, taken from the lily,
a flower popular at Easter
Lil, Lila, Lilah, Lilia, Lilias,
Lilis, Lilla, Lillia, Lillis, Lilly,
Lily

Linda: Latin, "she who is pretty"
Lindi, Lindie, Lynda, Lynde

Lindsay: Old English, "from the
island of the linden trees"
Lindsey, Lindsy, Linsey

Linnea: Scandinavian, "lime tree"
Linea, Lynea, Lynnea

Lisa: Hebrew, often a diminutive
of Elizabeth, but increasingly a
proper name in its own right
Leeza, Lise, Liset, Lisetta,
Lissa, Lysa

Lisabeth: Hebrew, usually
a variation of Elizabeth,
"consecrated to God"
Beth, Liz, Liza

Livia: Latin, usually a diminutive
of Olivia
Livie, Livvey, Livvie, Livy

Liz: Usually a diminutive of
Elizabeth
Liza, Lizetta, Lizette, Lizzie,
Lizzy

*Lois: Greek, "she who is
desirable"

Lois was the grandmother of Timothy. (See 2 Timothy 1:5.)

Lola: Spanish, usually a diminutive of names such as Dolores, Laurel, and Louise, but increasingly a proper name in its own right

Lolita: Spanish, "little sad one"
Lita, Lolo, Lulita

Lona: Latin, "lioness"
Lonee, Loni, Lonna, Lonni

Lora: Latin, one of the many diminutives of Laurel

Lorelei: Old German, "temptress"
Laralei, Loralei

Lorena: English, one of the many variations of Laurel, from the laurel plant

Loretta: English, one of the many variations of Laurel
Lauretta, Lorella, Lorelle

Lori: English, one of the many variations of Laurel
Loree, Lorie, Lory

Lorine: English, one of the many variations of Laurel
Loreen, Lorinda

Loris: Greek, often a diminutive of Chloris

Lorice, Lorisa

Lorna: Latin, one of the many variations of Laurel

Lorraine: Latin, "she who sorrows"
Lo, Loraine, Lorinda, Rainie

Lottie: Usually a diminutive of Charlotte
Lotti, Lotty

**LOTTIE MOON
(1840–1912)**

gave her life in service to Christ as a missionary to China.

Louella: A combination of Lou, from Louis, "noted warrior," and Ella, "elf-like"
Luella

Louise: Old German, "strong warrior"
Aloise, Lou, Louisa, Lu, Luisa (Spanish), Luise

Luann: Hebrew, "strong warrior"
Lu, Luana, Lu Ann, Luanna

Lucia: An Italian variation of Lucille, "she who brings light"
Luciana

Lucille: Latin, "she who brings light"

Lucie, Lucilla, Lucinda, Lucy

Lucretia: Latin, "worthy of praise"

Lulu: Usually a diminutive for names such as Louise, Luann, Lucinda, etc.

Lupe: Spanish, usually a diminutive of Guadalupe

Lurleen: A modern variation of Lorelei, "temptress"

Lurlene, Lurline

*Lydia: Greek, "she who comes from Lydia" (a former country in Asia Minor)

Lyda, Lidia

Lydia's story can be found in Acts 16:12–15 and Philippians 1:1–10.

Lyla: English, a feminine variation of Lyle, "from the island"

Lynette: A variation of Lynn— the "ette" ending is usually a diminutive

Linetta, Linette, Lynetta, Lynette

Lynn: A diminutive of Linda, but more recently a proper name in its own right

Lin, Lyn, Lynella, Lynelle, Lynna

Lyris: Greek, "she who plays the lyre"

Mabel: Latin, "she who is lovable"—a diminutive of Anabel

Amabel, Amable, Amaybelle, Mabelle (French), Mable, Maybel, Maybelle, Mayble

MABEL SHAW (1889–1973)

was first single woman missionary sent by the London Missionary Society to Central Africa. She was also an author.

Mackenzie: Scottish Gaelic, "son of the wise ruler"—a name for both boys and girls

Mackenzie, MacKensie, McKenzie, McKensie

Madeline: Hebrew, "tower of strength"; Greek, "woman from Magdala" (a town on the Sea of Galilee)

Mada, Madaleine, Madalena

(Spanish), Madalyn, Maddie, Maddy, Madelaine, Madeleine, Madelena, Madelene, Madelina, Madge, Magdala, Magdalee, Magdalena, Magdalene

Madge: A diminutive of Madeline, Margaret

Madison: Old English, "son of the mighty warrior"—a boys' name also used for girls

Madonna: Latin, "my lady"
Madona

Madra: Spanish, "mother"
Madre

Mae: A variation of May, "month of May"

***Magdala:** Hebrew, "a tower"— see Madeline

***Magdalene:** Hebrew, "a tower"— see Madeline
Magdalena
Mary Magdalene was a demon-possessed woman who became a Christian and was the first to see the resurrected Jesus. (See John 20:1–18.)

Maggie: A diminutive of Margaret
Maggi, Maggy

MAGDALENA HERBERT
(1878–1938)

was a missionary to the Comanche Indians in Oklahoma.

Magnilda: Old German, "strong in warfare"

Magnolia: From the flower named after French botanist Pierre Magnol

Mahalia: Hebrew, "tender one"
Mahala, Mahalah, Mahalee, Mahali, Mahaliah, Mahalla, Mehalia

MAHALIA JACKSON
(1911–1972)

was one of America's foremost gospel singers. The granddaughter of a slave, she was awarded a Lifetime Achievement Grammy Award.

Mahogany: Spanish, "rich, strong"—also the name of a kind of wood
Mahagony, Mahogani, Mohogany

Maila: Hawaiian variation of Myra, "wonderful"

Maimuna: Swahili, "she who is blessed"

Maire: Scottish variation of Mary, "bitter"

Maisie: A diminutive of Margaret, a Scottish variation of Margery and Margaret

Maisey, Maizie, Mazey, Mazie

Majesta: Latin, "majesty"

Makaleka: Hawaiian variation of Margaret, "pearl"

Makela: Hawaiian variation of Marcella, from Marcia, "fearless, brave, warlike"

Malaika: Swahili, "angel"

Malaka: Hawaiian variation of Martha, "lady, woman"

Maliana: Hawaiian variation of Marian—see that entry

Mallory: Old German, "army counselor"

Mal, Mallorie, Malori, Malorie, Malory

Malvina: Gaelic, "refined, polished"

Mal, Malva, Mavina, Melvina, Melvine

Mandisa: Xhosa (South Africa), "sweet"

Mandy: A diminutive of Amanda

Manda, Mandee, Mandie, Mandy

Manuela: Hebrew, "God is with us"—a Spanish feminine variation of Emmanuel

Manuelita

*Mara: A variation of Mary, "bitter"

Marah

Mara was the name given to the Israelites' first campsite after the Red Sea crossing because of the bitter water found there. (See Exodus 15:22–27.)

Marcella: Latin, "belonging to Mars, warlike"—a feminine variation of Marcel, Marcus

Marcela (Spanish), Marcele, Marcelle (French), Marcha, Marcia, Marcie, Marcille, Marcy, Marsha, Marshe

Marcenya: A modern name, origin and meaning uncertain

Marcia: Latin, "fearless, brave, warlike"—feminine variation of Mark

Marcella, Marci, Marcille, Marcina, Marcy, Marsiella

Marcy: A diminutive of Marcella

Marcey, Marci, Marcie, Marsie

Mare: Irish variation of Mary, "bitter"

Mair, Maire

MARGARET OF NAVARRE (1492–1549)

also known as Marguerite of Navarre, was the sister of King Francis I and a supporter of the Reformation in France.

MARGARET BAXTER (1615–1691)

was the wife of Puritan preacher and writer Richard Baxter.

Margaret: Greek, "pearl"

Greta, Gretchen (German), Gretel, Gretta, Madge, Mag, Maggi, Maggie, Maggy, Marga, Margareta, Margarete, Margarette, Margarita (Italian, Spanish), Margarite, Marge, Margaretta, Margarie, Margerita, Margery, Marget, Margette, Margie, Margita, Margorie, Margory, Margret, Margy, Marje, Marji, Marjie, Marjorey, Marjorie (Scottish),

Marjy, Meg, Megan (Irish), Meggi, Meggy, Meghan, Peg, Peggi, Peggie, Peggy—additional variations are possible

Margarita: A variation of Margaret, "pearl"

Margery: A diminutive of Margaret

Marge, Margi, Margie, Margy, Marje, Marji, Marjorey, Marjorie, Marjy

Marguerite: French, a variation of Margaret, "pearl"

Margarite, Marguerita

MARIA ASPDEN (d. 1900)

joined the China Inland Mission in 1891 and died a martyr in the Boxer Rebellion on July 12, 1900.

Maria: Latin and Spanish, a variation of Mary, "bitter"

Mariah, Marie, Mariya, Marja, Marya (Slavic), Mayra, Mayria

Mariam: Greek, a variation of Mary, "bitter"

Marian: French combination of Mary, "bitter," and Ann, "she who is full of grace"; also a variation of Mary

Mariam, Mariana, Mariane, Marianne, Marion, Maryann, Maryanne

MARIA TAYLOR (1832–1905)

was the wife of James Hudson Taylor. Together, they served as missionaries in China and founded the China Inland Mission.

Marianne: French combination of Marie, from Mary, "bitter," and Ann, "she who is full of grace"

Mariana (Spanish), Mariane, Mariann, Marianna (Italian), Marianne, Maryann, Maryanna, Maryanne

Maribel: A combination of Mary, "bitter," and Belle, "she who is beautiful"

Maribelle, Marybelle, Meribel, Meribella, Meribelle

Maridel: A variation of Mary

Marie: French variation of Mary

Maree, Maretta (Italian), Marrie

Mariel: French variation of Mary

Marietta: Italian variation of Mary

Marigold: From the flower of the same name

Marilyn: A combination of Mary, "bitter," and Lynn, "she who is pretty"

Maralin, Maralynn, Marilin, Marillyn, Marilynne, Marrilyn, Marylin

Marina: Latin, "from the sea"

Marena, Marinna, Marna, Marne, Marni, Marnie

Marion: French variation of Mary—also a name given to boys

Marian, Maryan, Maryonn, Maryonne

MARION HARVEY (d. 1681)

was a young woman martyr of the Scottish Reformation.

MARION SCOTT STEVENSON

was a Scottish missionary to Gikuyu, Kenya, in the early 1900s.

Maris: Latin, "of the sea"

Marisa, Marise, Marisea, Marisee

Marisa: A variation of Maris, "of the sea"

Mareesa, Mari, Marisa (Russian), Marissa, Maryse (Dutch)

Marisol: A combination of Mary, "bitter," and the masculine name Sol, "sun, sunshine"

Marissa: A variation of Maris, "of the sea"

Maressa, Marisa, Marisse, Merissa, Morissa

MARJORY BONAR
(1808–1889)

was the mother of Scottish minister and hymn writer Horatius Bonar.

Marjorie: A variation of Margery, diminutive of Margaret

Marge, Margerey, Margerie, Margery, Margey, Margi, Margie, Margy, Marje, Marjerey, Marjerie, Marji, Marjie, Marjori, Marjory, Marjy

Marla: A variation of Marlene— see that entry

Marlah

Marlene: A combination of Mary, "bitter," and Magdalene, "a tower"

Marla, Marlane, Marlayne, Marlea, Marlee, Marleen, Marlena (German), Marley, Marlie, Marline, Marlyn, Marlynn, Marylynne

Marlo: A possible variation of the masculine name Marlow, "hill near the lake"—also, sometimes a diminutive of Marlene

Marloe, Marlow, Marlowe

Marsha: A variation of Marcia, "fearless, brave, warlike"

Marta: Spanish variation of Martha, "lady, woman"

MARTHA BROOKS
(1608–1680)

was the first wife of Puritan preacher and writer Thomas Brooks.

*Martha: Aramaic, "lady, woman"

Marta, Marth, Marthe, Marthena (Spanish), Marthine, Marti, Martie, Marty, Mattie

Martha was the sister of Mary

and Lazarus.
(See John 11:20, 30.)

Martina: Latin, "warlike"—a feminine variation of Martin

Marta, Marteena, Martie, Martine (French), Marty

Marva: Hebrew, "sage"

MARY SLESSOR
(1848–1915)

was a Scottish missionary to Africa who was affectionately known as "Ma" Slessor. In addition to winning Africans to Christ, she helped found an institute that offered training in trades and medical work.

---

*Mary: Hebrew, "bitter"

Mae, Maira (Irish), Mara (Slavic), Marabel, Marabelle, Mare, Maree (French), Mari, Maria, Mariam, Marian, Mariann, Marianna, Marianne, Maridel, Marie, Mariel, Mariella, Marielle, Marietta, Mariette, Marilee, Marilyn, Marion, Marita, Marja (Swedish), Marjorie (Scottish), Marya, Maryann, Maryanne, Marylin— additional variations are possible

There are six Marys in the New Testament: 1. Mary, the mother of Jesus (Luke 1–2); 2. Mary Magdalene (John 20:1–18); 3. Mary, the mother of James and Joseph (Mark 15:40); 4. Mary, the sister of Martha and Lazarus (John 11); 5. Mary, the mother of John Mark (Acts 12:12); and 6. Mary of Rome (Romans 16:6).

MARY MÜLLER
(1805–1898)

was the wife of preacher and orphanage founder George Müller.

Maryann: A combination of Mary, "bitter," and Ann, "she who is full of grace."

Mariann, Marianne, Maryanna, Maryanne

MARY ANN ALDERSEY
(1797–1868)

was the first woman missionary to China.

Marybeth: A combination of Mary, "bitter," and Beth, a diminutive of Elizabeth,

"consecrated to God"
Maribeth

Maryellen: A combination of Mary, "bitter," and Ellen, a diminutive of Helen, "light"
Mariellen

Marylou: A combination of Mary, "bitter," and Louise, "strong warrior"
Marilou, Maryl, Meryl

Mathna: Swahili, "praise"

Matilda: Old German, "she who is a battle maiden"
Mathilda, Matilde (French), Matti, Mattie, Matty, Tilda, Tildie, Tildy

Mattea: Hebrew, "gift of God"—a feminine variation of Matthew
Mathea, Mathia, Matthea, Matthia

MAUDE CARY
(1808–1889)

was a missionary who went to Morocco in 1901 and worked with the Muslims there for fifty years, learning Arabic, as well as the difficult Berber language.

Maud: A variation of Matilda,

"she who is a battle maiden"
Maude, Maudie

Maura: Irish variation of Mary, "bitter"
Moira, Mora, Morah

Maureen: Irish Gaelic, "little Mary"
Maura, Maurene, Maurine, Moreen, Morena (Spanish), Morene, Moria

Mawuli: Ewe (Ghana), "there is a God"

Mawusi: Ewe (Ghana), "in the hands of God"

Maxine: Latin, "greatest, renowned"—a feminine variation of Maximilian
Max, Maxeen, Maxena, Maxene, Maxi, Maxie, Maxina, Maxine, Maxy

Maxy: A feminine variation of Max, from Maxwell, "Mack's stream," or Maximilian, "greatest, distinguished one"
Maxi, Maxie

MAY ROSE NATHAN
(d. 1900)

was a missionary martyred during the Boxer Rebellion in China.

May: Latin, "month of May"
Mae, Maia, Maye, Mei

Mead: Old English, "meadow"
Meade, Meide

Meara: Irish/Gaelic, "mirth, joy"
Meera, Mira

Megan: Irish/Gaelic variation of Margaret, "pearl"
Meagan, Meaghan (Welsh), Meg, Meghan, Meghanna, Meghanne

Meira: Hebrew, "light"—a feminine variation of Meir

Melanctha: Greek, "dark flower"

Melanie: Greek, "dark, black"
Mel, Mela (Polish), Melaine, Melana (Russian), Melani, Melania, Melannie, Melany, Mellanie, Melli, Mellie, Melly

Melba: Greek, "soft"
Malva, Mellba, Melva

Melelina: Hawaiian, a variation of Marilyn, from Mary, "bitter," and Lynn, "she who is pretty"

Melika: Hawaiian, a variation of Melissa, "honeybee"

Melina: Greek, "she who is beautiful"

Malina, Mallina, Meleana, Meleena, Mellina

Melinda: Latin, "mild, gentle one"
Linda, Lindy, Lynda, Malinda, Malinde, Malynda, Melinde, Mellinda, Melynda

Melissa: Greek, "honeybee"
Lissa, Mel, Meleesa, Melesa, Melicia, Melisa, Melise, Melisha, Melisse, Mellie, Mellisa, Melly, Milli, Millie, Milly

Melody: Greek, "song"
Melodee, Melodey, Melodie, Melodye

Melosa: Spanish, "sweet as honey"

Melvina: Celtic, "like a chieftain"—a feminine variation of Melvin
Malva, Malvinda, Melveen, Melvene, Melvine

Mercedes: Spanish, "mercies"
Mercede, Mercedez

Mercy: Middle Engish, "compassion, mercy"
Mercey, Merci, Mercia, Mercie

Meredith: Old Welsh, "protector of the sea"
Meradith, Meredithe, Meri, Merry

Merry: Old English, "joyful, lighthearted, happy"

Marylee, Merie, Merri, Merrie, Merrielle, Merrilee, Merrily

Merryanne: A combination of Merry, "joyful, lighthearted, happy," and Anne, "she who is full of grace"

Meryl: A variation of Muriel, "sea-bright"

Merrell, Merril, Merryl, Meryle

Meyya: Swahili, "Mary"

Mia: Italian, "mine"

Mea, Meya

Michaela: See Michal

*Michal: Hebrew, "Who is like the Lord?"—a feminine variation of Michael

Micah, Michael, Michaela, Michaeline, Michal, Michele, Micheline, Michelle

Michal was King Saul's youngest daughter and King David's first wife. (See 1 Samuel 14:49; 18:27.)

Michelle: Hebrew, "Who is like the Lord?"—a feminine variation of Michael

Chelle, Macelle, Machelle, Mechelle, Meshella, Micaela, Michaela, Michaeline, Michele, Michelina, Micheline, Michell, Mishaelle, Mishella, Mychelle, Myshell, Myshella

Miguela: Spanish, feminine variation of Miguel, from Michael, "Who is like God?"

Mikala: Hawaiian, a variation of Michelle, "Who is like the Lord?"

*Milcah: Hebrew, "queen, counsel" There are two Milcahs in the Old Testament. (See Genesis 24:15; Numbers 26:33.)

Mildred: Old English, "gentle counselor"

Mil, Milda, Mildrid, Milli, Millie, Milly

> ### MILDRED CABLE
> ### (1878–1952)
>
> served as a missionary in China and the Gobi Desert for thirty-six years, then worked for the British and Foreign Bible Society.

Milena: Hawaiian, a variation of Myrna, "she who is polite, gentle"

Mimi: French variation of Miriam, "bitter, strong"

Mina: German, "love"
Mena, Minette, Minna, Minnette, Minnie

MINA S. EVERETT (1857–1936)

spent most of her life as a Southern Baptist missionary in the frontier regions of the American West, establishing churches and schools. She also served in Brazil and Mexico.

Mindy: Latin, "mild, gentle one"—a diminutive of Melinda
Minda, Mindee, Mindi, Mindie

Minerva: Greek, "she who is wise"
Minnie, Minny, Myna

Minna: Old German, "Will-helmet"—a diminutive of Wilhelmina
Mina, Minda, Minetta, Minette, Minne, Minnie, Minny

Minnie: A diminutive of Mary

and Wilhelmina
Minnee, Minny

MINNIE SUE ANDERSON (1892–1967)

was an author and a missionary to Nigeria.

Mira: A diminutive of Miranda
Mirella, Mirelle, Mirielle, Mirra, Myra

Mirabel: Latin, "great beauty"
Meribel, Meribell, Meribelle, Mira, Mirabella, Mirabelle

Miranda: Latin, "she who is extraordinary"
Maranda, Meranda, Mira, Miran, Mirandala, Mirra, Mirranda, Myra, Myranda, Randa, Randi, Randie, Randy

*Miriam: Hebrew, "bitter, strong"
Mariam, Meriam, Mimi (French), Mirriam, Myriam
Miriam, the sister of Moses, watched over his safety as he floated along the Nile River in a basket. (See Exodus 2:4.) A second Miriam was a daughter of Ezra. (See 1 Chronicles 4:17.)

Mishaela: A modern variation of Michelle, "Who is like the Lord?"

Missy: A diminutive of Melissa, "honeybee"
Missie

Misty: Old English, "mist"
Mysti

Moana: Hawaiian, "ocean"

Moani: Hawaiian, "gentle breeze"

Moira: Irish variation of Mary, "bitter"
Maura, Moyra

Molly: Irish, a variation of Mary
Mollee, Molley, Molli, Mollie

Mona: Irish Gaelic, "noble one" — also a diminutive of Ramona
Moina, Monah, Monica, Monique, Monna, Moyna

Monica: Latin, "adviser, counselor"
Mona, Monika, Moniqua, Monique, Monnica

MONICA
(c. 331–381)

was the mother of early church theologian and writer Augustine of Hippo.

Monique: French variation of Monica, "advisor, counselor"

Montana: Latin, "mountainous"

Morgan: Welsh, "dweller by the sea"
Morgana, Morgane, Morganica, Morganne, Morgen, Morgin

Moriah: Hebrew, "God is my teacher"
Mariah, Moraiah, Moria, Moryah

Morna: Irish, "beloved, affection"
Myrna

Morrow: Origin and meaning unknown

MORROW COFFEY GRAHAM
(1892–1981)

was the mother of evangelist Billy Graham.

Moselle: A feminine variation of Moses, possibly "saved" or "the one drawn out (of the water)"
Mosella, Mozelle

Mudiwa: Shona (Zimbabwe), "beloved"

Muna: Swahili, "hope"

Muriel: Irish Gaelic, "sea-bright"
Merial, Meriel, Merryl, Meryl, Meryle, Murial, Muriella, Murielle

Myra: Latin, "wonderful"—a feminine variation of Myron, "fragrant oil"
Maira, Mira, Myree

Myrna: Irish Gaelic, "she who is polite, gentle"
Meirna, Merna, Mirna, Mirne, Morna, Moyna

Myrtle: Greek, "myrtle"—a flowering shrub
Mertle, Mirtle, Myrta, Myrtia, Myrtie

N

*Naamah: Hebrew, "pleasant, sweetness"
Naava, Naavah, Nama, Nava
(See Genesis 4:22; 1 Kings 14:21.)

Nabila: Swahili, "noble"

Nada: A diminutive of Nadezhda (Russian), "hope"
Nada, Nadia, Nadie, Nadja, Nady, Nadya

Nadine: Slavic, "hope"—a variation of Nada
Nada, Nadean, Nadeen, Nadena, Nadene, Nadia, Nadie, Nadina, Nadiya, Nadya, Nadyna, Nadyne

Nadiya: Swahili, "generous"

Nafia: Swahili, "gift"

Nafisa: Swahili, "precious gem"

Naima: Swahili, "she who is graceful"

Nakawa: Swahili, "she who is beautiful"

Nan: A diminutive of Nancy
Nan, Nana, Nance, Nancee, Nancey, Nanci, Nancie, Nancy, Nanella, Nanelle, Nanette (French), Nania, Nanine, Nanna, Nannette (French), Nannie, Nanny

Nancy: Hebrew, "graceful"—a variation of Ann
Nance, Nancee, Nanci, Nancie, Nanice, Nanncy, Nannie, Nanny, Nansee, Nansey

Naneki: Hawaiian, a variation of Nancy, "graceful"

Nanette: French, a diminutive of Nan
Nannette

Nani: Hawaiian, "beautiful"

Nanyanika: Ewe (Ghana), "God's gift"

*Naomi: Hebrew, "pleasant"

Naoma, Naome, Naomia, Naomie, Noami

Naomi was the mother-in-law of Ruth. Her story can be read in the book of Ruth.

Nariko: Japanese, "gentle child"

Nastasia: Greek, "resurrection"—a diminutive of Anastasia

Nastassia, Nastassya

Nasya: Hebrew, "miracle of God"

Nasia

Natalie: Latin, "child born at Christmas"

Nat, Nata, Natala, Natalee, Natalene, Natalia (Russian), Natalina (Polish), Nataline, Natalya, Natilie, Nattie, Natty, Talia, Talya

Natasha: Russian, a diminutive of Natalie

Nastassia, Natacha, Natascha,

Nathania: Hebrew, "a gift", or "given of God"—a feminine variation of Nathan

Nataniella, Natanielle, Nathaniella, Nathanielle, Netania, Netanya

Nayo: Yoruba (Nigeria), "we have joy"

Neala: Irish Gaelic, "champion"—a feminine variation of Neal

Neale, Nealla, Neila, Neile, Neilla, Neille

Neida: A modern name, possibly a variation of Nita, "grace"

Nell: A diminutive of Helen

Neila, Neilla, Nel, Nella, Nellene, Nellie, Nelly

Nellie: See Nell and Helen

Nell, Nelley

Nellwyn: Old English, "friend of Nell"

Nell, Nellwynn

Nessie: Greek, "pure"—a diminutive of Agnes

Nessa, Nessi, Nessy

Nettie: A diminutive of -ette in names such as Annette

Netta, Netty

Neva: Spanish, "covered in snow, snowy"

Nevada, Nevara, Neve, Nevia

NETTIE FOWLER McCORMICK (1835–1923)

was a Christian philanthropist who helped many become trained for ministry and mission work.

Ngina: Kikuyu (Kenya), "a servant"

Ngozi: Ibo (Nigeria), "blessing"

Nicole: Greek, "victorious people"—a variation of Nicholas

Nichelle, Nichola, Nichole, Nicholette, Nicholle, Nicia, Nicki, Nickie, Nickola, Nicky, Nicola (Italian), Nicole, Nicolea, Nicolla, Nicolle, Nicolli, Niki, Nikita (Russian), Nikki, Nikky, Nikola, Nikole, Nycole, Nykole—additional variations are possible; some of the spelling variations above are used for both boys and girls

Nike: Greek, "victory"

Nika

Nikita: Russian, a variation of Nicole, "victorious people"

Nikki: A variation of Nicole

Nickie, Nicky, Niki, Nikkey, Nikky

Nina: Spanish, "girl"

Neena, Nena, Ninette, Ninnette, Ninya, Nyna

Nisi: Hebrew, "emblem"

Nissi

Nissa: A modern name, origin and meaning uncertain

Nita: Spanish, "grace"—a diminutive of names such as Anita, Juanita

Anita

Nkechi: Ibo (Nigeria), "this is for God"

*Noah: Hebrew, "rest, comfort"

Noa, Noë

Noah was one of the five daughters of Zelophehad. (See Numbers 26:33.)

Noel: French, "Christmas"—a name for both boys and girls

Noela, Noeleen, Noelene, Noeline, Noell, Noella, Noelle (French), Noleen

Noelani: Hawaiian, "heavenly mist"

NOLLIE TEN BOOM
(1890–1953)

was the sister of Corrie ten Boom, a Dutch Christian Holocaust survivor whose family helped many Jews escape from the Nazis during World War II. Nollie's given name was Arnolda.

Nollie: See Olive

Nomble: Xhosa (South Africa), "beautiful"

Nona: Latin, "the ninth"
Nonah, Noni, Nonie, Nonna, Nonnah

Noni: Swahili, "she who is a gift of God"

Nora: Latin, "woman of honor"— also a diminutive of Eleanor
Norah, Norella, Norelle

Noreen: Irish variation of Norma, "pattern, precept"
Norina, Norine

Norma: Latin, "pattern, precept"
Noreen, Normie, Normina

Nura: Swahili, "brightness"

Nurisha: Swahili, "shine light upon"

Nyameke: Akan (Ghana), "gift from God"

Nydia: Latin, "from the nest"
Neda, Nedda, Needia, Nidia

Nyimbo: Swahili, "song"

Nysa: Latin, "goal, aim"
Nissa, Nisse, Nyssa

O

Oceana: A modern name that means "ocean, sea"
Oceanna

Octavia: Latin, "eighth"—a feminine variation of Octavius
Octaviana, Octavianne, Octavie (French), Ottavia (Italian), Tavi, Tavia, Tavie, Tavy

Odele: Possibly German, "rich," or Greek, "song"
Odela, Odelet, Odelina, Odeline, Odella, Odelle, Odellette

Odelia: Hebrew, "praise God"
Odele, Odella, Odellia, Odilia, Otha, Othelia, Othilia

Odessa: Greek, "long voyage"
Odissa, Odyesa, Odyssia

Olabisi: Yoruba (Nigeria), "multiplied joy"

Olena: Russian version of Helen, "light"

Alena, Elena, Lena, Lenya, Olenya, Olina, Olinia

Olethea: A variation of Alethea— Latin, "truth"

Oleta

Olga: Russian, "peace," or Scandinavian, "holy"

Elga, Helga, Olva

PRINCESS OLGA OF KIEV (c. 902–969)

was a Russian ruler who is credited with promoting Christianity. She was the grandmother of Vladimir I, who Christianized what is now Ukraine and southern Russia.

Oliana: Polynesian, "Oleander"

Oleana, Olianna

Olinda: Old English, "holly"

Olive: See Olivia

Olivia: Latin, "olive tree, olive branch"

Liva, Livia (Hebrew), Nola, Nollie, Olia, Oliva, Olive, Olivet, Olivete, Olivette (French), Olivya, Olva

Olubayo: Yoruba (Nigeria), "greatest joy"

Oluremi: Yoruba (Nigeria), "God consoles me"

Olympia: Greek, "from Mount Olympus"

Olimpia, Olympias, Olympie

Omorose: Fon (Benin), "beautiful child"

Oneida: Iroquois (American Indian), "standing rock"

Onella: Greek, "light"

Opal: Sanskrit, "a precious stone"

Opali, Opalina, Opaline

Ophelia: Greek, "help"

Also a famous character in Shakespeare's *Hamlet*.

Ofelia, Ofilia, Ophelie

Oralia: Latin, "golden"

Aurelie, Oralee, Oralie, Orelle, Oriel, Orielle, Orlena, Orlene

Oriana: Latin, "dawn"

Oria, Oriane, Orianna, Orlanna

Orlanda: Old German, "fame of the land," feminine variation of Orlando

*Orpah: Hebrew, "fawn"

Ophra, Ophrah, Oprah, Orpa, Orpha

Orpah was a daughter-in-law of Naomi. (See Ruth 1:4–14.)

Orsa: Latin, "bear"—a variation of Ursula

Orsalina, Orsaline, Orselina, Orseline, Orssa, Ursa

Ortensia: Italian, a variation of Hortense

Ortensa

Oseye: Fon (Benin), "she who is happy"

Ovelia: Spanish, a variation of Ophelia, "help"

P

Pacifica: Latin, "to pacify, to make peace"

Page: French, "young attendant"

Padget, Padgett, Paget, Pagett, Paige

Palma: Latin, "palm tree"

Palmeda, Palmer, Palmira, Palmyra, Pelmira

Paloma: Spanish, "dove"

Palloma, Palometa, Palomita, Peloma

Pamela: Greek, "loving, kind, all honey"

Pam, Pama, Pamala, Pamalla, Pamelia, Pamelina, Pamella, Pamelyn, Pamilla, Pammi, Pammie, Pammy, Pamyla

> **PATIENCE BROOKS**
> **(1608–1680)**
>
> was the second wife of Puritan preacher and writer Thomas Brooks.

Pansy: French, "thought"—also the name of a flower

Pansey, Pansie

Paola: Italian, a feminine variation of Paolo, (Latin) "little"

Paris: The place name of the capital of France

Parris, Parrish

Pat: A diminutive of Patricia, "noble one"

Patience: Latin, "to suffer"

A virtue name popular among

the Puritans.

Patia, Patsy, Patty

Patricia: Latin, "noble one"—a feminine variation of Patrick

Pat, Patrica, Patrice (French), Patrizia (Italian), Patsy, Patte, Pattee, Pattey, Patti, Pattie, Patty, Tricia, Trish, Trisha

> ### PATRICIA MARY ST. JOHN (1919–1993)
>
> was a missionary who served in Morocco for twenty-seven years and founded a school for nurses. She was also a beloved and successful writer of children's books, including the best-selling *The Tanglewoods' Secret* (1948).

Paula: Latin, "petite"—a feminine variation of Paul

Paola (Italian/Spanish), Paolina, Paule, Pauleen, Pauletta, Paulette, Paulina, Pauline, Paulyne

Paulette: See Paula

Peace: Latin, "peace"

A virtue name popular among the Puritans.

Pearl: Latin, "pearl, a jewel"

Pearla, Pearle, Pearleen, Pearlette, Pearlie, Pearline, Perl, Perla, Perle, Perlette

Peggy: A diminutive of Margaret

Peg, Peggie

Peleka: Hawaiian, a variation of Bertha, "she who is radiant"

Pelekila: Hawaiian, a variation of Priscilla, "ancient, worthy"

Penelope: Greek, "weaver"

Pen, Penalopa, Penna, Penney, Pennie, Penny

Peninah: Hebrew, "pearl"

Penina

Penny: Greek, "weaver"—a diminutive of Penelope

Penee, Pennee, Penney, Pennie

Pepita: Spanish, "she shall add"

Pepa, Pepi, Peppie, Peppy, Peta

Pernella: French, a variation of the Greek word for "rock" and a feminine variation of Peter

Perpetua: Latin, "perpetual"

Perry: Middle English, "pear tree"

Perrey, Perri, Perrie

Petra: Greek, "rock"—a feminine variation of Peter

Patrine, Pet, Peta, Peterina, Petria, Petrina, Pietra (Italian)—additional variations are possible

PETRA MALENA "MALLA" MOE (1863–1953)

was a Norwegian who was influenced by American evangelist Dwight L. Moody and became an evangelist in Africa.

Petunia: North American Indian, "petunia flower"

Phares: Hebrew, "bursting forth"—derived from the biblical name Perez

Pheodora: Russian, from the Greek for "gift of God"—a feminine variation of Theodore

Fedora, Feodora, Fyedora

Philana: Greek, "adoring"

Filania, Filanna, Phila, Philena, Philene, Philina, Philine, Phillina

Philantha: Greek, "lover of flowers"

Filanthia, Philanthia, Philanthie

Philene: A feminine variation of Phil or Philip, "lover of horses"

Philiberta: Old English, "very brilliant"—a feminine variation of Filbert

Filberta, Filiberta, Philberta, Philberthe

Philippa: Greek, "lover of horses"—a feminine variation of Philip

Felipa (Spanish), Filipa, Filipia, Filippa (Italian), Pelipa, Pelippa, Philipa, Philippe, Phillipa

Philomena: Greek, "she who is friendly, loving"

Filomena, Mena

Philyra: Greek, "lover of music"

*Phoebe: Greek, "pure, shining, radiant"

Febe, Pheabe, Phebe, Pheby, Phoeboe

Phoebe was a deaconess who carried Paul's epistle to the Romans to the church at Rome. (See Romans 16:1–2.)

Phyllida: Greek, "leafy branch"—a variation of Phyllis

Fillida, Phillida, Phillyda

Phyllis: Greek, "leafy branch"

PHYLLIS THOMPSON
(1906–2000)

served in remote inland China as a missionary for fifteen years, then went on to write forty-four books, including biographies.

Filis, Fillis, Fillys, Fyllis, Philis, Phillis, Philys, Phylis, Phylliss

Pippa: Greek, "lover of horses," a diminutive of Philippa
Pippy

Placidia: Latin, "she who is serene"
Placida

Poleke: Hawaiian, a variation of Paulette, from Paula, "petite"

Polly: A variation of Molly and a diminutive of Mary
Pollee, Polley, Polli, Pollie, Pollyanna

Pomona: Latin, "fruit"

Poppy: Latin, "poppy flower"

Preciosa: Spanish, "she who is precious"

Preye: Ibo (Nigeria), "God's gift or blessing"

Prima: Latin, "first"
Primalia, Primetta, Primina, Priminia

Primrose: Latin, "first rose"
Primarosa, Primorosa

Prisciliana: Spanish variation of Priscilla, "ancient, worthy"

*Priscilla: Latin, "ancient, worthy"
Cilla, Cyla, Prisca, Priscella, Priscille, Prisilla, Prysilla
Priscilla and her husband, Aquila, encouraged the apostle Paul. (See Acts 18:26.)

Prudence: Latin, "good sense, foresight"
A virtue name popular among the Puritans.
Pru, Prudenca, Prudi, Prue

Pualani: Hawaiian, "royal flower"

Pulika: Swahili, "obedience"

Purity: Middle English, "purity"
A virtue name popular among the Puritans.

Q

Queen: Old English, literally queen
Quanda, Queena, Queene, Queenette, Queenie

Querida: Spanish, "dear, beloved"

Quinn: Irish Gaelic, "she who is wise"

Quin

Quintessa: Latin, "essence"

Quintie, Tess, Tessa, Tessie

Quintina: Latin, "fifth"

Quenta, Quentina, Quinta, Quintana, Quintessa

R

*Rachel: Hebrew, "ewe, little lamb"

Rachael, Racheal, Rachele (Italian), Rachelle (French), Rae, Rahel (German), Raquel (Spanish), Raquela, Ray, Raychel, Shell, Shelley, Shellie, Shelly

Rachel was the wife of Jacob and the mother of Joseph and Benjamin. (See Genesis 25:16–20; 29:18; 30:23–24.)

Radhi: Swahili, "forgiveness"

Radhiya: Swahili, "she who is content"

Rae: Old English, "doe"

LaRae, Raeann, Ray, Raye, Rayna

Rafaela: Spanish, a feminine variation of Rafael, "God has healed"

> ### RACHEL SAINT
> ### (1914–1994)
>
> was an evangelical Christian missionary to Ecuador. Her brother, Nate, was among the missionaries killed with Jim Elliot (Elisabeth Elliot's husband) by the Huaorani (Auca) people in South America in 1956.

Rahima: Swahili, "compassionate"

Rahimu: Swahili, "mercy"

Raina: A variation of Regina, "queen, noble woman"

Rainah, Raine, Rainelle, Rainey, Rana, Rane, Ranelle, Raya, Rayana, Rayna, Reyna

Raissa: Old French, "thinker"

Raisa, Razel

Ramona: Spanish, "wise protector"—a feminine variation of Raymond

Mona, Ramonda, Ramonna, Romona, Romonda

Ran: Japanese, "water lily"

Randy: Latin, "admirable"—a diminutive of Miranda

Randa, Randee, Randelle,

Randene, Randi, Randie

Ranielle: A modern name, possibly a variation of Danielle, from Daniel, "God is my judge"

Ranita: Hebrew, "song"
Ranice, Ranit, Ranite, Ranitra, Ranitta

Raphaela: Hebrew, "God heals"—a feminine variation of Raphael, "God has healed"
Rafa, Rafaela, Rafaele, Rafaelia, Rafaella, Rafella, Rafelle, Raphaella, Raphaelle

Raquel: Spanish, a variation of Rachel, "ewe, little lamb"
Raquelle

Rashida: Swahili, "righteous"

Raven: Old English, literally, raven—a large black bird
Ravenna, Ravenne, Rayven

Raya: Hebrew, "she who is a friend"

Rayanne: A combination of Ray, from Raymond, "wise guardian, and Anne, "she who is full of grace"

Razina: Swahili, "strong, patient"

REBECCA ST. JAMES (1977–)

is a Christian pop rock singer, songwriter, speaker, and author. She has won multiple Dove Awards and a Grammy.

Reba: A diminutive of Rebecca
Reyba, Rheba

*Rebecca: Hebrew, "bound"
Becca, Becka, Beckee, Beckey, Beckie, Becky, Beka, Bekka, Bekki, Bekkie, Raba, Rebeca (Spanish), Rebecka, Rebeka, Rebekah, Rebekkah, Rebeque (French), Reveka (Slavic), Revekah, Revekka, Riva, Rivi, Rivkah
Rebekah was the wife of Isaac and the mother of Jacob and Esau. (See Genesis 22:23; 24:67; 25:26.)

Regina: Latin, "queen, noble woman"
Gina, Raina, Raine, Rani, Rayna, Reggi, Reggie, Régine (French), Reina, Reine, Reinetta, Reinette, Reyna, Rina

Rehani: Swahili, "promise"

Rehema: Swahili, "compassion"

Remedios: Spanish, "help, remedy"

Rena: Hebrew, "joy, song"
Reena, Rene, Renee, Reneta, Renette, Renita, Rina

Renata: Latin, "reborn"—the Latin variation of Renée (French)
Ranae, Ranay, Renae, René, Renée, Renelle, Renetta, Renette, Renie, Renisa, Renise, Renita, Rennae, Rennay, Rennie

René: Greek, "peace"—a diminutive of Irene; a name for both boys and girls
Reney, Renie, Rennie

Renée: French, "reborn"
Ranae, Ranay, Ranée, Renae, René, Renelle, Renie, Rennie, Renny

RENÉE OF FRANCE
(1510–1575)

was a Christian noblewoman who helped Protestants facing persecution during the Reformation, including John Calvin.

Renita: Latin, "resistant"
Reneeta, Renyta

Reubena: Hebrew, "behold, a son"—a feminine variation of Reuben
Reuvena

Rhea: Greek, "motherly"
Rea, Rhia, Ria

Rheanna: A modern name of which the origin and meaning are uncertain
Reann, Reanna, Rheana, Rheanne

Rheta: Greek, "well-spoken"

*Rhoda: Greek, "a rose, from Rhodes"
(See Acts 12:14.)

Rhona: Old Norse, "rough island"
Rhona, Roana

Rhonda: Greek, possibly "grand"
Rhodeia, Rhodia, Rhodie, Rhody, Roda, Rodi, Rodie, Rodina, Ronda

Ria: A diminutive of Victoria
Rea

Ricarda: Old German, "powerful ruler"—a feminine variation of Richard
Rica, Ricarda, Richarda, Richardella, Richardene, Richardette, Richardina,

Richardyne, Richel, Richela, Richelle, Richette, Ricki, Riki

Richelle: A feminine variation of Richard, "strong ruler"

Rickie: a diminutive of Frederica
Ricki, Ricky, Rika, Riki, Rikki, Rikky

Rilla: Low German, "small brook"
Rella, Rilletta, Rillette

Risa: Latin, "laughter"
Riesa, Rise, Rysa

Rissa: A diminutive of names such as Clarissa and Marissa

Rita: A diminutive of Margarita
Reeta, Reida, Reita, Rheeta, Rheta, Rieta, Ritta

Riva: Hebrew, "bound"—see Rebecca
Reba, Reeva, Reva, Rifka, Rivi, Rivka, Rivkah, Rivke

*Rizpah: Hebrew, "hot stone" (See 2 Samuel 21:8–14.)

Roanna: A variation of Rosanne, from Rose and Anne, "she who is full of grace"
Ranna, Roanne, Ronni, Ronnie, Ronny

Roberta: Old English, "bright, famous"—a feminine variation of Robert
This popular name has many variations:
Berta, Bertie, Berty, Bobbe, Bobbee, Bobbie, Bobby, Bobbye, Bobette, Bobi, Reberta, Roba, Robbee, Robbey, Robbi, Robbie, Robby, Robeena, Robella, Robelle, Robena, Robetta, Robette, Robin, Robina, Robinette, Robinia, Robyn, Robyna, Robynna, Ruperta (Spanish)

Robin: Old English, "shining with fame"—a diminutive of Robert; a name for both boys and girls
Robee, Robbey, Robbi, Robbie, Robbin, Robby, Robbyn, Robena, Robene, Robenia, Robi, Robina, Robine, Robinia, Robyn, Robyna, Robynette

Rochelle: French, "little rock"
Roch, Rochell, Rochella, Rochette, Roschella, Roschelle, Roshelle, Shell, Shelley, Shelly

Roderica: Old German, "renowned ruler"—feminine variation of Roderick
Rica, Roderiga, Roderiqua, Roderique, Rodriga

Rolanda: Old German, "fame of the land"—a feminine variation of Roland

Orlanda, Orlande, Rolande, Rollande

Roline: Old German, "man"—a diminutive of Caroline
Rolene, Rolleen, Rollene, Rollina, Rolline, Rolyne, Rolynne

Roma: Latin, "eternal city"
Romelle, Romilda, Romina, Romma

Romaine: French, "from Rome"—a feminine variation of Romain
Romane, Romayne, Romeine, Romene

Romola: Latin, "she who is from Rome"
Romala, Roman, Romana, Romella, Romelle, Rommola, Romolla

Rona: Old Norse, "rough island"
Rhona, Ronalda, Ronel, Ronella, , Ronna, Ronnelle

Ronnell: A feminine variation of Ron and Ronald, "mighty power"
Ronel, Ronelle, Ronnel

Ronni: A feminine variation of Ronald, "mighty power"
Ronalda, Ronee, Ronette, Roni, Ronna, Ronnee,

Ronnella, Ronnelle, Ronney, Ronnie, Ronny

Rory: Irish Gaelic, "red king"—a name used for both boys and girls
Rori

Rosa: A Spanish variation of Rose

Rosabel: A combination of Rose and Belle, "beautiful rose"
Rosabella, Rosabelle

Rosalie: An Irish variation of Rose
Rosalee, Rosaleen, Rosaley, Rosalia, Rosalina, Rosaline, Rosalyne, Roselia, Rosella, Roselle, Rozalia, Rozalie, Rozele, Rozelie

ROSALIND GOFORTH (1864–1942)

was the wife of Jonathan Goforth. Together, they served as missionaries in China and Manchuria. She wrote the classic book *How I Know God Answers Prayer.*

Rosalind: Spanish, "beautiful rose"
Ros, Rosalen, Rosalin, Rosalina, Rosalinda, Rosalinde, Rosaline, Rosalinn,

Rosalyn, Roselin, Roselina, Roselinda, Roselinde, Roseline, Roselyn, Roslyn, Roz, Rozali, Rozalia, Rozalin—additional variations are possible

Rosalyn: A combination of Rose and Lynn, "she who is pretty"

Rosalin, Rosalynn, Roselynn, Roslyn, Rozlynn

Rosamond: Old German, "famous protector"

Ros, Rosamonde, Rosemonda, Rosemonde (French), Roz, Rozamond, Rozamonda

Rosana: A combination of Rose and Ana, "she who is full of grace"

Rose: From *rosa*, the Latin name for the flower

Rhodes, Rhodia, Rhody, Rhonda, Rosa (Italian/ Spanish), Rosaleen, Rosalia, Rosalie, Rosalin, Rosalina, Rosaline, Rosanie, Rosario, Roselia, Roselina, Roseline, Rosella, Roselle, Rosena, Rosene, Rosetta (Italian/ Spanish), Rosette (French), Rosey, Rosi, Rosie, Rosina, Rosita, Roslyn, Rosy, Roza, Rozalie, Roze, Rozella, Rozelle, Rozy—additional variations are possible

ROSE PATIENCE GRENFELL (1849–1906)

was the wife of George Grenfell. Together, they served as missionaries in Africa.

Roseanne: A combination of Rose and Anne, "she who is full of grace"

Roanna, Roanne, Rosanna, Rosannah, Rosanne, Roseann, Roseanna, Rozanna, Rozanne

Rosemary: Latin, "dew of the sea"

Rosemaree, Rosemarey, Rosemaria, Rosemarie, Rosmarie, Rozemary

Rowena: Old English, "well-known friend"

Ranna, Rena, Ronni, Ronnie, Ronny, Rowe

Roxanne: Persian, "dawn," or brilliant one"

Rox, Roxana, Roxane, Roxann, Roxanna, Roxene, Roxey, Roxiane, Roxianne, Roxie, Roxine, Roxy, Roxyann, Roxyanna

Ruby: Latin, "red"—a red gemstone

Rubee, Rubetta, Rubette,

Rubey, Rubi, Rubia, Rubie,
Rubina, Rubya

Rufina: Latin, "red-haired"—a
feminine variation of Rufus
Rufeena, Rufeine, Ruffina,
Ruphyna

Rukiya: Swahili, "she who rises
high"

*Ruth: Hebrew, "friend,
companion"
Ruthe, Ruthelle, Ruthi,
Ruthie, Ruthina, Ruthine

Ruth was a loyal daughter-in-
law who moved to Israel with
her mother-in-law, Naomi.
Eventually, she became the wife
of Boaz. You can read their
story in the book of Ruth.

RUTH BELL GRAHAM
(1920–2007)

was born in Quinjiang,
China, the daughter of
medical missionaries. She
was the wife of evangelist
Billy Graham and the
mother of five children.

Ruthann: A combination of Ruth,
"friend, companion," and Ann,
"she who is full of grace"
Ruthanna, Ruthanne

Ruzuna: Swahili, "calm"

S

Sabiha: Swahili, "she who is
graceful"

Sabina: Latin, "Sabine woman
(Italy), woman from Sheba"
Sabine, Sabinna, Sabyna,
Savina, Savine, Sebina,
Sebinah, Zabinah

Sabra: Hebrew, "to rest"
Sabrah, Sebra

Sabrina: Latin, "from the border"
Brina, Sabreena, Sabrinna,
Sabryna, Sebreena, Sebrina,
Zabrina

Saburi: Swahili, "patience"

Sadie: Hebrew, "princess"—a
diminutive of Sarah
Sada, Sadah, Sadelle, Sadye,
Saida, Saidee, Saidey, Saidie,
Saydie, Sydell, Sydella, Sydelle

Safiya: Swahili, "pure"
Safiyah

Sage: Latin, "wise, healthy"
Saige, Sayge

Saida: Swahili, "happy"

Saiha: Swahili, "good"

Sakina: Swahili, "she who is calm"

Sala: Swahili, "prayer"

Salama: Swahili, "peace"

Salina: Latin, "by the salt water"
Saleena

Sally: Hebrew, "princess"—a diminutive of Sarah
Sal, Saletta, Sallee, Salletta, Sallette, Salley, Sallianne, Sallie, Sallyann

*Salome: Hebrew, "peaceful"
Sahlma, Salima, Salma, Salmah, Saloma, Salomea, Salomey, Salomi, Selima, Selma, Selmah, Solome, Solomea

There are two Salomes in the New Testament: one was the daughter of Herodias, who requested that John the Baptist be put to death. (See Matthew 14:6–11.) The other was the mother of James and John, who were asked by Jesus to become His disciples. (See Matthew 10:2.)

Salvia: Latin, "whole, healthy"
Sallvia, Salvina

Samala: Hebrew, "requested of God"
Samale, Sammala

Samantha: Aramaic, "she who listens"—a feminine variation of Samuel
Sam, Samantha, Samey, Sami, Sammee, Sammey, Sammie, Sammy, Simantha, Symantha

Samara: Hebrew, "guarded by God"
Sam, Samaria, Samarie, Sammara, Sammy, Semara

Samuela: Hebrew, "heard by God"—a feminine variation of Samuel
Samella, Samelle, Samuella, Samuelle

Sandra: Greek, "helper, defender of mankind"—a diminutive of Alexandra
Sandee, Sandi, Sandie, Sandrea, Sandrella, Sandrelle, Sandria, Sandrina, Sandrine, Sandy, Sondra, Sonndra, Zandra, Zondra

Sandy: A diminutive of Sandra—a name for both boys and girls
Sandee, Sandi, Sandie

*Sapphira: Greek, "sapphire"—a deep blue gemstone
Safira, Saphira, Sapir, Sapira, Sapphira, Sephira

Sapphira was the wife of Ananias. The couple,

unfortunately, chose to act deceptively when they sold some land and gave only part of the money to the Lord. They were punished with death. (See Acts 5:1–10.)

*Sarah: Hebrew, "princess"

Sara, Sarai, Saraia, Sarena, Sarette, Sari, Sarina, Sarine, Sarita, Saritia, Sarra, Sarrah, Sera, Serah, Serita, Shara, Zara, Zarah, Zaria, Zarita (Spanish)

Sarah was the wife of Abraham and the mother of Isaac. (See Genesis 11:29; 21:1–7.)

Sarah Edwards (1703–1758)

was the wife of Jonathan Edwards, an eminent American preacher, theologian, and missionary.

Sarah Gwynne Wesley (1726–1822)

was the wife of English hymn writer and preacher Charles Wesley.

Sasha: Russian, a diminutive of Alexandra

Sacha, Sascha

Savannah: Spanish, "treeless plain, meadow"

Savana, Savanna, Sevanna

Scarlett: Middle English, "deep red"

Scarlet, Scarletta, Scarlette

Seba: Greek, "from Sheba"

Sabah, Sheba, Shebah

Sebastiane: Latin, "honorable, respected"—a feminine variation of Sebastian

Sebastiana, Sebastianne

Seema: Hebrew, "precious, treasure"

Cima, Cyma, Seemah, Sima, Simah

Sekelaga: Nyakyusa (Tanzania), "rejoice"

Selena: Greek, "the moon"

Celene, Celie, Celina, Celinda, Celine, Salena, Salina, Sela, Selena, Selina, Selinda

Selma: Celtic, "fair"

Anselma, Sellma, Selmah, Zelma, Zelmah

Selwyn: Old English, "friend of the family"

Selwin, Win, Winnie, Winny,

Wyn, Wynn

Senalda: Spanish, "a sign"

September: From the name of the ninth month of the year

Septima: Latin, "seventh"

*Serah: Hebrew, "abundance"
Sera
(See Genesis 46:17.)

Seraphia: A variation of Seraphim, "burning, ardent"

SERAPHIA
(d. c. 125)

was a slave girl of Antioch who shared the gospel with her mistress, Sambine. Both women were later martyred for their faith.

Seraphim: Hebrew, "burning, ardent"
Sarafina, Serafina, Seraphine

Serena: Latin, "she who is calm, serene"
Cerena, Reena, Rena, Sarina, Saryna, Serene, Serenity, Serenna, Serina, Seryna, Sirena

Serwa: Ewe (Ghana), "noble woman"

Shaina: Hebrew, "she who is beautiful"
Shaine, Shana, Shanee, Shani, Shanie, Shanya, Shayne

Shaleen: A modern name of which the origin and meaning are uncertain
Shalene, Shaline, Shelene

Shalom: Hebrew, "peace"—a greeting sometimes used as a name
Shalome, Shalva, Shalvah, Shelom, Shilom, Sholome

Shana: Hebrew, "the Lord is gracious"—a feminine variation of Sean
Sean, Seana, Scanna, Shana, Shanna, Shannah, Shaun, Shauna, Shaunee, Shaunie, Shawn, Shawna

Shandra: modern variation of Sandra, "helper, defender of mankind"

Shani: Swahili, "marvelous"

Shannon: Irish Gaelic, "wise one"—a name for both boys and girls
Channa, Shana, Shane, Shani, Shanna, Shanon

Sharee: A variation of Sherry, "dear, cherished"

Shari: Hungarian, a variation of Sarah, "princess"

Sharlene: Old Gaelic, "man"—a feminine variation of Charles

Sharleen, Sharlina, Sharline, Sharlyne

Sharon: Hebrew, "princess," "of the plain"

Shara, Sharan, Sharen, Sharene, Shari, Sharie, Sharla, Sharyn, Sheran, Sherri, Sherry

Shasta: A name of which origin and meaning are uncertain; the name of a mountain in northern California

Shea: Irish Gaelic, "majestic"— a name for both boys and girls

Shae, Shay, Shaye, Shayla, Shealyn, Shealynn

Sheba: Hebrew, "from Sheba"— also a variation of Bathsheba, "daughter of promise"

Saba, Sabah, Scheba, Shebah, Sheeba, Shieba

Sheena: Hebrew, "the Lord is gracious"

Sheenah, Sheina, Shena

Sheila: Irish, a variation of Cecilia

Seila, Selia, Shayla, Sheila, Sheilah, Shela, Shelia, Shiela

Shelby: Old English, "estate on the ledge"

Shel, Shelbea, Shelbee, Shelbey, Shelbi, Shelbie, Shellby

Shelley: Old English, "sloping meadow"

Schelley, Shell, Shellee, Shelli, Shellie, Shelly

*Sherah: Hebrew, "female relative"

Sheerah

(See 1 Chronicles 7:24.)

Sherry: French, "dear, cherished"

Sharee, Shari, Sharie, Sharrie, Sheree, Sherey, Sheri, Sherie, Sherina, Sherree, Sherrey, Sherri, Sherye

Sheryl: A variation of Shirley, "from the bright meadow"

Cheralyn, Cheralynn, Cherilyn, Cherilynn, Cheryl, Sheralin, Sheralyn, Sherileen, Sherill, Sherilyn, Sherrell, Sherrill, Sherryl, Sheryll

Shifra: Hebrew, "she who is beautiful"

Schifra, Shifrah

Shina: Japanese, "faithful"

Shiri: Hebrew, "my song"

Shira, Shirah, Shirit

Shirley: Old English, "from the bright meadow"

Sher, Sheree, Sheri, Sherlee, Sherli, Sherlie, Sheryl, Shirlee, Shirlene, Shirline

Shona: A feminine variation of Sean, from John, "God is gracious"

Shaina, Shaine, Shana, Shanie, Shonah, Shone, Shoni, Shonie, Shuna

Shoshana: Hebrew, "rose"

Shosha, Shoshanah, Sosaana, Sosannah

*Shua: Hebrew, "rich, noble" (See 1 Chronicles 7:32.)

Shukura: Swahili, "she who is grateful"

Shulamith: Hebrew, "peace"

Shula, Shulamit, Sula, Sulamith

Sibyl: Greek, "prophetess, oracle"

Cybele, Cybil, Cybilla, Sabilla, Sabylla, Sibel, Sibell, Sibella, Sibelle, Sibil, Sibilla, Sibyll, Sybel, Sybella, Sybill, Sybilla, Sybille

Sidonie: Latin, "fine cloth"—*Sidon* is a place name in the Middle East

Sidaine, Sidonia, Sidony, Sydona, Sydonah, Sydonia

Sierra: Spanish, "saw" (for cutting), "mountain range"

Ciera, Cierra, Siera, Sierah, Sierrah, Sierre

Sigfreda: Old German, "peaceful victory"

Sigfreida, Sigfrida, Sigfrieda, Sigfryda

Sigourney: A name of which the origin and meaning are unknown

Sigornee, Sigournee, Sigournie

Sikia: Swahili, "harmony"

Silvia: Latin, "from the forest"—a variation of Sylvia

Silva, Silvann, Silvanna, Silvie, Silvy, Silvya, Sylvia, Sylvie

Simcha: Hebrew, "joy"

Simchah

Simone: Hebrew, "one who hears"—a feminine variation of Simon

Shimona, Shimonah, Simeona, Simona, Simonia, Symona

Sivia: Hebrew, "deer"
Sivya

Socorra: Spanish, "aid, help"
Secorra, Socaria, Succora

Sofia: See Sophia

Solane: Spanish, "sunshine"
Solenne

Soledad: Spanish, "solitude"

Sondra: A variation of Sandra, "helper, defender of mankind, which is a diminutive of Alexandra
Saundra, Sohndra, Zaundra, Zohndra, Zondra

Sonia: Russian, a diminutive of Sophia
Sohnia, Sonja, Sonje, Sonya

Sophia: Greek, "she who is wise"
Sofia, Sofie, Sofiya (Russian), Sofy, Sofya, Sonia, Sonja, Sonya, Sophey, Sophie, Sophy, Zofia (Polish)

Sorcha: Irish Gaelic, "bright, shining"

Sorrel: From the botanical name
Sorel, Sorelle, Sorrell, Sorrelle

Spring: Old English, "springtime"

Ssanyu: Uganda, "happiness"

Stacy: Irish variation of Anastasia—"resurrection"
Stace, Stacee, Stacey, Staci, Stacia, Stacie, Stasey, Stasha, Stasia, Stasie, Stasey, Stasy, Stasya (Russian), Taci, Tacie, Tacy

Star: Old English, literally, star
Starla, Starlene, Starletta, Starlette, Starr

Stella: Latin, "star"
Estella, Estelle, Stela, Stelle

Stephanie: Greek, "crowned one"—a feminine variation of Stephen
Fania, Fanya, Stefa, Stefana, Stefania, Stefanie, Steffa, Steffanie, Steffenie, Stepfanie, Stepha, Stephana, Stephania, Stephene, Stephine, Stevana, Stevena, Stevie, Stevey— additional variations are possible

Stevie: A feminine variation of Steve and diminutive of Stephanie

Stina: Greek, "anointed, Christian"—a diminutive of Christina
Stine

Stormy: Old English, "tempest"
Stormey, Stormie

Subria: Swahili, "patience rewarded"

Sue: See Susan

Summer: Old English, the name of one of the four seasons
Somer, Sommers, Sumer, Summers

Sunny: English, "bright, cheerful"
Sunnee, Sunnie, Sunshine

Surayya: Swahili, "she who is noble"

Susan: Hebrew, "graceful lily"
Sue, Sueann, Susana, Susanetta, Susann, Susanna, Susannah, Susanne, Suse, Susee, Susette (French), Susi, Susie, Susy, Suzan, Suzana, Suzane, Suzanna, Suzanne, Suze, Suzee, Suzetta, Suzette (French), Suzie, Suzy, Zanna, Zannie

*Susannah: Hebrew, "graceful lily"
Suesanna, Susana, Susanna, Suzanna, Zanna, Zannah, Zanne, Zannie
Susanna was among the women whom Christ healed. She showed her appreciation

by joining the other women who followed Christ and the disciples and who helped with their sustenance. (See Luke 8:2–3.)

SUSANNAH SPURGEON (1832–1903)

was the wife of English preacher C. H. Spurgeon. She started and ran the Book Fund, a ministry that supplied books to poor ministers.

SUSANNA ANSLEY WESLEY (1669–1742)

was an author, a teacher, and the mother of nineteen children, including John Wesley and Charles Wesley.

Suzanne: French, a variation of Susan, "graceful lily"
Susanna, Susanne, Suzane, Suzannah, Suzette, Suzzanne, Zanne, Zannie

Suzette: See Susan

Swana: Old English, "swan"

Sybil: A variation of Sibyl,

"prophetess, oracle"

Sibyl, Sibylla, Sybel, Sybella, Sybelle, Sybill, Sybilla

Sydney: Old French, "Saint Denis"

Cydney, Sidney, Sidnie, Sydnie

Sylvia: Latin, "from the forest"

Silva, Silvana, Silvania, Silvanna, Silvia, Silviana, Silvianne, Silvie, Sylva, Sylvana, Sylvanna, Sylviana, Sylvianne, Zilvia, Zylvia

Syntyche: Hebrew, "fortunate"

Syntyche was among the women in the church at Philippi. (See Philippians 4:2.)

T

Tabita: Swahili, "graceful"

*Tabitha: Aramaic, "a gazelle"

Tabatha, Tabbee, Tabbey, Tabbi, Tabbie, Tabby, Tabita, Tabytha

Tabitha (also known as Dorcas) was raised from the dead by the apostle Peter. (See Acts 9.)

Tacita: Latin, "silent one"

Tacey, Tacia, Tacie, Tacye

Taffy: Welsh, "beloved"

Tavi, Tavita, Tevita

Talia: Hebrew, "dew from heaven"

Tali, Tallie, Tally, Talya, Thalia

*Talitha: Aramaic, "maiden, little girl"

Taleetha, Taletha, Talicia, Talisha, Talita

(See Mark 5:41.)

*Tamar: Hebrew, "palm tree"

Tama, Tamara, Tamarah, Tamera, Tamma, Tammara, Tammi, Tammy, Tamora, Tamra, Tamrah, Thamar, Thamara, Thamera

Tamar was Judah's daughter-in-law, who is part of the lineage of David and Christ. (See Genesis 38:12–30; Matthew 1:3.) A second Tamar was the daughter of King David (see 2 Samuel 13:1–19), and a third Tamar was the daughter of David's son Absalom (see 2 Samuel 14:27).

Tamara: See Tamar

Tammey, Tammi, Tammie, Tammy

Tamika: A modern name of which the origin and meaning are uncertain

Tameka, Tamieka, Tamike, Tamique, Temika, Tomika,

Tonica, Tonique

Tammy: A diminutive of Tamara

Tami, Tamie, Tammee, Tammey, Tammi, Tammie

Tamsin: Hebrew, "twin"—a variation of Thomasina

Tamasin, Tamasine, Tamsine, Tamsinne, Tamsyn, Tamsynne, Tamzen, Tamzin

Tamu: Swahili, "she who is sweet"

Tanisha: A modern name of which the origin and meaning are uncertain

Taneesha, Taniesha, Tanitia, Tannicia, Tannisha, Teneesha, Tinecia, Tynisha

Tansy: Greek, "immortality"

Tansee, Tansey, Tansia, Tanzey, Tanzie

Tanya: Russian, "fairy princess"

Tahnya, Tana, Tania, Tanita, Tanja, Tonya

***Taphath:** Hebrew, "a drop of myrrh"

Taphath was one of the daughters of King Solomon. (See 1 Kings 4:11.)

Tara: Irish Gaelic, "rocky hill"

Tarah, Tari, Taria, Tarra,

Tarrah, Taryn, Terra

Taraji: Swahili, "faith"

Taralynn: A combination of Tara, "rocky hill," and Lynn, from Linda, "she who is pretty"

Taralyn, Taralynne

Tari: See Tara

Taryn: A variation of Tara, "rocky hill"

Taran, Tarin, Tarina, Tarnia, Tarryn, Taryna

Tasha: Russian, "Christmas child"—also a diminutive of Natasha

Tahsha, Tashey, Tashi (Slavic), Tashina, Tasia, Taska, Tasya

Tatum: Old English, "cheerful"—a feminine variation of Tate

Tata, Tate

Tauna: A modern name of which the origin and meaning are uncertain

Taylor: Middle English, "tailor"

Tailor, Tayler

Teague: Irish Gaelic, "poet"

Teagan, Tegan, Teigan, Teigen, Teigue

Tecia: Greek, "fame, of God"

Teccia, Tekia, Tekli, Telca,
Telka, Thekla

Telisa: A modern name, possibly
based on Lisa, which is often a
diminutive of Elizabeth

Temira: Hebrew, "tall"

Temora, Timora

Temperance: Latin, "moderation"
A virtue name popular among
the Puritans.

Tendayi: Shona (Zimbabwe),
"give thanks"

Teodora: Spanish, a feminine
form of Teodoro, which is a
variation of Theodore, "gift of
God"

Terema: Swahili, "cheerful"

Terena: A feminine variation of
Terence

Tareena, Tarena, Tarina,
Tereena, Terenia, Terenne,
Terina, Terrena, Terrene,
Terriell, Terriella, Terrin,
Terrina, Teryl, Teryll

Teresa: See also Theresa

Terasa, Terasina, Terasita,
Terecena, Teresia (Spanish),
Teresina, Teresita (Spanish),
Teresse, Tereza, Terezita,
Terosina, Terrie, Terry, Tersa,

Tersia, Tesa, Tesia, Tess, Tessa,
Tessie, Tessy

> **TERESA OF AVILA**
> **(1515–1582)**
>
> was a Christian mystic,
> writer, and monastic
> reformer of the Middle Ages.

Terra: Latin, "earth"

Tera, Terah, Terrah

Terri: A diminutive of Theresa

Terea, Teree, Terell, Terella,
Teri, Terie, Terree, Terrey,
Terry (this variation also used
for boys), Terrye

Tertia: Latin, "third"

Tercia, Tersha, Tersia

Tess: A variation of Tessa and a
diminutive of Teresa

Tessa: A diminutive of Teresa

Tess, Tessie, Tessy, Teza

Tessie: See Teresa

Thaddea: A feminine variation of
Thaddeus, "courageous, tender"

Tada, Taddie, Thada, Thadda,
Thaddie, Thadee

Thalassa: Greek, "from the sea"

Talassa

Thalia: Greek, "to flourish"

Talia, Thaleia, Thalie, Thalya

Thelma: Greek, "nursing"

Telma, Thellma

Themba: Zulu (South Africa), "trusted"

Theodora: Greek, "gift of God"—a feminine variation of Theodore

Dora, Fedora, Feodora (Russian), Fyodora, Tedda, Teddey, Teddi, Teddie, Teodora, (Spanish), Teodosia (Italian), Theda, Theo, Theodosi, Theodosia, Todora

THEODORA
(d. c. 120)

was a woman martyred under Emperor Decius for refusing to offer sacrifices to Roman idols.

Theophania: Greek, "God's appearance"

Teofanie, Teophania, Teophanie, Theofania, Theophanie

Theophila: Greek, "God-loving"

Teofila, Teophila, Theofila

Theresa: Greek, "harvester"

Resa, Taresa, Tera, Terasa, Teresa, Terese, Teresia, Tereza, Teri, Terri, Terrie, Terry, Tess, Tessa, Tessi, Tessie, Tessy, Therese, Tresa, Treza, Zita— additional variations are possible

THEODOSIA ALLEINE
(1634–1668)

was the wife of Puritan minister Joseph Alleine.

Thomasa: Greek, "twin"—a feminine variation of Thomas

Thomasina, Thomasine, Toma, Tomasa, Tomasina, Tomasine, Tommi, Tommie, Tommy

Thora: Old Norse, "thunder"—a feminine variation of Thor

Thordia, Thordis, Tyra

Tia: Spanish, "aunt"

Thia, Tiana, Tiara

Tiara: Latin, "headdress"

Tyara

Tiberia: Latin, "the River Tiber"

Tibbie, Tibby, Tyberia

Tierra: Spanish, "earth"

Tiffany: Old French, "appearance of God," from Theophania

Teffan, Teffany, Thefania, Theophania, Tifara, Tiff, Tiffan, Tiffaney, Tiffani, Tiffanie, Tiffie, Tiffney, Tiffy, Tiphani, Tiphanie, Tiphara, Tyffany

Tilda: A diminutive of Matilda

Thilda, Thilde, Tildie, Tildy, Tilley, Tillie, Tilly

Timothea: Greek, "honoring God"—a feminine variation of Timothy

Thea, Tim, Timi, Timmey, Timmi, Timmie, Timotheya

Tina: A diminutive of names ending with -tina or -tine, but increasingly a proper name in its own right

Teena, Teenie, Teina, Tena, Tine, Tiny

Tira: Hebrew, "enclosure"

*Tirzah: Hebrew, "pleasantness"

Thersa, Thirsa, Thirza, Thirzah, Thursa, Thurza, Thyrza, Tierza, Tirza, Tyrzah (See Numbers 26:33.)

Tisha: A diminutive of names ending with -ticia

Ticia, Tish

Tita: Greek, "of the giants"— possibly a feminine variation of Titus, "honor"

Teeta, Tyta

Tivona: Hebrew, "fond of nature"

Tibona, Tiboni, Tivoni

Toby: Hebrew, "God is good"

Thobie, Thoby, Toba, Tobe, Tobee, Tobelle, Tobey, Tobi, Tobiah, Tobye

Tomasa: Spanish, a feminine variation of Tomás, from Thomas, "twin"

Tamasa, Tomana, Tomasena, Tomasina, Tomaza, Tomeseta

Toni: Latin, "priceless"—a diminutive of Antoinette

Tona, Tonee, Toney, Tonia, Tonie, Tony, Tonya

Topaz: Latin, a gemstone that is found in various colors—blue, brown, and yellow

Topaza

Tori: Latin, "victory"—a diminutive of Victoria

Torey, Toria, Torie, Torrey, Torrye, Tory

Tosan: Shekiri (Nigeria), "God knows the best"

Tracy: A diminutive of Theresa—a name for both boys and girls

Trace, Tracee, Tracey, Traci, Tracie, Trasey

Tricia: A diminutive of Patricia

Trichia, Tris, Trisa, Trish, Trisha, Trisia, Trissina

Trina: A diminutive of Katrina

Treena, Treina, Trenna, Trinette, Trinnette

Trinity: Latin, "triad"

Tini, Trini, Trinidad, Trinidade, Trinita, Trinitee, Trinitey

Trisha: See Patricia

Trixie: Latin, "bringer of gladness"—a diminutive of Beatrice

Trix, Trixee, Trixey

Trudy: Old German, "beloved"—a diminutive of Gertrude

Truda, Trude, Trudey, Trudi, Trudie, Trudye

*Tryphena: Greek, "delicate"

Tryphena was one of two women whom the apostle Paul commended for devoted service to the church in Rome. (See Romans 16:12.)

*Tryphosa: Greek, "delicate"

Tryphosa may have been a twin sister of Tryphena. Paul praised her for her wonderful labors for the Lord. (See Romans 16:12.)

Tsifira: Hebrew, "crown"

Tumaini: Swahili, "hope"

Twyla: Middle English, "woven of double thread"

Tuwyla, Twila, Twilla

Tyana: A modern name of which the origin and meaning are uncertain; possibly a variation of Dana, "she who is from Denmark," or Dyana, "divine one"

Tyler: Old English, "maker of tiles"— a name for both boys and girls

Tyller

U

Udele: Old English, "prosperous"

Uda, Udella, Udelle, Yudella, Yudelle

Ula: Celtic, "sea jewel"

Eula, Ulla, Yulla

Ulrica: Old German, "power of the

home"—a feminine variation
of Ulrich

Rica, Ricka, Ula, Ulka, Ullrica,
Ulrika, Ulrike

Una: Latin, "one, unity"

Euna, Ona, Oona, Unah

Unity: Middle English, "unity"

A virtue name popular among
the Puritans.

Unita, Unite, Unitey

Urania: Greek, "heaven"

Ourania, Ouranie, Urainia,
Uraniya, Uranya

Urbana: Latin, "of the city"—a
feminine variation of Urban

Urbanna

Ursula: Latin, "little bear"

Orsa, Orsala, Orsola (Italian),
Ulla, Ursa, Ursala, Ursel,
Urselina (Spanish), Ursella,
Ursina, Ursine, Ursola, Ursule,
Ursulette, Ursulina, Ursuline

Uzuri: Swahili, "beauty"

V

Val: A diminutive of names such
as Valentina and Valerie

Valentina: A feminine variation

of Valentine, "strong, brave"

Teena, Teina, Tena, Tina,
Val, Vale, Valentia, Valentine,
Valida, Valina, Vallatina, Valli,
Vallie, Vally

Valerie: Latin, "strong"

Val, Valari, Valaria, Valarie,
Vale, Valeree, Valerey, Valeria
(Italian), Valeriana (Spanish),
Valery, Vallarie, Valleree,
Vallerie, Vallery, Vallie,
Vallorie, Vallory, Valorie—
additional variations are
possible

Valonia: Latin, "shallow valley"

Vallonia, Vallonya, Valonya

Valora: Latin, "courageous"

Vallora, Valloria, Vallorie,
Vallory, Valoria, Valorie,
Valory, Valorya, Valoura,
Valouria

Vanessa: A name invented by
Jonathan Swift for his poem
"Cadenus and Vanessa" (1713)

Nessa, Nessi, Nessie, Nessy,
Van, Vanesa, Vanesse, Vanetta,
Vanna, Vannessa, Vannie,
Vanny, Venesa, Venessa,
Venetta, Vinessa

Vania: A feminine variation of
Ivan, the Russian version of
John, "gift of God"

Vanya

Varda: Hebrew, "rose"

Vardia, Vardina, Vardis

*Vashti: Persian, "beautiful"

Vashti was the wife of King
Ahasuerus of Persia, but
after falling out of favor with
the king, she was replaced by
Esther. This fascinating story
is found in Esther 1–2.

Velma: A diminutive of
Wilhelmina

Bellma, Vehlma

Venetia: Latin, "kindness,
forgiveness"

Vanecia, Vanetia, Venecia,
Veneta, Venetta, Venezia,
Venice, Venise, Venita

Venus: Latin, "love, loveliness"

Venusa, Venusina, Venusita

Vera: A diminutive of Veronica

Veira, Veradis, Verasha,
Verena, Verene, Veria, Verita

Verena: Old German, "defender"

Varena, Varina, Vera, Veradis,
Vereena, Verene, Verina,
Verine, Verna, Veryna

Verna: Latin, "springtime,
springlike"

Verda, Verne, Verneta,
Vernetta, Vernette, Vernice,
Vernie, Vernise, Vernisse,
Vernita, Virna, Vyrna

Verona: A diminutive of Veronica

Verone

Veronica: Latin, "true likeness"

Roni, Ronica, Ronika,
Ronne, Ronnee, Ronni,
Ronnie, Veira, Vera (Slavic),
Veronice, Veronicka, Veronika,
Veroniqua

Vespera: Latin, "evening star"

Vesperina

Vicky: A diminutive of Victoria

Vicci, Vickey, Vicki, Vickie,
Vicky, Vikkey, Vikki, Vikky

Victoria: Latin, "the victorious"—a
feminine variation of Victor

Toria, Torie, Toya, Vic,
Vicci, Vici, Vickee, Vickey,
Vicki, Vickie, Vicky, Victoire
(French), Victoriana, Victorie,
Victorina, Viktoria, Viktorina,
Vitoria (Spanish), Vittoria
(Italian)

Vida: Hebrew, "loved one"—a
diminutive of Davida

Veda, Vidette, Vieda, Vita,
Vitia

Vienna: A modern name of
which origin and meaning are

uncertain—possibly a place name

Vigilia: Latin, "wakefulness"

Vilhelmina: A variation of Wilhelmina, from William, "resolute protector"

Vilhelmine, Villhelmina

Vilma: Russian, a diminutive of Vilhelmina

Wilma

Vina: A diminutive of Davina

Vena, Veina, Vinetta, Vinette, Vinia, Vinica, Vinita, Vinya

Vincentia: A feminine variation of Vincent, "conqueror"

Vicenta, Vicentia, Vincenta, Vincetta, Vinette

Vinette: A feminine variation of Vinny, from Vincent, "conqueror"

Viola: A variation of Violet

Violet: Latin, "a violet flower"

Vi, Viola, Viole, Violetta, Violette, (French)Viollet, (French)Voilletta, Vyolet

Virginia: Latin, "maiden, virgin"

Genia, Genya, Gigi, Gina (Italian), Ginger, Ginia, Ginni,

Ginnie, Ginny, Ginya, Jinia, Jinnie, Jinny, Virgie, Virginie (French), Virgy, Virgye— additional variations are possible

Vita: Latin, "life"

Vitas, Vitella, Vitia

Viva: Latin, "full of life"

Vivca, Vivva, Vyva

Vivian: Latin, "living"

Vi, Viv, Vivia, Viviana, Viviane, Vivianna, Vivianne, Vivie, Vivien, Vivina, Vivyan, Vivyana

Vonette: A variation of Yvonne, "knight of the lion"

VONETTE ZACHARY BRIGHT
(c. 1921–)

was the cofounder of Campus Crusade for Christ with her husband, Bill Bright, in 1951.

Vonna: A variation of Yvonne, "knight of the lion"

Vynn: A variation of Vina—see that entry

Vynetta, Vynette

W

Wainika: Hawaiian, a variation of Juanita, "God's gracious gift"

Walanika: Hawaiian, a variation of Veronica, "true likeness"

Walda: Old German, "powerful warrior"—a feminine variation of Walter

Wallis: Old English, "from Wales"—a feminine variation of Wallace
Walless, Wallie, Walliss, Wally, Wallys

Wambui: Kikuyu (Kenya), "singer"

Wanaka: Hawaiian, a variation of Wanda, "wanderer"

Wanda: Old German, "wanderer"
Vanda (Czech), Vonda, Wahnda, Wandy, Wenda, Wendaline, Wendi, Wendy, Wendye

Wangai: Kikuyu (Kenya), "born from God"

Wendy: From *Peter Pan* by James Barrie (1880–1937)—also a diminutive of Gwendolyn
Wenda, Wendee, Wendey, Wendi, Wendie, Wendye

Wenona: Old English, "provider of bliss"
Wenonah, Winona, Wynona

Whitney: Old English, "from the white island"
Whitnea, Whitnee, Whitni, Whitnie, Whitny

Wilhelmina: A feminine variation of William, "resolute protector"
Billie, Elma, Helma, Helmina, Mina, Minnie, Minny, Valma, Velma, Vilhelmina, Vilma, Wilene, Wilhemine (Danish), Willa, Willamina, Willamine, Willandra, Willemina, Willetta, Willette, Williamina, Willmina, Wilma, Wilmena, Wilmette, Wilmina, Wylma— additional variations are possible

Willow: Middle English, "willow tree"

Wilma: A diminutive of Wilhelmina
Valma, Vilma, Willma, Wilmina, Wylma

Wilona: Old English, "desired"
Wilone

Winifred: Old English, "friend of peace"
Freda, Freddi, Freddie, Freddy,

Fredi, Fredy, Wenefreda,
Wina, Winafred, Winefred,
Winefreda, Winfrieda,
Winifryd, Winnie, Winnifred,
Wyn, Wynelle, Wynette,
Wynifred, Wynn, Wynne,
Wynnifred

Winnie: A diminutive of
Winifred

Winona: Native American Indian
(Sioux), "firstborn daughter"
Wenona, Wenonah, Winnie,
Winoena, Winonah, Wynona

Wren: Old English, literally, wren

Wyetta: A feminine variation of
Wyatt, "small fighter"

Wynelle: A variation of Wynne,
"she who is fair, pure"

Wynne: Old Welsh, "she who is
fair, pure"
Win, Winne, Winnie, Winny,
Wyn, Wynelle, Wynn

X

Xanthe: Greek, "golden yellow"
Xantha

Xaviera: Basque, "new house"—a
feminine variation of Xavier

Xenia: Greek, "hospitable"
Cena, Xeenia, Xena, Xene,
Ximena, Zeena, Zena, Zenia,
Zina, Zyna

Xin: Chinese, "elegant"

Xylia: Greek, "of the woods"
Xylina, Xylona, Zylina

Y

Yaffa: Hebrew, "she who is lovely"
Jaffa, Yaffah

Yakira: Hebrew, "precious"
Yakirah

Yancey: A name of which the
meaning and origin are
uncertain—possibly a Native
American word meaning
"Englishman"
Yancee, Yancie, Yancy

Yedida: Hebrew, "dear friend"
Yedidah

Yelena: Latin, "lily"

Yemina: A feminine variation of
Benjamin, "son of the right
hand"

Yetta: Old English, "to give,
giver"—a diminutive of
Henrietta
Yette

Ynez: Greek, "pure"—a Spanish

variation of Agnes

Ines, Inez, Ynes, Ynesita

Yolanda: Greek, "violet flower"

Iola, Iolanda, Iolande, Jolanna, Jolanne, Yalinda, Yalonda, Yola, Yolande, Yolane, Yolantha, Yolanthe, Yolette, Yollande

Yonina: Hebrew, "dove"

Jona, Jonina, Yona, Yonah, Yonina, Yoninah, Yonita

Yosepha: Hebrew, "Jehovah increases"—a feminine variation of Joseph

Josefa, Josepha, Yosefa

Yoshe: Japanese, "lovely"

Yoshi: Japanese, "good"

Ysabel: Hebrew, "pledged to God"—a variation of Elizabeth

Yabella, Yabelle, Ysabell, Ysabella, Ysabelle, Ysbel

Ysanne: A modern combination of Ysabel, "pledged to God," and Anne, "she who is full of grace"

Ysande, Ysanna

Yvette: A diminutive of Yvonne

Ivett, Ivetta, Ivette, Yevette, Yvedt, Yvetta

Yvonne: French, "knight of the lion"

Evona, Evonne, Ivetta, Ivona (Russian), Ivone (Portuguese), Ivonne, Vonna, Yevette, Yve, Yvetta, Yvette

Z

Zabina: A variation of Sabina, "Sabine woman (Italy), woman from Sheba"

Zahavah: Hebrew, "gilded"

Zachava, Zachavah, , Zahava, Zehavah, Zehavit

Zahra: Swahili, "blossom"

Zaina: Swahili, "she who is beautiful"

Zakiya: Swahili, "she who is smart"

Zalira: Swahili, "flower"

Zandra: A variation of Sandra, "helper, defender of mankind," and a diminutive of Alexandra, from Alexander, "he who defends"

Zahndra, Zandie, Zandy, Zanndra, Zohndra, Zondra

Zanna: A diminutive of Susanna

Zana, Zanne, Zannie

Zara: Hebrew, "dawn"
Zaira, Zarah, Zaria, Zarina,
Zarinda

Zarifa: Swahili, "graceful"

Zawadi: Swahili, "a gift has come"

Zelda: A diminutive of Griselda
Selda, Zeilda, Zelde

Zelia: Hebrew, "she who is
zealous"
Zele, Zelie, Zelina

Zelma: Old German, "helmet
of God"—a diminutive of
Anselma
Zelima, Zellma

Zena: Greek, "welcoming"—a
variation of Xenia
Zeena, Zeenia, Zeenya,
Zenia, Zenya, Zina

Zephyr: Greek, "west wind"
Sefarina, Sefira, Sephira, Zefir,
Zefiryn, Zephira, Zephirine,
Zephyra, Zephrine

Zera: Swahili, "dawn"

*Zeruiah: Hebrew, "balsam from
Jehovah"
(See 1 Chronicles 2:16.)

Zetta: Hebrew, "olive"
Zayit, Zeta, Zetana

Zevida: Hebrew, "gift"
Zevuda

Zhane: A modern name of which
the origin and meaning are
uncertain

Zhi: Chinese, "character"

Zhin: Chinese, "treasure"

Zhuo: Chinese, "brilliant"

Zia: Latin, "grain"
Zea

*Zibiah: Hebrew, "a female
gazelle"
(See 2 Kings 12:1.)

*Zillah: Hebrew, "shadow"
Zila, Zilla, Zylla, Zyllah
(See Genesis 4:19–23.)

Zina: Swahili, "beautiful"

Zinnia: Latin, the name of a
popular and colorful flower
Zeenia, Zina, Zinia, Zinnya,
Zinya

*Zipporah: Hebrew, "little bird"
Sippora, Sipporah, Zipora,
Ziporah, Zippora
Zipporah was the wife of
Moses. (See Exodus 2:21.)

Zita: Greek, "seeker"—a

diminutive of names such as
Rosita
Zeeta, Zyta

Ziva: Hebrew, "to shine brightly"
Zeeva, Zeva, Ziv, Zivit

Zoe: Greek, "life"
Zoee, Zoeline, Zoelle, Zoey,
Zoie

Zoila: Spanish, a feminine
variation of Ziolo, which is
derived from the Greek Zoe

Zola: Italian, "lump of earth"

Zona: Latin, "belt, girdle"—the
name given to the belt in the
constellation of Orion
Zonia

Zora: Slavic, "golden dawn"
Zahrah, Zarya, Zorah,
Zorana, Zoreen, Zorene,
Zorina, Zorine, Zorna, Zorra,
Zorrah, Zorya, Zoya

Zuna: Bobangi (Nigeria),
"abundance"

Zuri: Swahili, "beautiful"

Zuwena: Swahili, "good"

Boys' Names
A-Z

A

*Aaron: Hebrew, "enlightened one"

Aaran, Aaren, Aarin, Ahren, Aron, Arran, Arrand

Aaron was one of the most important men of the Old Testament. He was the brother of Moses and the first high priest of Israel. Read about him in the books of Exodus, Leviticus, Numbers, and Deuteronomy.

Abbott: Hebrew, "father"

Abbey, Abbot, Abott

*Abel: Hebrew, "breath of life"

Abe, Abell, Avel

Abel was the second son of Adam and Eve and was murdered by his older brother, Cain. Read Abel's story in Genesis 4:1–15 and Hebrews 11:4; 12:24.

Abelard: Old German, "noble one"

Abelhard

*Abiah: Hebrew, "God is my father"

Abia, Abiel, Abija, Abijah

There were four men in the Bible named Abiah. (See 1 Samuel 8:2; 1 Chronicles 3:10; 1 Chronicles 7:8; Luke 1:5.) Also, one woman was named Abiah. (See 1 Chronicles 2:24.)

*Abner: Hebrew, "father of lights"

Ab, Abbie, Abby, Ebner

Abner served under his cousin Saul as captain of the Hebrew army. (See 1 Samuel 14:50–51; 17:55–57.)

*Abraham: Hebrew, "father of a multitude"

Abe, Abie, Abrahm, Abram, Ibrahim (Arabic)

Abraham was one of the most important patriarchs in the Old Testament. He was noted for believing God and thereby being justified by his faith. (See, for example, Romans 4:3.) Abraham was also known as a "friend of God" (see, for example, James 2:23), and in offering up his son Isaac, he became a model of God the Father, who offered up His

Son for the atonement of our sins. Read about Abraham primarily in Genesis 11–25.

ABRAHAM LINCOLN (1809–1865)

was the sixteenth president of the United States and one of the most beloved men in American history.

Ace: Latin, "one"—usually a nickname or an endearment
Acey

*Adaiah: Hebrew, "he who is pleasing to God"
Adia, Adiah
Adaiah was a popular Hebrew name, and several minor characters in the Old Testament were called Adaiah.

Adair: Scottish, "from the brook by the oak grove"
Adaire, Adare, Adaren, Aderrick

*Adam: Hebrew, "made from the earth"
Adamo (Italian), Adams
Adam was the first human created by God.
(See Genesis 1–3.)

ADAM CLARKE (1762–1832)

was an English Methodist pastor and a popular Bible commentator.

Addis: Old English, "child of Adam"
Ad, Addison, Addy

*Adlai: Hebrew, "God's justice"
(See 1 Chronicles 27:29.)

Adler: Old German, "he who is brave"

Adolph: Old German, "noble wolf"
Adolf, Adolfus, Adolphus, Dolf, Dolph, Dolphe, Dolphus

ADONIRAM JUDSON (1788–1850)

was a renowned missionary to India and Burma.

*Adoniram: Hebrew, "God is mighty!"
Ad
(See 1 Kings 4:6; 5:14.)

Adrian: Latin, derived from the

area of Adrian, Italy

Adrien, Adrion

ADONIRAM JUDSON (A. J.) GORDON (1836–1895)

was given his first and middle names in honor of the missionary of that name. A. J. Gordon was a popular Baptist pastor in Boston, the founder of Gordon College and Divinity School, and the author of several books on the Christian life.

*Adriel: Hebrew, "God, my majesty"

Adrial

(See 1 Samuel 18:19; 2 Samuel 21:8.)

*Aeneas: Greek, "he who is praiseworthy"

Aeneas was a paralytic man healed by the apostle Peter. (See Acts 9:33–34.)

*Agabus: Hebrew, "locust"

(See Acts 11:28; 21:10–11.)

Aidan: Latin, "he who helps"

Aden, Adin, Aiden, Aydan

AIDEN WILSON (A. W.) TOZER (1897–1963)

was a pastor with the Christian and Missionary Alliance denomination and the author of several classic Christian books, most notably *The Knowledge of the Holy* and *The Pursuit of God*.

Aiken: English, "from the oak"

Ainsley: Scottish, "from my meadow"

Ainsleigh, Ansley

Akins: Yoruba (Nigeria), "he who is courageous"

Akens

Alain: French, a variation of Alan, "attractive man" or "fair one"

Alair: Latin, "he who is joyful"—a variation of Hillary

Alaire, Alare

Alan: Celtic, "attractive man" or "fair one"

Al, Alain (French), Alano (Spanish), Allan, Allen, Allyn

Alaric: German, "ruler"

Al, Alar, Larry

Aldo: Italian, "rich man"

Aldous: Old German, "wise man"
Al, Aldis

Aldred: Old English, "he who is wise"
Eldred

Aldrich: Old English, "wise man"
Aldric, Aldrick, Aldridge, Eldric, Eldrick, Eldridge

***Alexander:** Greek, "he who defends"
Al, Alec, Alejandro (Spanish), Aleksander, Alessandro (Italian), Alex, Alexis, Lex, Sandy

At least three Alexanders are named in the Bible. (See Mark 15:21; Acts 4:6; 19:33—Some scholars say this is the same Alexander later referenced in 2 Timothy 4:14.)

> **ALAN REDPATH**
> (1907–1989)
>
> was a popular British pastor, speaker, and author.

Alastair: Irish variation of Alexander, "he who defends"
Alastar, Alistair

Alban: Latin, "fair-complected one," or from the area of Alba, Italy
Albany, Alben, Albin

Albert: Old German, "he who is brilliant"
Al, Alberto (Spanish), Bert, Bertie, Berty, Elbert

> **ALBERT BENJAMIN (A. B.) SIMPSON**
> (1844–1919)
>
> was the founder of the Christian and Missionary Alliance denomination and the author of many excellent books on the Christian faith.

> **ALEXANDER CAMPBELL**
> (1788–1866)
>
> was an evangelist and the cofounder of the Disciples of Christ denomination.

Alden: Old English, "he who is friendly"
Aldan, Aldin

Alfred: Old English, "wise counselor"

Al, Alf, Alfie, Alford, Alfredo, Alvord

ALEXANDER CRUDEN (1699–1770)

was an early compiler of the concordance to the Bible that bears his name, which is still in print.

Algernon: Old French, "noble warrior"
Alger, Elger, Elgernon

Allard: Old German, "he who is determined"
Alard

Allison: Old German, "he who is pious"
Al, Alison, Ally

Aloysius: Old German, "well-known warrior"

*Alpheus: Hebrew, "transient"
Alf, Alphaeus
(See Matthew 10:3; Mark 2:14; 3:18; Luke 6:15; Acts 1:13.)

Alphonse: Old German, "he who is ready for battle"
Al, Alf, Alfie, Alfonso (Italian),

Alonzo (Spanish), Alphonsus

Alton: Old English, "from the old town"
Allton, Altan, Alten

*Alvah: Hebrew, "injustice"
Alva
(See Genesis 36:40; 1 Chronicles 1:51.)

*Alvan: Hebrew, "he who is sublime"
(See Genesis 36:23; 1 Chronicles 1:40.)

Alvin: Hebrew, "he who is beloved"
Al, Alwin, Alwyn, Vin, Vinny

Amadeo: Italian, "loved God"
Amado, Amador

Amadeus: Latin, "lover of God"

Ambrose: Greek, "immortal one"
Ambrosio

Ames: French, "he who is friendly"
Possibly from the Latin word for love, *amor*, in which case Ames can be considered a masculine variation of the feminine name Aimee/Amy.

*Ammiel: Hebrew, "kinsman of God"

Amiel
(See Numbers 13:12;
2 Samuel 9:4–5;
1 Chronicles 3:5; 26:5.)

Amory: Latin, "he who is loved"
Amery

*Amos: Hebrew, "he who bears a
burden"
Amos was one of what are
called the "minor" prophets of
the Old Testament. See the
book bearing his name.

*Ananiah: Hebrew, "God has
answered my plea"
(See Nehemiah 8:4; 10:22.)

ANDRAÉ CROUCH
(1942–)

is a popular Christian singer,
songwriter, and pastor. His
well-known songs include
"My Tribute (To God Be the
Glory)," "Through It All," and
"The Blood Will Never Lose
Its Power."

Anastasias: Greek, "resurrection"
Anas, Anastasius, Stace,
Stacey

Anatole: Greek, "from the east"
Anatolio

André: A French variation of
Andrew, "strong, masculine"

Andrae: Greek, "man, warrior"
Andreas (Greek), Andres
(Spanish)

*Andrew: Greek, "strong,
masculine"
Anders (Scandinavian),
Andrae (French), André
(French), Andreas (Greek),
Andres (Spanish), Andry,
Andy, Drew
Andrew was the first of the
disciples chosen by Jesus and
the brother of Peter. (See
Matthew 4:18; 10:2.) Andrew
died a martyr's death, and
tradition suggests he was
crucified upon an X-shaped
cross.

ANDREW MURRAY
(1828–1917)

was a South African pastor
and writer of many books on
the Christian life still read by
Christians today.

Angelo: An Italian variation of
angel, "messenger from God"
Angel, Angelos

Angus: Scottish, "he who is
strong"

*Annas: Hebrew, "the grace of God"

Anas

(See Luke 3:2; John 18:13, 24; Acts 4:6.)

Ansel: French, "he who is a nobleman"

Ancel, Ancil, Ansell

Anselm: Old German, "he who is protected by God"

Anselmo (Spanish)

Anson: Old German, "divine one"

Anthony: Latin, "deserving of high honor"

Antoine (French), Anton (Slavic), Antonio (Italian), Antony, Tony

*Ara: Hebrew, "he who is strong"

(See 1 Chronicles 7:38.)

*Aram: Hebrew, "exalted"

(See Genesis 10:22–23; 22:21; 1 Chronicles 1:17; 7:34; Matthew 1:3–4.)

Aran: Asian/Thai, "he who is from the forest"

Archer: Latin, "bowman"

Arch, Archie

Archibald: Old German, "he who is bold"

Arch, Archer, Archie

Arden: Latin, "he who is ablaze with passion"—from the same root as the word *ardent*

Ardan, Ardin, Ardy

Argus: Greek, "fully aware one"

Argyle: Irish, "from Ireland"

Aric: Old German, "one who rules"

Arick, Arric, Arrick, Rick, Ricky

*Ariel: Hebrew, "lion of God"

Ari, Arie, Arriel, Arye

(See Ezra 8:16–17; 2 Samuel 23:20; 1 Chronicles 11:22.)

Arlan: Irish, "he who pledges or promises"

Arlen, Arlin, Arlyn

Arley: Old English, "he who hunts"—usually associated with hunting via archery, or a bowman

Arleigh, Arlie

Arlo: Spanish, "the barberry tree"

Armand: A Germanic variation of Herman, "warrior"

Arman, Armando (Spanish), Mandy, Manny

Armstrong: Old English, literally, as it sounds, "strong of arm"

*Arnan: Hebrew, "he who is strong"
(See 1 Chronicles 3:21.)

Arnold: Old German, "the glory of the eagle"
Arend, Arne, Arnie, Arnoldo

Arsenio: Greek, "manly"
Arsen, Arsene, Arsenius

*Artemus: Greek, "complete"— some references connect this name to the Greek goddess Artemis
Art, Arte, Artemas, Artemis, Artie
(See Titus 3:12.)

Arthur: English, "sturdy, like a rock; firm, unmovable"
Art, Artie, Artur, Arturo (Italian), Arty

Arvin: Old German, "he who is friendly"
Arv, Arvie, Arvind

*Asa: Hebrew, "healer"
Asa was the great-grandson of Solomon and a forebear of Jesus Christ. (See Matthew 1:7–8.) He was also the third king of Judah.

*Asaiah: Hebrew, "Jehovah is the cause"
There are several minor Old Testament references to men with this name, the meaning of which gives glory to God.

*Asaph: Hebrew, "he who gathers, collects"
Asaf
There are three Asaphs in the Bible. The most notable was the Levite appointed by King David to be a director of choral music for the people of God. (See 1 Chronicles 6:39; 15:17–19; 16:5–7; 25:1–9.)

Ash: Old English, from the tree of the same name
Ashby, Ashton

*Asher: Hebrew, "blessed one"
Ash
Asher was the eighth son of Jacob. (See Genesis 30:13; 35:26; 49:20; Deuteronomy 33:24–25.)

Ashley: Greek, "starlike"
Ash, Aston (from the ash-tree village)

*Ashur: Hebrew, "free man"
(See 2 Samuel 2:9.)

Atherton: Old English, "village by the spring"

Athol: Possibly a Scottish place name

Atholl

Attica: Greek, a place name for a region in southern Greece

Atticas, Atticus

The variant name Atticus was made popular in recent decades from the protagonist (Atticus Finch) of the classic Harper Lee novel *To Kill a Mockingbird.*

Aubrey: Old German, "ruler"

Awbrey

August: Latin, "he who is respectable" or, literally, august

Agostino, Augie, Augustin, Augustine, *Augustus (see Luke 2:1; Acts 25:21; 27:1), Austin.

AUGUSTINE
(354–430)

was the bishop of Hippo, a town on the North African coast. Sixteen centuries after his death, his writings endure. Most notable are *Confessions* and *The City of God.*

AUGUSTUS TOPLADY
(1740–1778)

was an English clergyman and hymn writer, best remembered for "Rock of Ages."

Austen: Latin, "majestic"

Augey, Augie, Austin, Austino, Gus

Averill: Old English, "he who hunts the boar"

Ave, Averell

Avery: English, "ruler"

Ave

Avi: Hebrew, "God is my father"

Abi, Aviel

Axel: Hebrew, "father of peace"

Ax, Axe, Axell

Aylwin: German, "he who is beloved"—a variation of Alvin

*Azariah: Hebrew, "he who hears the Lord"

Az, Azaria, Azzy

There are at least thirty Azariahs in the Bible. It was a very common name, particularly in the Old Testament.

*Aziel: Hebrew, "God is mighty"
Az, Azzy
Aziel was a Levite who played the lyre in the tabernacle. (See 1 Chronicles 15:20.)

Azizi: Swahili, "he who is dear"
Azzizi, Azzy

Azriel: Hebrew, "God is my helper"

B

Baden: German, "bather"
Bay, Bayden

Bailey: Old French, "steward"— from the same root as the word *bailiff*
Bail, Baily, Bale, Bayley

Bain: Irish, possibly a diminutive for Bainbridge, "fine bridge"
Bane, Bayne

Baird: Irish, "poet" or "entertainer"
Bard, Bayard (can also mean "he who has red hair")

Baldwin: Old German, "treasured friend"

Ballard: Latin, "dancer"

Bancroft: Old English, "from the bean field"

Bank, Banky, Bink, Binky

Banner: English, "flag-bearer"
Ban, Banny

Bao: Asian/Vietnamese, "to place a bid"

*Barabbas: Hebrew, "a father's son"
Barabbas was the prisoner doomed to die on the cross, until the angry crowds demanded his freedom instead of Christ's.
(See Matthew 27:16–26.)

*Barak: Hebrew, "sudden light" (as in a flash of lightning)
Barack, Barrak
Barak was a mighty warrior under the judge Deborah. Read about Barak in Judges 4:6 and Hebrews 11:32.

Baraka: Swahili, "he shall be blessed"

*Barnabas: Hebrew, "son of encouragement"
Barn, Barna (Italian), Barnaby, Barney
Barnabas was the apostle Paul's companion on many of his journeys.
(See Acts 4:36; 9:37.)

Barnett: Old English, "he who is noble"

Barn, Barney

Baron: Latin, "warrior"

Barron

Barrett: Old German, "bearlike"

Barret

Barry: Irish, "valiant spearsman"

Baris, Barris, Bary, Berry

Barth: Usually a diminutive of Bartholomew.

It has also been used as a proper name, honoring Karl Barth, an influential twentieth-century theologian.

*Bartholomew: Hebrew, "son of the farmer"

Bart, Barth, Bartley

Bartholomew was one of Jesus's twelve disciples. He was also known by the name Nathanael. (See Matthew 10:3; Mark 3:18; Luke 6:14; Acts 1:13.)

*Bartimaeus: Hebrew, "son of Timaeus"

Bart, Tim

Bartimaeus was the blind begger healed by Jesus. (See Mark 10:36; Luke 18:35.)

Barton: Old English place name, possibly "the town where barley is grown"

Bart, Bartie, Barty

*Baruch: Hebrew, "he who is blessed"

(See Nehemiah 3:20; 10:6; 11:5; Jeremiah 32:12–16.)

Basil: Greek, "kingly"

Basc, Basile, Basel, Vasily (Russian)

BASIL THE GREAT
(330–379)

was born into a wealthy landowning family known for their Christian faith. He became the bishop of Caesarea in 370.

Baxter: Old English, "baker"

Bax, Baxy

Beal: Old French variation of Beau, "handsome man"

Beaman: Old English, "one who keeps bees"

Beeman, Beman, Bemon

Beauregard: Old French, "handsome man"

Beau, Bo

Beck: Old English, "stream" or "brook"

Bela: Slavic, "white"

Belah

Benedict: Latin, "blessed"

Ben, Benedictus, Benito (Italian), Bennet, Bennett

*Benjamin: Hebrew, "son of the right hand"

Ben, Benji, Benn, Benny, Benyamin

Benjamin was the youngest son of Jacob and Rachel and the first of the Israelite tribe bearing his name. Rachel died giving birth to him. She had named him Benomi ("son of sorrows"), but Jacob later changed his name to Benjamin. There are also several other Benjamins mentioned in the Old Testament.

BENJAMIN (BEN) CARSON (1951–)

is a noted neurosurgeon and the author of *Gifted Hands* and *Think Big*.

Benson: English, "son of Ben"

Ben, Bensen

BERNARD OF CLAIRVAUX (1090–1153)

was a medieval Christian mystic and ardent proclaimer of the love of God. His hymns include "Jesus, the Very Thought of Thee" and "O Sacred Head Now Wounded."

Bentley: Old English, "from the meadow with rough grass"

Ben, Bent

Benton: Old English, "from the town with rough grass"

Ben, Bent

*Beriah: Hebrew, "God has created"

(See 1 Chronicles 8:13, 21.)

Berkeley: An Old English place name referring to "the forest of birch trees" or "the meadow where the birch trees grow"

Barclay, Berk, Berkley

Bernard: Old German, "true warrior"

Barnard, Barney, Barny, Bern, Bernardo (Spanish), Bernerd, Bernie

Bertram: Old German, "bright raven," or sometimes "glorious shield"

Bert, Bertie, Berton, Bertrand, Burt

Bevan: Welsh, "son of Evan"
Bev, Beven, Bevin, Bevon

Beverly: Old English, "from the beaver meadow"
Bev, Beverley

**GEORGE BEVERLY SHEA
(1909–)**

was one of the most beloved gospel singers of the twentieth century. He frequently sang for the Billy Graham Crusades.

**BIL KEANE
(1922–2011)**

was the originator of the popular comic strip *The Family Circus*.

**WILLIAM "BILL" BRIGHT
(1921–2003)**

was the author of the popular evangelistic tract *The Four Spiritual Laws* and the founder of Campus Crusade for Christ, a successful ministry that began as an effort to reach college students with the gospel.

Bien: Asian/Vietnamese, "from the great sea"

Bijay: Asian/Bengali, "he who overcomes"

Bill: Old German, usually a diminutive of William
Bil, Billy, Will, Willy

**WILLIAM "BILLY" GRAHAM
(1918–)**

is one of the most successful and widely known evangelists of all time. Through his crusades and his many books, literally hundreds of thousands—if not millions—have come to know Christ.

**WILLIAM "BILLY" SUNDAY
(1862–1935)**

was a baseball player before he was converted to Christ. He went on to become one of America's more famous and successful evangelists.

Binh: Asian/Vietnamese, "vase"

Bjorn: Scandinavian, a variation of Bernard, "true warrior"

Blade: Old English, literally, as a knife blade, "sharp, swordlike"

Blaine: Irish, "thin one"
Blane, Blaney, Blayne

Blair: Irish, "from the field"

Blaise: French, "fiery, aflame"
Blase, Blaze (English)

BLAISE PASCAL
(1623–1662)

was a French mathematician and scientist who, upon converting to Christianity, became a noted apologist.

Blake: Old English, "white"
Blakely, Blakeley

Bo: Usually a diminutive of Beauregard

*Boaz: Hebrew, "strong, manly"
Boaz was an Old Testament model of Christ the Redeemer. Read his heroic story in the book of Ruth, chapters 2–4.
Bob, Bobbie, Bobby (usually diminutives of Robert)

Boniface: Latin, "doer of good deeds" or "of handsome appearance"

Booth: Old English, "small dwelling"
Boothe

Borden: Old English, "from the valley of the boar"
Bord, Bordy

Boris: Slavic, "fierce in battle, mighty warrior"
Borris

Boswell: French, "the town near the forest"
Bosworth, Boz

Bowen: Welsh, "son of Owen"
Bow, Bowe, Bowie

Boyce: Old French, "from the forest"
Boice, Boise, Boyse

Boyden: Scottish, "fair-haired one"
Boyd

Bradley: Old English, "large meadow or field"
Brad, Braden, Bradford, Bradwell, Brady

Brainard: Old English, "ravenlike"
Brainerd

Brand: Middle English, "fiery one"—as in a firebrand
Brandt, Brant, Brantly

Brandon: Old English, "from the beacon hill"
Bran, Brand, Brandan, Brannon (Irish)

Breck: Irish, "freckled one"

Brede: Scandinavian, "glacial"

Brendan: Irish, "man of the sword"
Bren, Brenden, Brennan, Brennen

Brent: Old English, "from the hill"

Bret: Scottish, "from Brittany"
Brett, Brit, Britt, Britton

Brian: Irish, "honorable man"
Brien, Brion, Bryan, Bryant, Bryon

Brice: Welsh, "bright, alert one"
Bryce

Brick: English, "bridge"
Bridger

Brock: Old English, "badgerlike"
Brocke, Brocker

Broderick: Welsh, "son of renown"
Brodrick, Rick, Rickie, Ricky

Brody: German, "he with the unusual beard"—or Gaelic, "ditch"

Brod, Brode, Brodie

Bronson: Old English, "son of Brown"
Bron, Bronnie, Bronny

Brook: Old English, "stream"—literally, a brook
Brooks

Bruce: Old French, "from the woods"

Bruno: Old German, "darkly complected man"

Buck: American, "male deer"—usually a nickname or diminutive
Bucky

Dud: American, "friend"—usually a nickname or diminutive
Budd, Buddy

Burgess: Old English, "town dweller"

Burk: German, "castle"
Berk, Bourk, Burk, Burke

Burl: Old English, "knotty wood; tuft of wool"
Berl, Berle, Byrl

Burns: Scottish, "from the fountain"

Byrne, Byrnes

Burton: English, "he who is famous"—or a place name

Berton, Burt

Buster: American, usually a nickname or diminutive

Butch: American, usually a nickname or diminutive

Buzz: American, usually a nickname or diminutive

Buzzy

Byrd: Old English, "birdlike"

Bird

Byrne: Old English, "by the brook"

Bern, Berne, Burne, Burns, Byrn

Byron: Old German, "cottage dweller"

Biron, Byran

C

Cable: Old French, "rope," literally, cable

Cabe, Cabel

Cade: Welsh, "warrior"

Caid, Caide

*Caesar: Latin, "long-haired one"

Cesar (Spanish), Cesare (Italian)

*Cain: Hebrew, "possessed"

Caine, Kane

Cain was Adam and Eve's firstborn son. His jealousy of his younger brother, Abel, due to God's acceptance of Abel's sacrifice and rejection of Cain's, resulted in the first murder in human history, which is also the first murder noted in the Bible. (See Genesis 4.)

Calder: Irish, "from the stony stream"

Cal, Cald, Cale

*Caleb: Hebrew, "adventuresome" or "faithful"

Cal, Cale, Kaleb

Brave Caleb was one of the spies sent out by Moses to survey the Promised Land. (See Numbers 13 and 14.)

CALVIN MILLER
(1936–)

is a popular pastor, speaker, and author of many books, including his classic trilogy *The Singer.*

Calvin: Latin, "bald one"
Cal, Calv, Kalvin, Vin, Vinnie, Vinny

Cameron: Scottish, "one with the crooked nose"
Cam, Cammy, Kameron

Campbell: Scottish, "he who has a crooked mouth," or perhaps "smile"
Cam, Campy

Carey: Irish, "from the fortified city"
Cary, Kerry

> ### CARL F. H. HENRY
> ### (1913–2003)
>
> was an important leader in twentieth-century evangelical Christian circles. He also served as editor of *Christianity Today* magazine from 1956 to 1958.

Carl: Considered by many to be a variation of Charles, "masculine, manly, virile"
Carlson, Carlton, Karl

Carlin: Irish, "champion"
Carl, Carlyn

Carlisle: Old English, "from the tower of the castle"
Carlyle

Carlo: Spanish and Italian variations of Charles, "masculine, manly, virile"
Carlos

Carmichael: Scottish, "friend of Michael"

Carmine: Latin, "song"
Carm, Carmen

Carney: Irish, "warrior"
Carn, Carny

Carroll: Irish, "champion"
Caro, Carol, Karrell

Carson: Old English, "son of Carr"
Carse, Carsen

Carter: Old English, "one who drives a cart"

Carver: Old English, "one who carves wood"

Cary: Celtic, "he who is dark"
Carey, Kerry

Case: Irish, "he who is full of courage"
Casey, Kase, Kasey

Cash: Latin, "he who is proud"

Caspar: German, "imperial one"
Cas, Casper, Cass, Cassie,
Jaspar, Jasper, Kaspar, Kasper

Cassidy: Irish, "clever one"
Cass, Kassidy

Cassius: Latin, "he who is vain"—
though this is a negative
connotation, it might be
better construed as "he who is
confident"
Cass, Cassio

Cato: Latin, "he who is wise"

Cecil: Latin, "blind one"
Cec

Cedric: Old English, "he who
leads in battle"
Ced, Cedrick, Rick, Ricky

*Cephas: Greek, "small rock"
Cephas (Peter) was the name
that Jesus gave to Simon, the
brother of Andrew. (See John
1:42.)

Chad: Irish, "valiant warrior"
Chadd, Chade, Chadwick

Chai: Asian (numerous
languages), "tea"

Chaim: Hebrew, "life"

Chance: Middle English, "good
fortune"—for a Christian, this
might be construed as "he who
is blessed"
Chan, Chanse

Chandler: Old English,
"candlemaker"
Chan, Chaney

Chaney: French, "oak"
Chane, Cheney

Changa: African, "he who is
strong"

Channing: Old English, "he who
is wise"
Chan

Charles: Old German, "masculine,
manly, virile"
Charles has many variations
and diminutives, both
masculine and feminine and in
various languages.
Carlo (Italian), Carlos
(Spanish), Charley, Charlie,
Chaz, Chazz, Chick, Chip,
Chuck, Chucky

Charlton: A variation of Charles,
"masculine, manly, virile"
Charl, Charleston

CHARLES GRANDISON FINNEY
(1792–1875)

was one of the most influential revivalists in American history. *The Autobiography of Charles G. Finney* has motivated many Christians to lead holy lives. His other works include the popular *Revival Lectures*.

CHARLES HADDON SPURGEON
(1834–1892)

was converted at age fifteen and became one of the most successful evangelists of all time. His Metropolitan Tabernacle in London seated six thousand congregants.

Chase: Old French, "he who seeks"

Chauncey: Latin, "official of the church"
Chaunce, Chauncy

Chester: Latin, "from the soldier's camp"
Ches, Cheston, Chet

CHUCK COLSON
(1931–2012)

was a key figure in the Watergate scandal involving former President Richard Nixon. Colson served seven months in prison after pleading guilty on obstruction of justice charges. While incarcerated, he became a Christian, and, afterward, he founded the hugely successful Prison Fellowship in 1976. His story is told in his best-selling book *Born Again*.

Chilton: Old English, "farm by the brook"
Chilt, Chilty

Christian: Greek, "anointed one"—literally, a Christian
Chris, Chrystian, Cristian, Kris, Kristian

Christopher: Greek, "Christ-bearer"
Chris, Christos, Kris, Kristopher, Toph, Topher

Chuck: A diminutive of Charles

Chung: Asian/Chinese, "he who is wise"

Clair: Latin, "clear"
Clare (when spelled this way, usually a diminutive of Clarence)

Clancey: Irish, "redheaded man"
Clancy

Clarence: Latin, "clear, pure"
Clar, Clare, Clarry

Clark: Greek, from the word for "clerk," particularly a clerk in the Old English church
Clarke

*Claudius: Latin, "he who is lame"
Claud, Claude, Claudel, Claudio (Spanish)
(See Acts 11:28; 18:2; 23:26.)

Clayton: Old English, "town near the clay beds" or "formed of clay"
Clay

Cleary: Irish, "he who is wise"

Cleavon: English, "from the cliff"

*Clement: Latin, "he who shows mercy to others"—from the same root as the word *clemency*
Clem
Clement was a co-laborer with the apostle Paul. (See Philippians 4:3.)

CLEMENT OF ALEXANDRIA (155–220)

was born in Athens to pagan parents but converted to Christianity. He wrote widely in his role as a teacher in Alexandria.

CLEMENT OF ROME (d. 101)

was an early Christian father and leader of the church in Rome. Some of his writings remain in use today for teaching how the church functioned in its earliest years.

Cleon: Greek, "he who is well-known"

*Cleopas: Greek, "glory"
Cleophas, Clopas
(See the reference to Cleopas in Luke 24:18 and to Cleophas in John 19:25.)

Cleveland: Old English, "from the cliff"
Cleve

Clifford: Old English, "from the

cliff"

Cliff, Cliffy

Clifton: Old English, "from the
town on the cliff"

Cliff, Clift

Clinton: Old English, "from the
town on the hill"

Clint

Clive: Old English, often a
diminutive for Clifford,
Clifton, or Cleveland, but
increasingly a proper name in
its own right

**C. S. (CLIVE STAPLES)
LEWIS
(1898–1963)**

was a British professor at the
University of Cambridge and
a vibrant Christian author
of such classics as *Mere
Christianity* and *The
Chronicles of Narnia.*

Clovis: Old German, "celebrated
warrior"

Clyde: Welsh, "distant noise"

Cody: Old English, "pillow,
cushion"

Code, Codey, Codie, Kody

Colby: Old English, a place name

Cole: Greek, originally a
diminutive for Nicholas—or
Old English, "he who is dark-
skinned"

Kole, Koll

Coleman: Old English, "he who
makes coal"

Cole, Colman

Colin: Irish, "young man"—also,
formerly a diminutive of
Nicholas, but increasingly a
proper name in its own right

Colan, Colen, Collin, Collins

Collier: Old English, "miner"

Collyer, Colyer

Colton: Old English, "from the
dark town"

Conan: Irish, "worthy of praise"

Conant, Conley, Konan,
Konant

Conn: Old English, often a
diminutive of Conan, Connor,
Conrad, Conroy, Conway, but
increasingly a proper name in
its own right

Connor: Scottish, "he who is wise"

Con, Conor, Konnor

Conrad: Old German, "wise
counselor"

Con, Konrad

Conroy: Irish, "he who is wise"
Con, Roy

Constantine: Latin, "he who is
reliable" or "constant"
Con, Conn, Constant, Costa,
Konstantine, Stan

**CONSTANTINE I
(285–337)**

ceased the persecution of
Christians in the Roman
Empire and became an active
patron of the Christian
church. In 325, he organized
the historic Council of
Nicaea.

Conway: Celtic, "hound from the
plains"
Con

Cooper: Old English,
"barrelmaker"
Coop

Corbett: Latin, "raven, warrior"
Corban, Corbin, Corby, Cory

Corcoran: Irish, "he with the
ruddy complexion"
Corky

Cordell: Old French, "one who
makes ropes"
Cord

Corey: Irish, "he who lives in the
hollow"
Cory, Korey, Kory

Corin: Irish, "spearman"
Corrin, Korin, Korrin, Koryn

*****Cornelius**: Latin, "war crier"
Corn, Cornall, Cornel, Cornell
Cornelius was a Roman
centurion who was converted
to Christ, along with his
family, through the ministry of
Peter. (See Acts 10.)

Cort: Old German, "he who is
bold"
Corty, Kort

Cosmo: Greek, "of the universe"—
from the same root as the
word cosmos
Cos, Cosimo (Spanish)

Courtney: English, "from the
court"
Corey, Cort, Cory, Court,
Courtenay (French)

Craig: Irish, "rocky"—from the
same root as the word *crag*,
meaning "a rock formation"

Crandall: An Old English place name meaning "dale (valley) of the cranes"
Cran, Crandell

Crawford: Old English, "he who is from the ford of the crows"

Creighton: An Old English place name meaning "rocky area"
Cray, Crayton

Crispin: Latin, "curly-headed one"

*Crispus: Greek, "curly-headed one"
Crispus, the leader of the synagogue at Corinth, was baptized by the apostle Paul upon his conversion to Christ. (See Acts 18:8; 1 Corinthians 1:14.)

Cruz: Spanish, "cross"

Cullen: Irish, "young animal"
Cullan, Culley, Cullin

Curran: Irish, "heroic one"
Curan, Currey, Curry

Curtis: Latin, "small one"
Curt, Curtiss, Kurt, Kurtis

Cuthbert: Old English, "he who is brilliant"
Bert

Cyprian: Greek, "he who is from Cyprus"

Cyrano: Greek, "from the Greek city of Cyrene"

Cyril: Greek, "lordly one"

*Cyrus: Persian, "sun"
Cy
Cyrus was the founder of the Persian Empire and was responsible for allowing the Jews to return to their homeland after their captivity in territories under the control of Babylon/Persia.

CYRUS SCOFIELD (1843–1921)

was a Congregational minister, the author of several books, and the editor of the still widely used *Scofield Study Bible*.

D

Dace: Irish, "from the south"
Dacey, Dacian, Dacias, Dacy

Dale: Old German, "one who lives in the valley (dale)"
Dallan, Dalle, Dayely, Dayle

Dallas: Celtic, "he who lives by the waterfall"

Daly: Gaelic, "he who offers wisdom"

Daley

Damian: Greek, "he who tames"

Daman, Damien, Damion, Damon

***Dan:** Hebrew, "he who judges"

Dan was the fifth son of Jacob. The tribe of Dan is named for him. (See Genesis 30:6; Exodus 31:6.) The name Dan in this Old Testament usage is complete in itself and does not serve as a diminutive for Daniel. However, Dan may also be used as a diminutive, as seen below.

Dana: Old English, "he who is from Denmark"

Dain, Dane, Dayn

***Daniel:** Hebrew, "God is my judge"

Dan, Danal, Danby, Danforth, Dannel, Danno, Danny

Read the compelling story of the prophet Daniel in the book of the Bible that bears his name.

Dante: Latin, "he who endures"

Donte

Darby: Irish, "he who is free"

Darcy: Irish, "dark one"

Darce, Darcey

Daren: Irish, "magnificent"

Darin, Darren

***Darius:** Greek, "prosperous"

Darias, Dario, Darios

Three men named Darius are mentioned in the Bible. (See Ezra 4:5, 24; Nehemiah 12:22; Daniel 5:31; 6:9; 9:1; 11:1.)

Darrell: French, "dear one"

Darryl, Daryl, Derrell, Deryl

***Dathan:** Hebrew, "of the law"

Dathen, Dathon

(See Numbers 16; 26:9; Deuteronomy 11:6; Psalm 106:17.)

Daudi: Swahili, "he who is dearly loved"

***David:** Hebrew, "beloved one"

Dave, Davey, Davian, Davion, Davis, Davon, Davy

David is one of the most beloved men of the Bible and is best described as a "man after God's heart." (See 1 Samuel 13:14; Acts 13:22.) Read his story in various books of the

Old Testament, particularly 1 and 2 Samuel, 1 and 2 Kings, and 1 and 2 Chronicles. David also wrote many of the Psalms, some of which reflect incidents in his life.

DAVID BRAINERD (1718–1747)

in his short life, worked among the American Indians and wrote an extensive diary, which is still in print and has inspired Christians for more than 250 years.

DAVID LIVINGSTONE (1813–1873)

was a Scottish missionary to Africa.

Davis: Scottish, "David's son"

Dawson: Old English, "son of David"
Daw, Dawes, Daws

Dean: Old English, "valley"
Dino (Italian)

Dedric: Old German, "one who rules"
Dedrick, Rick, Ricky

DAWSON "DAWS" TROTMAN (1906–1956)

was the founder of the Navigators, a successful evangelistic ministry that has a global influence.

Del: Old English, "valley"— sometimes a diminutive for Delbert and similar names but often used as a proper name in its own right
Dell

Delany: Gaelic, "from he who challenges"
Del, Delain, Delane

Delbert: Old English, "brilliant as the sunshine"
Bert, Del, Dil, Dilbert

Delmar: Latin, "from the sea"
Del, Delmer, Delmore

*Demas: Greek, "he who rules"— also, possibly a diminutive of Demosthenes
Demos, Dimas

Demas was an early companion of the apostle Paul (see Colossians 4:14; Philemon 24) but later forsook the apostle for *"this present world"* (2 Timothy 4:10).

*Demetrius: Greek, "he who follows [the false goddess] Demeter"

Demitri, Dmitri, Dmitrios

There are two men named Demetrius in the New Testament. (See Acts 19:24, 38; 3 John 12.) The latter man was a believer who was highly commended by the apostle John.

Dempsey: Irish, "he who is proud"

Denby: Scandinavian, "from Denmark"

Danby, Den, Denny

Dennis: Greek, "follower of [the false god] Dionysius"

Den, Denis, Dennison (son of Denny), Denny, Denys

Denton: Old English, "he who comes from the town in the valley"

Denver: Old English, "lush valley"

Denzel: English, "from Cornwall"

Denzil, Denzyl

Derek: Old German, "one who rules"

Darrick, Derric, Derrick, Dirk, Rick, Ricky

Deron: Hebrew, "he who is free"

Derry: Irish, "redheaded one"

Desi: Latin, "he who is desired"— often a diminutive of Desiderio

Des, Desiderio

Desmond: Latin, "created one"

Des, Desmund

Devin: Irish, "poet"

Devan, Devon

Devlin: Irish, "courageous"

Dewey: Irish, "dearly prized"

Dewitt: Welsh, "he who is blond"

DeWitt

Dexter: Latin, "easily movable"

From the same root as *ambidextrous* (adept with either the right or left hand)

Dex

Dick: Usually a diminutive of Richard

Dickson: English, "son of Dick"— Dick is usually a diminutive of Richard

Dick, Dickinson, Dicky, Dixon

Diego: Spanish, a variation of James, from Jacob, "he who supplants another"

Dietrich: German, "he who prospers"
Diederick, Dieter

DIETRICH BONHOEFFER
(1906–1945)

was a German pastor who resisted the Nazis and was hanged for his stance against Hitler's regime. Among his popular books are *The Cost of Discipleship* and *Life Together*.

Digby: Irish, "from the town by the dike or ditch"

Dillon: Irish, "man of faith"
Dill, Dillan, Dilly, Dylan

Dino: Usually, an Italian variation of Dean, "valley"

Dion: Usually, a diminutive of Dionysius, but increasingly a proper name in its own right
Deion, Deon

*Dionysius: Greek name for their ancient god of wine

Deion, Deon, Dion
(See the reference to the early Christian convert Dionysius in Acts 17:34.)

Dirk: Old German, "one who rules"—often a diminutive of Derrick, Theodoric, and Roderick

Dolph: Old German, usually a diminutive of Adolph, Rudolph, or Randolph
Dolf, Dolfus, Dolphus

DOLPHUS WEARY
(1946–)

has been a tireless worker for racial reconciliation in the body of Christ. His story is told in his book *I Ain't Coming Back*.

Dominic: Latin, "he who belongs to the Lord"
Dom, Domingo (Spanish), Dominick, Nick, Nicky

Donald: Celtic, "powerful ruler"
Don, Donal, Donaldo (Spanish), Donel, Donner, Donnie, Donny, Donovan

Donato: Italian, "gift from God"
Don, Nat

Dooley: Irish, "dark warrior"

Doran: Greek, "gift from God"
Dore, Dorian, Dorien, Dorran, Dory

Dougal: Scottish, "dark stranger"

Douglas: Irish, "dweller by the brook"
Doug, Douglass

Dow: Irish, "one with dark hair"
Dowe, Dowell

Doyle: Irish, "dark stranger"—usually an Irish variation of Dougal

Drake: Middle English, "serpent"

Drew: Usually a diminutive for Andrew
Dru

Driscoll: Celtic, "melancholy one"

Drury: Old French, "he who loves"

Duane: Irish, "dark one"
DeWayne, Dwain, Dwaine, Dwayne

Dude: Usually a nickname, but occasionally a proper name

Dudley: Old English, "from the field"

Duff: Scottish, "dark one"
Duffy

Dugan: Irish, "dark one"
Doogan, Duggan

Duke: Latin, "one who leads"—usually a nickname, but occasionally a proper name

Duncan: Scottish, "warrior"

Dunstan: Old English, "strong fortress"

Durant: Latin, "he who endures"
Durand, Durante, Ran, Randy

Durward: Old English, "he who guards the gate"
Ward

Dustin: Old German, "courageous warrior"
Dustan, Dustyn, Dusty

DWIGHT L. MOODY (1837–1899)

was one of America's most successful evangelists. He founded the famed Moody Bible Institute in Chicago in 1887 as the Chicago Evangelization Society.

Dutch: Literally, "from the Netherlands"

Dwayne: See Duane

Dwight: German, "fair one"

Dylan: Welsh, "from the sea"
Dilan, Dillan, Dillon

E

Earl: Old English, "noble one"
Earle, Erle, Errol, Erroll

Eban: Hebrew, "rock"
Eb, Eben

Ebenezer: Hebrew, "the Lord is my rock"
Eb, Eben

Eberhard: Old German, "strong like the boar"
Eb, Eberhardt, Evard, Everard

*Eden: Hebrew, "he who is a delight"
Edan
(See 2 Chronicles 29:13; 31:15.)
Many names that begin with Ed-, as in the names below, have Anglo-Saxon roots. This prefix in such names is indicative of "prosperity."

Edgar: Old English, "prosperous guardian"
Ed, Eddie, Medgar (German)

Edmund: Old English, "prosperous guardian"
Ed, Eddie, Edmond, Edmundo (Italian), Esmond (French)

Edric: Old English, "prosperous leader"
Ederic, Ederick, Edrick, Rick, Ricky

Edson: Old English, literally, "Ed's son"
Ed, Eddie, Edison

Edward: Old English, "prosperous guardian"
Duarte (Portugese), Ed, Eddie, Eduardo (Spanish)

E. V. (EDWARD VICTOR) HILL (1933–2003)

was the pastor of Mt. Zion Missionary Baptist Church in the Watts section of Los Angeles, the founder of the World Christian Training Center, and a popular Christian speaker.

Edwin: Old English, "treasured or prosperous friend"
Ed, Eddie, Eddy

Efrem: See Ephraim

Egan: Celtic, "ardent one"

Egbert: Old English, "he who wields the shining sword"
Bert, Bertie, Berty

Eldon: Old English, "from the hill of God"
Eldan, Elden, Eldin

Eldred: Old English, "wise counselor"
Eldrid

Eldridge: Usually, a variation of Aldrich/Aldridge, "wise man"
Eldredge

*Elead: Hebrew, "God is witness"
(See 1 Chronicles 7:21.)

*Eleazar: Hebrew, "God has been my helper"
There are seven Eleazars in the Bible, one of whom was an ancestor of Christ. (See Matthew 1:15).

*Eli: Hebrew, "Jehovah is my God"
Elias (the New Testament form of Elijah), Elihu, Elijah,

Ely
(See 1 Samuel 1–4; 14:3.)

*Eliah: Hebrew, "God is Jehovah"
(See 1 Chronicles 8:27; Ezra 10:26.)

*Eliam: Hebrew, "the people of God"
Eliam was the father of Bathsheba, the consort of David. (See 2 Samuel 11:3.)

Elian: Spanish, meaning uncertain

*Eliel: Hebrew, "God is God"
There were ten Eliels in the Old Testament, including a fellow warrior with King David. (See 1 Chronicles 11:47.)

*Eliezer: Hebrew, "God is my helper"
There are eleven Eliezers in the Bible, including an ancestor of Joseph, Mary's husband. (See Luke 3:29.)

*Elihu: Hebrew, "He is God"
There are five Elihus in the Bible, most notably the youngest of Job's friends. (See Job 32:2–6; 34:1; 35:1; 36:1.)

*Elijah: Hebrew, "the Lord, my

God"—a variation of Eli, "Jehovah is my God"

Elijah was the greatest prophet of the Old Testament. (See 1 Kings 17–19; 2 Kings 1–3; 9–10.)

Eliot: French, "Jehovah is God"—a variation of Eli, "Jehovah is my God"

Elliot, Elliott

*Elisha: Hebrew, "the Lord is my salvation"

Elisha was a prophet and the successor to Elijah. (See 1 Kings 19:16–19; 2 Kings 2–13.)

Ellis: An English variation of Eli, "Jehovah is my God"

Ellison (son of Eli)

Elmer: Old English, "he who is noble"

Almer, Almo, Elmo

Elmo: Greek, "he who is easy to please"

Elroy: Latin, "royal one"

Roy

Elvin: Old English, "he who is elfish"

Elwin, Elwyn

Elvis: Scandinavian, "he who is wise"

Elvyn, Elwin, Elwyn

Elwood: English, "ancient forest"

Woody

Emery: Old German, "diligent worker"

Emerick, Emerson (son of Emery), Emory

Emil: German, "diligent worker"

Emile (French), Emilio (Spanish)

Emlyn: A Welsh place name

Em, Emelyn, Emlon, Emlyn

*Emmanuel: Hebrew, "God with us"

Emanuel, Immanuel, Manny, Manuel

Though not used as a proper name in the Bible, this term is the prophesied appellation for the coming Savior who would indeed be *"God with us."* (See Isaiah 7:14; Matthew 1:23.)

Emmet: Hebrew, "he who speaks the truth"

Em, Emett, Emmett, Emmit, Emmitt

*Enan: Hebrew, "from the fountain"

(See Numbers 1:15; 2:29; 7:78, 83; 10:27.)

*Eneas: Hebrew, "he who praises Jehovah," a variation of Aeneas (See Acts 9:33–34.)

Engelbert: Old German, "bright angel"
Bert, Berty, Ingelbert

*Enoch: Hebrew, "he who is dedicated"
(See Genesis 4:17–18; 5:18–23.)

*Enos: Hebrew, "man, mortal one"
Enosh
Enos was a son of Seth and a grandson of Adam and Eve. (See Genesis 4.)

Enrique: Spanish, a variation of Henry, "he who rules the home"
Rick, Ricky

*Epaphras: Greek, "he who is covered with foam," as in passion
(See Colossians 1:7; 4:12; Philemon 23.)

*Ephraim: Hebrew, "abundantly fruitful"
Efrem, Ephrem
(See Genesis 41:52.)

*Eran: Hebrew, "he who is watchful"
(See Numbers 26:36.)

Erasmus: Greek, "he who is friendly, lovable"

*Eri: Hebrew, "my watcher"
(See Genesis 46:16; Numbers 26:16.)

Eric: Scandinavian, "he who is powerful"
Erich, Erick, Erickson ("son of Erick"), Ericson ("son of Eric"), Erik, Rick, Ricky

ERIC LIDDELL (1902–1945)

was a gold-medal winner representing the United Kingdom in the 400-meter run at the 1924 Olympics in Paris. His inspiring story was told in the popular movie *Chariots of Fire*. He later served as a missionary to China.

Ernest: Old German, "intent, purposeful"
Ern, Ernesto (Spanish), Ernie

Errol: See Earl
Erroll

Erskine: Old English, "from the cliff"

Erwin: Old English, "lover of the sea"

Ervin

*Esau: Hebrew, "he who is hairy"

Esau was the elder twin brother of Jacob, who tricked him to gain his birthright and who also stole his blessing. (See Genesis 25–28.)

Esmond: Old English, "valued guardian"

Esteban: Spanish, a variation of Stephen/Steven, "crowned one"

Estevan, Steve

Estes: Italian, "from the east"

*Ethan: Hebrew, "he who is strong"

There are four Ethans in the Bible. The most notable was the wise Ezrahite. (See 1 Kings 4:31.)

Eugene: Greek, "of noble birth"

Gene

Eugene Peterson (1932–)

is a prolific Christian author and the creator of the popular paraphrase of the Bible entitled *The Message*.

Eusebius: Greek, "he who is godly"

Eustace: Greek, "fruitful"

*Eutychus: Greek, "he who is blessed"

Read the interesting story of Eutychus, who fell asleep during one of the apostle Paul's lengthy sermons and tumbled out of a window seat to his death, after which Paul raised him. (See Acts 20:7–12.)

Evan: Greek, "of noble birth"

Evans, Evin, Evyn

Evan Hopkins (1837–1918)

was a popular Bible teacher at the Keswick Conventions in late nineteenth-century England. His book *The Law of Liberty in the Spiritual Life* is considered to be a classic on the deeper Christian life.

Everard: Old German, "he who is strong"

Everett: A more common variation of Everard, "he who is strong"

Ev, Everet, Evert

*Ezekiel: Hebrew, "by the strength of the Lord"

Zeke

Ezekiel was an Old Testament prophet. See the book of the Bible that bears his name.

*Ezra: Hebrew, "he who helps"

Ezra was an Old Testament prophet. (See the book of Ezra, as well as 1 Chronicles 4:17 and Nehemiah 10:2–8.)

F

Fabian: Latin, "bean farmer"

Fabien (French), Fabio (Italian)

Fain: Old English, "he who is joyful"

Faine, Fane, Faniel, Fayne, Fein

Farley: Old English, "from the meadowlands"

Farleigh, Farly, Farr

Farran: English, "sojourner"

Farin, Faron, Farr, Farrin, Farron

Farrell: Irish, "heroic one"

Farrel, Ferrell

Farris: English, "he who is strong"

Faris, Ferris

Favian: Latin, "he who understands, perceives"

Felipe: Spanish, a variation of Philip, "lover of horses"

*Felix: Latin, "blessed one"

Feliciano, Felicio (Italian)

Felix was the Roman governor of Judea who was convicted by the gospel message through the preaching of the apostle Paul but did not respond to it. (See Acts 23:23–24:27.)

Fenton: Old English, "from the farm"

Fen, Fenny, Fent

Ferdinand: Old German, "adventurous one"

Ferd, Ferdy, Fernando (Spanish), Hernando (Spanish), Nando

Fergus: Irish, "masculine, virile"

Fergas, Ferguson (Fergus's son)

Fernando: See Ferdinand

Ferris: Celtic, "rock"

Faris, Farris

*Festus: Latin, from the same root as the word *festive*

Festus was, like Felix, above, a Roman governor of Judea. (See Acts 24:27; 25; 26:24, 32.)

Fidel: Latin, "he who is faithful," from the same root as the word *fidelity*
Fidelio (Italian)

Filbert: Old English, "he who is brilliant"
Bert, Philbert

Fillmore: English, "well-known"
Philmore

Findlay: Irish, "fair-complected one"
Fin, Findley, Finlay, Fyn, Fynn

Finian: Irish, "he who is fair-skinned"
Finnegan, Finnian

Firth: English, "from the forest"

Fitz: Old English, "son"
Whenever you see a name beginning with *Fitz-*, you can be assured that the meaning is "son of" the latter part of the name, as in the two entries below.

Fitzgerald: Old English, "son of Gerald"

Fitzpatrick: Old English, "son of Patrick"

Fleming: Old English, "he who is from the lowlands" or "from Flanders"
Flemming

Fletcher: Middle English, "arrowmaker"
Fletch

Flint: Old English, "stone"
Flynt

Flip: English, usually a nickname, though sometimes, a diminutive of Philip

Floyd: Celtic, "gray"

Flynn: Irish, "son of the red-haired man"
Flin, Flyn

Foluke: Yoruba (Nigeria), "he who is protected by God"— can be either masculine or feminine

Forbes: English, "he who is prosperous"

Forrest: Old English, literally, a forest
Forest, Forrester, Forster

Foster: Old English, a variation of

the occupational name Forrest, "he who works in the forest"

Fowler: Old English, "one who hunts fowl"

Francis: German, "free man"
Frances (usually the female variation of this name), Franchot (French), Francisco (Spanish), Franco (Italian), François (French), Frank, Franky

FRANCIS ASBURY (1745–1816)

is considered the father of American Methodism.

FRANCIS OF ASSISI (1182–1226)

was one of the most influential Christians of all time. His life was marked by service to the poor and a deep devotion to Christ.

Frank: English, sometimes a diminutive of Franklin or Francis but often a proper name in its own right
Frankie, Franky

FRANCIS SCHAEFFER (1912–1984)

was the cofounder (with his wife, Edith) of the L'Abri Fellowship in Switzerland. Among his many important books are *True Spirituality, He Is There and He Is Not Silent,* and *How Should We Then Live?*.

FRANÇOIS FÉNELON (1651–1715)

was a popular French clergyman and author.

FRANK LAUBACH (1884–1970)

was a pioneer in the field of literacy and the author of the classic book *Prayer, the Mightiest Force in the World.*

Franklin: Middle English, "he who is a free landholder"
Frank, Franklyn, Franky

Franz: A German variation of Francis, "free man"
Frantz

Frazer: Old English, "he who has curly hair"

Fraizer, Fraser, Frasier

Frederick: Old German, "peaceful ruler"

Fred, Freddie, Freddy, Frederic, Fredric, Fredrick, Rick, Ricky

Freeman: Old English, "free man"

Fremont: Old German, "free man"—usually a German variation of Freeman

Fritz: German, sometimes a diminutive of Frederick but occasionally a proper name in its own right—or simply a nickname

Fuller: Old English, an occupational name "one who shrinks cloth"

Fulton: Old English, "from the town near the open field"

G

Gable: Possibly a diminutive of Gabriel

*Gabriel: Hebrew, "God is my strength"

Gabby, Gabe, Gaby, Gavriel

Gabriel was the angel who interpreted Daniel's vision (see Daniel 8:16–26; 9:20–27) and proclaimed the births of John the Baptist (see Luke 1:11–20) and Jesus (see Luke 1:26–38).

Gage: Old French, "he who promises"

Gaige, Gaije

*Gaius: Latin, "he who rejoices"

There are five references to men named Gaius in the New Testament. It's uncertain if these were five distinct men; it's possible that they refer to the same man. (See Acts 19:29; 20:4 Romans 16:23; 1 Corinthians 1:14; 3 John 1:1.)

Gale: Old French, "gentlemanly"—from the same root as the word *gallant*

Gael, Gail, Gayle

Galen: Greek, "peaceful one"

Galin, Gaylan, Gaylen, Gaylin, Gaylon

Gallagher: Irish, "devoted helper"

Galvin: Irish, "small bird" (sparrowlike)

Galvan, Galven

*Gamaliel: Hebrew, "God is my rewarder"

(See Numbers 1:10; 2:20; 7:54; 10:23; Acts 5:34; 22:3.)

Gannon: Irish, "fair-complected one"

García: Spanish, "strong spearman"

Gardner: Latin, "one who works with the land"—from the same origin as the word *gardener*

Gard, Gardiner, Gardnar

Gareth: Welsh, "he who is gentle"

Garath, Garith, Garreth, Garry, Gary

Garfield: Old English, "from the battlefield"

Garland: French, "decorative wreath"

Gar, Garlan, Garlin, Garlind, Garr

Garner: Old German, "warrior who protects the weak"

Garrett: Old German, "mighty spearman"

Garet, Garett, Garret

Garrick: Old German, "one who rules with the spear"

Garson: French, "he who protects"

Garth: a Scandinavian variation of Gardner, "one who works the land"

Gary: Old German, "brave spearman"

Garey, Garry

Gavin: Welsh, "he who is like a hawk"

Gavan, Gaven, Gawain, Gawayne

Gaylord: Old French, "he who is joyous, happy, jolly"

Gaynor: Irish, "son of the fair-complected one"

Gaine, Gayner

Geary: Middle English, "he who is adaptable"

GEORGE WASHINGTON CARVER (1861–1943)

was born into slavery the same year the American Civil War began. A man of faith, he became a leading agriculturist, and his inventive work with the "lowly peanut" led him to greatness.

Gene: Usually a diminutive for Eugene

Geno, Gino

Geoffrey: Old German, "the peace of God"—a variation of Jeffrey, "kept by the peace of God"

Geof, Geoff, Jeff, Jeffery, Jeffrey

George: Greek, "worker of the land" (farmer, husbandman)

Georges (French), Georgio (Italian), Jorge (Spanish), Jorgen (Danish)

GEORGE VERWER
(1938–)

was converted to Christ at age seventeen and was led by God to start Operation Mobilization (OM), an outreach to foreign lands, enhanced by the ministry's ships—the *Logos*, and, later, the *Logos II*.

GEORGE FOX
(1624–1691)

was the founder of the Quakers (the Society of Friends).

GEORGE WHITEFIELD
(1714–1770)

was a contemporary of John Wesley and a great preacher and teacher of the Bible. It was Whitefield who popularized the large outdoor meetings that characterized the Great Awakening.

GEORGE MÜLLER
(1805–1898)

was a British Christian, active among the Plymouth Brethren. He's largely remembered for his faith in God to provide for the daily needs of the several orphanages he founded. His autobiography is still popular among Christians everywhere.

Gerald: Old German, "mighty spearman"

Geraldo (Spanish), Gerrald, Gerrold, Gerry, Jerry

Gerard: Old German, "courageous spearman"

Gerrard, Gerry, Jerry

Germain: French, "he who comes

from Germany"

Germaine

GERARD MANLEY HOPKINS (1844–1889)

was an English poet and priest. Among his most notable poems is the classic "God's Grandeur."

Gian: Italian, a variation of John, "God is gracious"

This name can be combined with other Italian variations to produce an attractive name. One example is Giancarlo (John Charles).

*Gideon: Hebrew, "mighty warrior"

The story of Gideon, God's *"mighty warrior,"* is recounted in Judges 6–8.

Gifford: Old German, "generous giver"

Giff, Giffard

Gilbert: Old German, "bright pledge or promise"

Bert, Gil, Gilberto (Italian), Gilburt

G. K. (GILBERT KEITH) CHESTERTON (1874–1936)

was the popular writer of the Father Brown mystery stories and several books on the Christian faith still popular today, including *Orthodoxy* and *The Everlasting Man*.

*Gilead: Hebrew, "he who is strong"

There are three men named Gilead in the Bible. Gilead is also a region of the nation of Jordan.

Giles: Greek, "protected by a shield"

Gil, Gilles

Gilman: Irish, "servant of Gil, Gil's man"

Gil, Gill

Gilmer: Old English, "notable hostage"

Gil, Gill

Gilroy: Irish, "he who serves royalty"

Gil, Gill, Gillroy

Gino: Italian, a variation of Gene,

from Eugene, "of noble birth"

Giovanni: Italian, a variation of John, "God is gracious"
Gian, Gianni, Van, Vanny

Giuseppe: Italian, a variation of Joseph, "God shall add"

Glade: Old English, "he who brings happiness"
Glades

Glen: Irish, "a glen or valley"
Glenn, Glyn, Glynn

Glendon: Scottish, "he who lives in the glen"
Glen, Glenden, Glenn

Goddard: Old German, "the firmness of God"
Gothart

Godfrey: Old German, "the peace of God"

*Goliath: Hebrew, "he who is sent away"
Read the story of the giant man whom David killed in 1 Samuel 17.

*Gomer: Hebrew, "to make complete"
(See Genesis 10:2–3; 1 Chronicles 1:5; Ezekiel 38:6.)

Gonzales: Spanish, "wolf"
Gonsalve, Gonzalo, Gonzo

Goodwin: Old German, "godly friend"
Godwin, Goodwyn

Gordon: Old English, "he who comes from the hill"
Gord, Gordan, Gorden, Gordie, Gordy

Gower: Welsh, "he who is pure"

Grady: Latin, from the same root as our word *grade*, meaning a step or level

Graham: Old English, "lavish home"
Graeham, Grahame

Granger: Middle French, "he who farms"
Grange, Gray

Grant: French, "he who bestows, or grants"
Grantley

Granville: Old French, "from the big town"
Grenville, Greville

Gregory: Greek, "watchman"
Greg, Gregg, Gregor

GREG LAURIE
(1952–)

is a popular pastor,
speaker, and author.

GREGORY OF NYSSA
(330–395)

was the bishop of Nyssa and
an important figure in the
fourth-century church.

Gresham: Old English, "from the village by the grazing land"

Griffin: Latin, "hook-nosed one"
Griff, Griffen

Griffith: Welsh, "powerful leader"
Griff, Griffyth

Grover: Old English, "one who comes from the grove"
Grove

Guido: Italian, "he who guides"

Guillaume: French, a variation of William, "resolute protector"

Guillermo: Spanish, a variation of William, "resolute protector"

Gunnar: Norse, "warrior"

Gunther: Scandinavian, "warrior"
Gunnar, Gunter (German),
Gunthar

Gustav: German, "God's staff"
Guss, Gussie, Gustaf
(Swedish), Gustave, Gustavo
(Spanish), Gustavus

Guy: Irish, "he who guides"
Guido (Italian), Guyon
(French)

H

Haddon: Scottish, "from the heather"
Haddan, Hadden, Hadyn

Hale: Old English, "whole, complete"
Hayle

Haley: Irish, "he who has a superior mind; bright man"
Hailey, Haily, Hale

Hallan: English, "he who dwells at the hall"
Halen, Hallin, Halyn

Hamilton: Old English, "from the privileged estate"
Hamel, Hamil

Hamlin: Old German, "he who

cherishes his home"
Hamblyn, Hamlyn

*Hamuel: Hebrew, "God is my warmth"
(See 1 Chronicles 4:26.)

*Hanan: Hebrew, "he who has grace"
There are several Hanans in the Bible, including a descendant of Saul and his son Jonathan. (See 1 Chronicles 8:38; 9:44.)

*Hananiah: Hebrew, "Jehovah is full of grace"
There are fourteen Hananiahs in the Bible, all of them minor characters.

*Haniel: Hebrew, "he who has the grace of God"
Hanniel
(See Numbers 34:23; 1 Chronicles 7:39.)

Hank: English, usually a diminutive of Henry

Hansel: German, usually a diminutive of Johannes, the German variation of John, "God is gracious"
Hans, Hannes

*Haran: Hebrew, "he who is strong"

There are three Harans in the Bible, all minor characters.

Harbin: German, "small and strong warrior"

Harden: Old English, "from the valley of the Hares"
Hardin, Hardyn

Hardy: Old English, "he who is enduring"

Harlan: German, "from the warriors"
Harland, Harlen, Harlin, Harlon

Harley: Old English, "from the long pasture"
Harleigh, Harly

Harold: German, "noted warrior"
Hal, Haroldo (Spanish), Harry

Harper: Old English, "he who plays the harp"

Harrison: Old English, "son of Harry"
Harris, Harry

Harry: Usually a diminutive of Harold, Harrison, or Henry but used occasionally as a proper name in its own right

Hart: Old German, "a male deer, a stag"
Harte, Hartley

Harvey: Old German, "ready warrior"
Harve, Herve (French), Hervey

Hasani: Swahili, "he who is handsome"
Hasain, Hasan, Hason

Haven: Old English, "place of safety, refuge"

Heath: Middle English, "he who comes from the heath"
Heathe, Heith

Heathcliff: Middle English, "he who comes from the cliff near the heath"

Hector: Greek, "he who is firm, resolute"

Hein: Asian/Vietnamese, "he who is gentle"—can be masculine or feminine

Henry: Old German, "he who rules the home"
Hank, Hendrick (Dutch), Henri (French)

Herbert: Old German, "illustrious warrior"
Bert, Hebert, Herb, Herbie

Herman: Old German, "warrior"
Harmon, Hermon

Herschel: Hebrew, "deer"
Herschell, Hershel

*Hezekiah: Hebrew, "God is my strength"
Hezekiah was a king of Israel whose prayer for additional years of life was granted by God. (See 2 Kings 20:1–11.)

Hiatt: Old English, "from the high gate"
Hi, Hyatt

Hillary: Latin, "he who is cheerful"
Hil, Hilaire (French), Hilarian, Hilario (Spanish), Hilary, Hill, Hillery

*Hillel: Hebrew, "he who is highly esteemed"
(See Judges 12:13–15.)

*Hiram: Hebrew, "he who is exalted"
Hi, Hyram
There are two Hirams in the Bible, both minor characters.

*Hodiah: Hebrew, "he who honors God"

Hod

(See 1 Chronicles 3:24.)

Hogan: Irish, "youthful one"

Holden: Old German, "he who is kind"

Hollis: Old English, "he who lives by the holly groves"

Holmes: Norwegian, "from the land by the waters"

Holm, Hume

Holt: Old English, "from the forested hill"

Homer: Greek, "he who is held hostage"

Horace: Latin, "he who keeps the time"

Horatio, Horatius

*Hosea: Hebrew, "he who has God's salvation"

Hosea was an Old Testamant prophet. See the book of the Bible that bears his name.

Houston: Scottish, "from Hugh's town"

Huston

Howard: Old German, "he who guards"

Howe, Howie

Hoyt: Norse, "of the soul"

Hubert: Old German, "he who is mentally sharp, bright"

Bert, Hobart, Huber, Hugh

Hugh: Old German, "wise one, mentally sharp"

Huey, Hughes, Hugo

Humbert: Old German, "notable Hun"

Humberto, Umberto (Italian)

Humphrey: Old German, "peacemaker"

Humphry

Hunter: Old English, "he who hunts"

Hunt, Huntley

Hyde: English, a land measurement of approximately 120 acres

Hyman: Hebrew, "life"—a variation of Chaim

Haim, Hy, Hymie

I

Ian: A Scottish variation of John, "God is gracious"

Ean, Iain

(Major) Ian Thomas
(1914–2007)

founded the ministry of
Torchbearers International
and had a worldwide
teaching ministry for many
decades. He wrote several
books, including *The Saving
Life of Christ.*

*Ichabod: Hebrew—a sad name,
signifying "the spirit of the
Lord has departed"

Ignatius: Latin, "full of
enthusiasm, eager"
  Ignace, Ignacio

Ignatius
(d. c. 110)

was a first-century Christian
who served as the bishop
of Antioch. His writings
provide much insight into
the function and beliefs of
the early church.

Igor: Norse, "he who is heroic"

Ike: Usually a diminutive for Isaac

Ilias: A Greek variation of Elijah,
"the Lord, my God"

Immanuel: See Emmanuel

Ingmar: Scandinavian, "noted son"
  Ing, Inge, Inger

Ingram: Old English, "angel,
messenger of God"

Innis: Irish, "he who is from the
island"
  Innes

Ira: Hebrew, "he who watches,
guards"

Ira Sankey
(1840–1908)

was a noted gospel singer
who traveled with evangelist
Dwight L. Moody.

*Iri: Hebrew, "he who is watched
by God"
(See 1 Chronicles 7:7.)

Irving: Irish, "he who is
handsome"
  Irv, Irvin, Irvine, Irwin

*Isaac: Hebrew, "he who laughs"
  Ike, Itzaak, Itzak, Izaak, Izak,
Izzy, Zak

Isaac was the son of Abraham, born through his wife Sarah, in fulfillment of God's promise to Abraham. Isaac's story begins in Genesis 17 and is one of the most dramatic in the Bible.

> ### ISAAC WATTS
> ### (1674–1748)
>
> was an English writer of more than 500 hymns, many of which are still beloved today. Best known are the popular Christmas carol "Joy to the World" and the year-round favorite "When I Survey the Wondrous Cross."

*Isaiah: Hebrew, "God is my salvation"

Isa, Isiah, Issiah

Isaiah was one of Israel's most important prophets. Many prophecies of the coming Messiah are recorded in the book of the Bible that bears his name.

*Ishmael: Hebrew, "God has heard"

Ishmael was the son born to Abraham through Hagar, Sarah's handmaiden. Ishmael eventually became the founder of the tribal people called the Midianites. (See Genesis 16–17.)

*Israel: Hebrew, "he who has prevailed with God" or "a prince of God"

Israel was the new name given to Jacob at Jabbok after he prevailed in wrestling the angel of God. (See Genesis 32:28.)

*Issachar: Hebrew, "he who is rewarded"

There are two Issachars in the Bible, one of whom was the ninth son of Jacob and the head of one of the twelve tribes of Israel. (See Genesis 30:18.)

Ivan: A Russian variation of John, "God is gracious"

Ivano, Ivo, Vanya

Ives: Old English, "hunter with a bow and arrow"—literally, an archer

Yves (French)

*Izziah: Hebrew, "God exalts" (See Ezra 10:25.)

J

*Jaanai: Hebrew, "God answers my prayer"

Janai
(See 1 Chronicles 5:12.)

*Jabez: Hebrew, "he is born of pain"

Jabe, Jay

Jabez was born into affliction, but his life was blessed because he prayed and trusted in God to enlarge his circumstances. (See 1 Chronicles 4:9–10.)

*Jabin: Hebrew, "God, the creator"

(See Joshua 11:1–14; Judges 4; Psalm 83:9.)

*Jachin: Hebrew, "God establishes"

There are three Jachins in the Bible, all minor characters.

Jack: Usually a diminutive of John, Jacob, or Jackson, but also often used as a proper name in its own right

Jackie, Jacko, Jackson (son of Jack), Jock

*Jacob: Hebrew, "he who supplants another"

Jack, Jacobus, Jake, Jakob

Jacob was the younger of twin brothers born to Isaac and Rebekah. He traded a bowl of food to his hungry twin, Esau, in exchange for Esau's birthright, and he also stole Esau's blessing. (See Genesis 25; 27:1–40.)

JACK HAYFORD (1934–) is a leading pastor in the Foursquare denomination and a prolific author. His works include *Prayer Is Invading the Impossible* and the popular worship chorus "Majesty."

Jacques: A French variation of Jacob, "he who supplants another"

JACOBUS ARMINIUS (1559–1609) was a Dutch theologian and pastor whose teachings have long been held in contrast to those of John Calvin.

*Jadon: Hebrew, "God has heard"

Jaden, Jay, Jaydon

(See Nehemiah 3:7.)

Jael: Hebrew, "mountain goat"

Yael

*Jahleel: Hebrew, "God is patient"
Jaleel
(See Genesis 46:14;
Numbers 26:26.)

Jaime: Spanish, a variation of
James, from Jacob, "he who
supplants another"

*Jairus: Hebrew, "God gives light"
(See Mark 5:22; Luke 8:41.)

Jake: Usually a diminutive of
Jacob, "he who supplants
another"

*Jakeh: Hebrew, "he who is
devout"
(See Proverbs 30:1.)

Jamal: Arabic, "he who is
handsome"
Jahmal, Jahmil, Jamaal, Jamar

*James: English, a variation of
Jacob, "he who supplants
another"
Jamie, Jaymes, Jim, Jimmie,
Jimmy
There are four men named
James in the New Testament.
Two of them were disciples
of Jesus. One of these was the
brother of John the disciple.
Jesus referred to the two
brothers as "Sons of Thunder"
(Mark 3:17). The second of
these was the son of Alphaeus.

(See Matthew 10:3; Mark
3:18; Luke 6:15.) The third
James was the father of the
disciple Judas (not Iscariot).
(See Luke 6:16.) The fourth
James was the half-brother of
the Lord Jesus. (See Matthew
13:55; Mark 6:3; Acts 12:17;
15:13; 21:18; 1 Corinthians
15:7; Galatians 1:19; 2:9, 12;
James 1:1.)

JAMES (JIM) ELLIOT (1927–1956)

was one of the five
missionaries to Ecuador
who were martyred by the
Huaorani (Auca) people,
whom they wished to reach.
Their story has been told
in books written by Jim's
widow, Elisabeth Elliot. Jim
penned the widely known
Christian motto, "He is
no fool who gives what he
cannot keep to gain what
he cannot lose."

Jameson: English, "son of James"
Jamison, Jim, Jimmie, Jimmy

Jamie: English, usually a
diminutive of James but also
often a proper name in its own
right

JAMES HUDSON TAYLOR
(1832–1905)

was a pioneering missionary to China. His book, *Hudson Taylor's Spiritual Secret*, is considered a classic on living the victorious Christian life.

Jamil: Arabic, "he who is handsome"
Jamal, Jameel, Jamel

*Jamin: Hebrew, "he who is highly favored"
Jamian, Jamien, Jamon, Jaymin
There are three Jamins in the Old Testament, all minor characters.

*Jamlech: Hebrew, "Jehovah is king"
(See 1 Chronicles 4:34.)

Jan: Usually, a Dutch variation of John, "God is gracious," but also a proper name in its own right

Janson: English, "son of Jan"
Jan, Jans, Janse, Janzen

*Japheth: Hebrew, "he who is beautiful"
Japeth, Japh, Japhet, Jay
Japheth was the second son of Noah. (See Genesis 5:3; 6:10; 7:13; 9:18–27; 10:1–32.)

*Jarah: Hebrew, "honey"
Jara, Jera, Jerah
(See 1 Chronicles 9:42.)

*Jared: Hebrew, "he who descends"—from the same root as *Jordan*
Jerad, Jered, Jareth, Jarrod
(See Genesis 5:15–20; 1 Chronicles 1:2; Luke 3:37.)

Jarman: Old German, "he who comes from Germany"

Jaron: Hebrew, "he who sings"
Jaran, Jaren, Jarin

Jarrett: Old English, "brave spearman"
Jaret, Jerrett, Jerry

Jarvis: Old German, "spearlike, sharp"

*Jashen: Hebrew, "he who sleeps"
(See 2 Samuel 23:32.)

*Jason: Greek, "he who heals"
Jase, Jasen, Jasin, Jay, Jayce, Jayson
(See Romans 16:21; Acts 17:5–9.)

Jasper: Persian, "treasure; spotted stone"

Jasper was a stone in the breastplate of the Old Testament high priest. (See Exodus 28:15–20.)

Jaspar, Jazz

*Jathniel: Hebrew, "God gives gifts"
(See 1 Chronicles 9:14; 26:2.)

*Javan: Hebrew, "made of clay"

Javan was a grandson of Noah. (See Genesis 10:2; 1 Chronicles 1:5–7; Isaiah 66:19.)

Jay: Often a diminutive of many "J" names, such as Jeremiah, Jason, and Jacob, but also a proper name in its own right

Jean: French, a variation of John, "God is gracious"

*Jeconiah: Hebrew, "established by God"
Jeconia, Jeconias
(See Matthew 1:11–12.)

*Jediah: Hebrew, "God knows"
Jed, Jedaiah, Jedia
There are several Jediahs in the Bible, all minor characters.

*Jedidiah: Hebrew, "God is my friend"
Jed, Jedediah, Jedi
(See 2 Samuel 12:25.)

Jeffrey: Old English, "kept by the peace of God"
Geoffrey, Jeff, Jefferson (son of Jeff), Jeffery, Jeffy

*Jehiah: Hebrew, "God lives"
(See 1 Chronicles 15:24.)

*Jemuel: Hebrew, "God is light"
(See Genesis 46:10; Exodus 6:15.)

Jens: A Scandinavian variation of John, "God is gracious"
Jenson ("son of Jens")

*Jeremiah: Hebrew, "God is exalted"
Jeremia, Jeremias, Jerry
There are several Jeremiahs in the Bible. The most notable is the prophet whose book in the Bible bears his name.

Jeremy: English, a variation of the Hebrew Jeremiah/Jeremias, "God is exalted"
Jaramy, Jeremey, Jerry

Jeriah: Hebrew, "God has seen"

*Jeriel: Hebrew, "founded of God" (See 1 Chronicles 7:2.)

Jermaine: French, "to sprout," from the same root as the word *germinate*—or "from Germany"

Germaine, Jermain, Jermane

Jerome: Greek, "sacred name"

Jerom, Jeron, Jerrome, Jerry

Jerry: Usually a diminutive of Gerald or Gerard

*Jesher: Hebrew, "he who is righteous"

Jesh, Jeshar (See 1 Chronicles 2:18.)

JERRY B. JENKINS (1949–)

is a hugely popular Christian author with more than one hundred sixty books to his credit, including the megaselling *Left Behind* series.

---

*Jesiah: Hebrew, "God exists" (See 1 Chronicles 12:6; 23:20.)

*Jesse: Hebrew, "he who is graced by God"

Jess, Jessie, Jessy

Jesse was the father of King David and thus an ancestor of the Lord Jesus Christ. He was also the grandson of Ruth and Boaz. (See 1 Samuel 17:12–14.)

JESSE OWENS (1913–1980)

was an American athlete who won four gold medals in track and field at the 1936 Olympic games in Berlin, Germany. His story is told in his autobiography, *Jesse*.

---

*Jesus: Hebrew, "God is my salvation"

Jesus Christ, the Savior of mankind, is, of course, the primary individual in the Bible. Jesus means "God is salvation," which was literally true, as God Himself came in the form of man to bear our sins. This name, in association with Jesus Christ, is the name *"that is above every name"* (Philippians 2:9). The name

Jesus can also be translated as Jeshua, Jehoshua, and Joshua. In modern times, the name Jesús (pronounced "hay-oose") has been extremely popular in Latin American cultures, far less so elsewhere.

*Jethro: Hebrew, "he who is prosperous"

Jethro was the father-in-law of Moses. (See Exodus 3:1; 4:18; 18:1–12.)

*Jibsam: Hebrew, "he who is sweet"

(See 1 Chronicles 7:2.)

Jim: Almost always a diminutive of James

Jimmie, Jimmy

*Joab: Hebrew, "God is my good father"

There are several Joabs in the Old Testament, mostly minor characters.

*Joachim: Hebrew, "the Lord is my judge"

*Joah: Hebrew, "God is my brother"

There are several Joahs in the Bible, mostly minor characters.

Joaquín: A Spanish variation of Joachim, "the Lord is my judge"

*Job: Hebrew, "he who is afflicted"

Jobe, Joby

Read Job's miraculous story of tragedy and restoration in the book bearing his name.

*Joda: Hebrew, "he who is hasty"

(See Ezra 3:9; Luke 3:26.)

Jody: English, usually a diminutive of Joseph but often a proper name in its own right

*Joed: Hebrew, "Jehovah is my witness"

(See Nehemiah 11:7.)

*Joel: Hebrew: "the Lord Jehovah is God"

There are several Joels in the Bible, including the prophet Joel. See the Old Testament book that bears his name.

JOHANN GUTENBERG (1398–1468)

was a German metalworker who developed a press with movable type, which revolutioned the printing process.

JOHN BUNYAN
(1628–1688)

was a preacher in seventeenth-century England who dissented from the practices of the Anglican church. His book *Pilgrim's Progress* is arguably the best-selling fictional work of all time.

JOHN CALVIN
(1509–1564)

was a key figure in the Protestant Reformation.

JOHN NEWTON
(1725–1807)

was a debauched slave trader until his conversion at age twenty-three. He's best remembered today for his hymn "Amazing Grace."

*Joha: Hebrew, "Jehovah lives"
  (See 1 Chronicles 8:16; 11:45.)

Johan: German, a variation of John, "God is gracious"
  Johann, Johannes

JOHN PERKINS
(1930–)

was born into poverty in Mississippi. Converted to Christ at age twenty-seven, he began helping and serving poor communities in his home state. His courageous story is told in his book *With Justice for All.*

*Johanan: Hebrew, "God is gracious"
  There are eleven Johanans in the Bible, all minor characters.

JOHN SUNG
(1901–1944)

was a native-born Chinese evangelist.

*John: Hebrew, "God is gracious"
  Giovanni (Italian), Hannes (Finnish), Hans (Scandinavian), Ian (Scottish), Ivan (Russian), Jack, Jackie, Jean (French), Jens (Danish), Johann (German), Johnny, Juan (Spanish), Sean (Irish), Yanni (Greek)—see also Jonathan

  The two most notable Johns in the Bible are John the Baptist and the apostle John. The great apostle was the author of several books in the Bible, including the gospel and the three epistles that bear his name, as well as the book of Revelation.

JOHN WESLEY
(1707–1788)

is one of the most influential theologians and preachers of all time. For generations, male sons have been blessed with the first and middle names John and Wesley.

*Joiakim: Hebrew, "Jehovah establishes"
(See Nehemiah 12:10, 26.)

*Jonah: Hebrew, "dove"
Jonah was, in a sense, the first missionary. The prophet was sent to Nineveh to call the people of the city to repentance. See the book bearing Jonah's name for the story of his mission.

*Jonan: Hebrew, "God has been gracious"
(See Luke 3:30.)

*Jonas: A variation of John, "God is gracious"

*Jonathan: Hebrew, "he who is a gift from the Lord"
Jon, Jonathon, Jonny
There are fourteen Jonathans in the Bible, the most notable being the great warrior and beloved friend of King David. Read about their friendship in 1 Samuel 18.

JONATHAN EDWARDS
(1703–1758)

is one of the most influential clergymen in American history. Many of his writings are still read today, including his well-known sermon "Sinners in the Hands of an Angry God."

JONATHAN GOFORTH
(1859–1936)

along with his wife, Rosalind (1864–1942), gave his life to Christ in service as a missionary to China. The couple suffered great hardship, but their efforts bore much fruit in advancing the gospel in Asia.

*Jorah: Hebrew, "he who teaches" (See 1 Chronicles 5:13; Ezra 2:18.)

*Joram: Hebrew, "God is on high"
There are five Jorams in the Bible, all minor characters.

Jordan: Hebrew, "descending" (apparently a reference to the descending waters of the Jordan River)
Jordy, Jordyn

Jorge: Spanish, a variation of George, "worker of the land"

*Jorim: Hebrew, "he who exalts the Lord" (See Luke 3:29.)

José: Spanish, a variation of Joseph, "God shall add"

*Joseph: Hebrew, "God shall add"
Giuseppe (Italian), Joe, Joey, José (Spanish), Josef (German), Yusseff (Hebrew)
There are several Josephs in the Bible. Two of them are key characters. In the Old Testament, Joseph, the beloved son of Jacob, was betrayed by his brothers, and yet that betrayal ultimately resulted in the preservation of his family. (See Genesis 37–50.) In the New Testament, Joseph was the husband of Mary, the mother of the Lord Jesus. (See Matthew 1:16–2:23; Luke 1:22–2:52.)

*Joses: Hebrew, "he who pardons"
There are three men with the name Joses in the Bible, all minor characters.

*Joshua: Hebrew, "my salvation is of God"
Josh, Joshuah
Joshua was the successor of Moses in leading the Hebrews into the Promised Land. Read his story in several books in the Old Testament, including Exodus, Numbers, Deuteronomy, Joshua, and Judges.

JOSH McDOWELL
(1939–)

is a Christian evangelist and apologist who has influenced many through his books and ministry. His book *Evidence that Demands a Verdict* (1972) has served as a documentation of the historical facts of the gospel accounts for nearly a generation.

*Josiah: Hebrew, "may God protect"

Josiah was one of the good kings of Judah. His reign began when he was eight years old. (See 1 Kings 13:2; 2 Chronicles 34:3.)

*Jotham: Hebrew, "God is perfect"

There are three Jothams in the Bible. (See Judges 9:5; 1 Chronicles 2:47; 2 Kings 15:32.)

Jovan: Slavic, a variation of John, "God is gracious"

Jovani, Jovann, Jovin

Juan: Spanish, a variation of John, "God is gracious"

*Jubal: Hebrew, "ram's horn" (See Genesis 4:21.)

*Judah: Hebrew, "he who is praised"

Judas (Latin), Judd, Jude

There are several men in the Bible with variations of this popular name. The most prominent Judah is the fourth son of Jacob and Leah, who was the head of the tribe bearing his name. (See Genesis 29:35; Numbers 26:19–21; 1 Chronicles 2:3–6.)

Julian: Greek, "he who is youthful"

Jule, Jules, Julien, Julio (Spanish), Julius

Julio: Spanish, a variation of Julian, "he who is youthful"

Junius: Latin, "he who is young"—a variation of Julian

Justin: Latin, "he who is upright, just"

Juss, Justis, Justiss, Justus, Justyn

K

*Kadmiel: Hebrew, "God is from of old"

Cadmiel

There are three Kadmiels in the Bible, all minor characters.

Kai: Welsh, "he who protects, secures," as with a lock and key

Kala: African, "he who is tall"

Cala, Kalla

Kalil: Arabic, "he who is a friend"

Kahlil

*Kallai: Hebrew, "God is fast" (See Nehemiah 12:20.)

Kalle: Scandinavian, "virile, masculine"

Cale, Kael, Kail, Kale, Kayle

Kane: Celtic, "he who is fair-complected"

Kain, Kaine, Kayne

Karl: German, a variation of Charles, "masculine, manly, virile"

Carl, Karel (Slavic), Karlis, Karol (Slavic)

KARL BARTH
(1886–1968)

was a very influential theologian and writer of the twentieth century.

Karsten: Slavic, a variation of Christian, "anointed one"

Kashka: Yoruba (Nigeria), "he who is friendly to others"

Kavan: Irish, "he who is attractive"

Caven, Kaven, Kavin, Kavyn

Kean: Old English, "sharp, keen"

Keane, Keenan, Keene

Keefe: Irish, "he who is attractive"

Keef, Kief, Kiefe

Keegan: Irish, "little determined one"

Keeley: Irish, "he who is attractive"

Keely

Keenan: Irish, "little ancient one"

Keen, Kienan

***Keilah:** Hebrew, "he who is enclosed"

(See 1 Chronicles 4:19.)

Keir: Celtic, "he who is dark-skinned"

Kerwin, Kerwyn

Keith: Welsh, "he who is from the wooded area"

KEITH GREEN
(1953–1982)

was a popular singer, evangelist, and exhorter during the days of the Jesus Movement. His inspiring story is told in his biography *No Compromise.*

Kellen: Irish, "victorious warrior"

Kell, Kellan, Kelly

Keller: Irish, "faithful friend"

Kelly: Irish, "courageous warrior"

Kelley

Kelsey: Old German, "he who lives by the water"

Kelcey, Kelsy

Kelvin: Scottish, "from the narrow brook"

Celvin, Kelvan, Kelwin

Kempton: Middle English, "from the warriors"

Kemp, Kemper

*Kemuel: Hebrew, "our God stands"

There are three Kemuels in the Bible, all minor characters.

*Kenan: Hebrew, "he who is begotten"

Kenan was grandson of Adam. (See Genesis 5:9.)

Kendall: Celtic, "he who comes from the valley"

Ken, Kendal, Kendell, Kenny

Kendrick: English, "strong ruler"

Ken, Kendric, Kenny, Kenrick, Rick, Ricky

Kennedy: Gaelic, "he who wears the helmet"

Kenner: Irish, "he who is of great courage"

Ken, Kennar, Kennard

Kenneth: Celtic, "he who is attractive"

Ken, Kenn, Kenny

KENNETH TAYLOR (1917–2005)

was a giant in the Christian publishing industry of the twentieth century. His paraphrase of the Bible, *The Living Bible*, brought easier access to the Word of God for millions of readers. He was the founder of Tyndale House Publishers, one of the largest Christian publishing companies in America today.

Kent: Celtic, "fair-complected one"

Kenton

Kenyon: Irish, "he who is fair-haired, towheaded"

Ken, Kenny

Kenzie: Scottish, "worthy master"

Kermit: Dutch, "he who is from the church"

Kerry: Irish, "he who is dark"

Carey, Cary, Keary

Kerwin: Celtic, "he who is dark-

skinned"
Keir, Kerwyn

Kevin: Celtic, "he who is gentle"
Kevan, Kevyn

Kiefer: A German variation of
Cooper, "barrelmaker"
Keefer

Kieran: Irish, "he who is dark"
Kier, Kiernan

Killian: Gaelic, "small warrior"
Kilian, Killy, Killyan, Kilyan

Kimball: Old English, "brave
warrior"
Kim, Kimble

Kimberly: An English place name,
referring to a meadow
Kim

Kincaid: Scottish, "he who leads
in battle"
Kinkade

King: Old English, "he who rules"

Kingsley: Old English, "he who is
from the king's meadow"

Kingston: Old English, "he who is
from the king's manor"

Kipp: Old English, "he who is
from the steep hill"

Kip, Kipper, Kippy

Kirby: Old English, "he who is
from the church village"
Kerby

Kirk: Scottish, "he who is from
the church"—sometimes a
diminutive of Kirkland or
Kirkham

Kit: Usually, a diminutive of
Christopher
Kitt

Kivi: Hebrew, "he who is
protected"
Akiva, Kiva

Klaus: A German diminutive of
Nicholas
Klaas, Klas

Knox: English, "he who is from
the hill"

Knute: Danish, "he who is kind"
Canute, Knut

Konrad: German, a variation of
Conrad, "wise counselor"

Kristopher: An alternate spelling
of Christopher, "Christ-bearer"
Kris, Topher

Kurtis: An alternate spelling of
Curtis, "small one"
Kurt

Kyle: Irish, "a narrow strip of land"
Kiel, Kile, Kiley, Ky, Kyler, Kylie

Kynan: Welsh, "he who rules"
Ky

Kyne: English, "he who has royal blood"

L

***Laban:** Hebrew, "he who is white"
Laban was the brother of Rebekah, the father of Rachel and Leah, and the father-in-law of Jacob. (See Genesis 24; 27–28.)

***Lael:** Hebrew, "he who is committed to God"
(See Numbers 3:24.)

Laird: Scottish, "lord"

Lamar: Old French, "from the sea"
Lamarr, Lemarr

Lambert: Old German, "beautiful land"
Bert, Bertie, Berty, Lamberto

***Lamech:** Hebrew, "he who overthrows"
There are two Lamechs in the Bible, including the father of Noah. (See Genesis 5:26–31; Luke 3:36.)

Lamont: French, "the mountain"
Lamond

Lance: Originally a diminutive of Lancelot but, more often, a proper name in its own right
Launce

Lancelot: Latin, "he who serves"
Lan, Lance, Lanny, Launce, Launcelot

Landers: French, "he who is from the grassy plains"
Lan, Land, Lander, Landess, Landis

Landon: Old English, "he who comes from the meadowlands"
Lan, Landan, Lanny

Lane: Middle English, "he who is from the lane, the simple road"
Laine, Layne

Lang: Scandinavian, "he who is tall"
Lange

Langston: Old English, "long town"

Lanh: Asian/Vietnamese, "he who is peaceful"

Larken: Irish, "he who is determined"

Lark, Larkin, Larkyn

Larnelle: Apparently, an American name with unknown roots

Larnel, Larnell

Larry: Usually a diminutive of Lawrence, Laurence, or Lars

Lars: Swedish, originally a diminutive of Lawrence but also a proper name on its own

Laris, Larris, Larson ("son of Lars")

Latham: Scandinavian, "from the barn"

Laurence: Latin, "he who wears the laurel wreath"

Lan, Lanny, Larren, Larry, Lars, Laurie, Lawrence

Lavan: Hebrew, "white"

Lavi: Hebrew, "lion"

***Lazarus:** Hebrew, "grace"

Lazar, Lazaro (Italian)

There are two men named Lazarus in the Bible. The first one is in Jesus' story about the poor man who died and was taken to Abraham's bosom, where he was separated from the rich man by a wide, unspannable gulf. (See Luke 16:19–31.) The other Lazarus was the brother of Mary and Martha. Jesus raised him from the dead and restored him to his sisters. (See John 11; 12:1–7.)

BROTHER LAWRENCE (1611–1691)

was originally named Nicholas Herman. He served many years in the French Army, and then, in midlife, he joined a religious order where he served as a simple layman—a cook in the order's kitchen—for the next thirty years. And yet, his small but powerful book, *The Practice of the Presence of God*, continues to encourage and refresh Christians more than three hundred years after his death.

Leaf: English, literally, a tree leaf

Leal: Latin, "he who is faithful"

Leander: Greek, "he who is as fierce as a lion"

Ander, Anders, Lee

Leben: Yiddish, "life"

Lee: Old English, "from the meadow"

Leigh

Leif: Scandinavian, "he who is dearly loved"

Leighton: Old English, "from the farm meadowlands"

Lee

Leith: Celtic, "wide"

Leland: Old English, "from the land of shelter"

*Lemuel: Hebrew, "he who is dedicated to God"

Lem, Lemmy

(See Proverbs 31:1, 4.)

Leon: Usually a diminutive of Leonard

LEONARD RAVENHILL
(1907–1995)

was a British evangelist during the latter half of the twentieth century who exhorted Christians to pray and to live holy lives.

Leonard: Old German, "he who is like unto the lion"

Len, Lenny, Leo, Leon, Leonardo, Leonid, Leonidas

Leopold: Old German, "he who is

bold as a lion"

Leo

Leroy: Old French, "he who is royal"

Leslie: Scottish, "from the meadow in the valley"

Les, Lesley

Lester: Old English, a place name meaning "coming from Leicester"

Les

Lev: Hebrew, "heart"

*Levi: Hebrew, "united one"

Levy

There are four Levis in the Bible, including the third son of Jacob through Leah. His descendants became the Levitical priesthood.

Lewis: English, "noted warrior"

Lew, Lewie, Louis

LEWIS SPERRY CHAFER
(1871–1952)

was the founder of the influential Dallas Theological Seminary. His several books include *Grace*, *He That Is Spiritual*, and *True Evangelism*.

Lex: Greek, "the word"—also a diminutive of Alexander
Lexy, Lexxy

Liam: Irish, a variation of William, "resolute protector"

Lincoln: Old English, "he who comes from the town by the waters"
Linc

Lindsay: Old English, "from the island of linden trees"
Lin, Lind, Lindsey, Lindy, Lyn

*Linus: Greek, "he with flax-colored hair"
(See 2 Timothy 4:21.)

Lionel: Latin, "he who is like unto the lion"

Llewellyn: Welsh, "he who is like unto the lion"

Lloyd: Celtic, "gray, dark-complected one"
Loyd

Locke: Norse, "he who is last"
Loch, Lock

Logan: Scottish, "from the small hollow"

Lombard: German, "he who is bearded"
Bard, Lombardo

Lon: English, usually a diminutive of Alonzo, Lawrence, or Leonard
Lonnie, Lonny

London: English, a place name, from the British city of the same name
Lon, Lonnie

Loren: Latin, a variation of Laurence, "he who wears the laurel wreath"
Lorin, Lorren

Lorenzo: Italian, a variation of Laurence, "he who wears the laurel wreath"
Lorenso, Lorentz, Lorry, Ren, Rennie

LORENZO DOW
(1777–1834)

was a hugely popular revivalist of the Second Great Awakening—so popular that, by the mid-nineteenth century, Lorenzo was a favorite name for male babies in the United States.

Lorne: Latin, a variation of Laurence, "he who wears the laurel wreath"

*Lot: Hebrew, "he who is hidden"
Lot was Abraham's nephew.
(See Genesis 12:1–6; 13–14;
19.)

Louis: Old German, "noted warrior"
Lewis, Lou, Louie

Lowell: Old English, "he who is praiseworthy"
Lovell, Lowe, Lowel

Lucas: A variation of Luke, "he who brings light," that has become popular as a proper name in its own right
Lukas, Luke

Lucian: Latin, "he who brings light"
From the same root as *Lucifer*, the angel of light who fell into condemnation due to pride. However, in relation to the original intention, the variations of this name should represent any child of God who will bring the true light of Christ to those who do not know Him.
Luciano (Italian), Lucien, *Lucius (see Acts 13:1; Romans 16:21)

Ludwig: German, a variation of Louis, "noted warrior"

Luigi: Italian, a variation of Louis, "noted warrior"

Luís: Spanish, a variation of Louis, "noted warrior"

**Luís Palau
(1934–)**

is an Argentine-born evangelist who has led hundreds of thousands to Christ in his extensive international ministry.

*Luke: Latin, "he who brings light"
Lucas, Lukas, Luken

Luke was a physician, a man of great learning, and a committed follower of Jesus Christ. In addition to the gospel bearing his name, the book of Acts was written by Luke.

**Lyman Beecher
(1775–1863)**

was the father of Henry Ward Beecher and Harriet Beecher Stowe, two of the most influential religious figures of the nineteenth century. Lyman Beecher was an ardent revivalist who helped to found the American Bible Society.

Luther: Old German, "he who is a renowned warrior"

Lyle: Old French, "from the island"

Lyman: Old English, "he who comes from the meadow"

Lyndon: Old English, "linden tree"
Linden, Lindin, Lyn

Lynn: Old English, "beside the flowing water"
Lin, Lyn

Lysander: Greek, "he who sets free"
Lysan, Sandy

***Lysias:** Greek, "he who sets free" (See Acts 23:26; 24:7, 22.)

M

***Maacah:** Hebrew, "compression"
Maachah
There are five Maacahs in the Old Testament. Perhaps the two most notable ones are Abraham's brother (see Genesis 22:24) and one of King David's mighty men (see 1 Chronicles 11:43).

Mabry: Old English, meaning uncertain

Mac: English, Irish, and Scottish prefix that means "son of"—also used as a stand-alone name
Mack, Mackey, Mackie

Macabee: Hebrew, "hammer"
Maccabee

Macadam: Scottish Gaelic, "son of Adam"
MacAdam, McAdam

Macallister: Scottish Gaelic, "son of Alistair"
MacAlister, McAlister, McAllister

Macdonald: Scottish Gaelic, "son of Donald"
MacDonald, McDonald

Mack: A diminutive of Mackenzie

Mackenzie: Irish Gaelic, "son of the wise ruler"—a name for both boys and girls
Mackenzie, MacKensie, McKensie, McKenzie

Mackinley: Irish Gaelic, "learned ruler"
MacKinlay, McKinlay, McKinley

Macon: Old English, "to make, create"
Makon

Macy: Old French, "Matthew's estate"

Mace, Maceo, Macey

Maddock: Old Welsh, "he who is benevolent"

Madoc, Madoch, Madock

Maddox: Old Welsh, "benefactor's son"

Maddocks, Madocks, Madox

Madison: Old English, "valiant warrior"

Maddie, Maddison, Maddy, Madisson

*Magdiel: Hebrew, "honor of God"

(See Genesis 36:43.)

Magee: Irish Gaelic, "son of Hugh"

MacGee, MacGhee, McGee

Magen: Hebrew, "protector"

Magnus: Latin, "he who is great"

Magnes, Magnusson, Manus

Maguire: Irish Gaelic, "son of the beige one"

MacGuire, McGuire, McGwire

*Mahlah: Hebrew, "mildness"

Mahalah

(See 1 Chronicles 7:18.)

Makaio: Hawaiian, a variation of Matthew, "gift of the Lord"

Makani: Hawaiian, "breeze"

Makimo: Hawaiian, a variation of Maximus, Latin, "the greatest"

*Malachi: Hebrew, "messenger of God"

Malachai, Malachie, Malachy, Malaki, Maleki

Malachi was an Old Testament prophet. You can read about him in the book of the Bible that bears his name.

Malakai: Hawaiian, a variation of Malachi, "messenger of God"

*Malchiah: Hebrew, "God is my king"

Malchijah

(See 1 Chronicles 6:40.)

*Malchiel: Hebrew, "God is my king"

(See 1 Chronicles 7:31.)

Malcolm: Scottish Gaelic, "servant of St. Columba"

Mal, Malkolm

Maleko: Hawaiian, a variation of Mark, "warlike"

Malin: Old English, "strong

warrior"

Mallen, Mallin, Mallon

Mallory: Old German, "army counselor"

Mallery, Mallorie, Malory

Maloney: Irish Gaelic, "pious"

Malone, Malonee, Malonie, Malony

Malvin: A variation of Melvin, "chief"

Malvyn

*Manasseh: Hebrew, "causing forgetfulness"

Manasseh and his brother, Ephraim, were sons of Joseph, the son of Jacob. Manasseh's descendants became one of the tribes of Israel. (See Genesis 41:51.) Manasseh was also the name of a wicked king of Israel. (See 2 Kings 21:1–2.)

Mandel: German, "almond"

Mandy, Mannie, Manny

Manfred: Old English, "man of peace"

Fred, Freddie, Freddy, Manifred, Mannie, Manny—additional variations are possible

Manley: Middle English,

"meadow" or "guardian of a pasture"

Manleigh, Manly, Mansfield, Manton

Manning: Old English, "to station, guard"

Mannyng

*Manoah: Hebrew, "rest, quiet"

Manoah was a godly man and the father of Samson. (See Judges 13.)

Mansfield: Old English, "field by the little river"

Manton: Old English, "man's town"

Mannton, Manten

Manuel: Spanish, a variation of Emmanuel, "God with us"

Mano, Manolo, Manny

Manville: Old French, "great town"

Mandeville, Manvel, Manvill, Manville

Marc: French, a variation of Mark, "warlike"

Marcel: Latin, "he who is a hard worker"

Marceau, Marcelin, Marcello (Italian), Marcellus, Marcelo (Spanish)

Marcos: Spanish variation of Marcus, "brilliant warrior, warlike"

Marcus: Latin, "brilliant warrior, warlike"

Marc, Marco, Marko, Markus

MARCUS WHITMAN (1802–1847)

was a physician who helped pioneer missionary work in the Oregon Territory in the 1830s and 1840s.

Marden: Old English, "sheltered place near the sea"

Marsden

Mario: Italian, a variation of Mark, "warlike"

Marianus, Marius, Meirion

Marion: Hebrew, "bitter, rebellious"—a name for both boys and girls

Mariano

*Mark: Latin, "warlike"

Marc (French), Marceau, Marcel, Marco, Marcos, Marcus, Mario, Marius, Marko, Markos (Greek), Markus, Marq—additional variations are possible

John Mark was a helper to Paul and Barnabas and a close companion of Peter. (See Acts 12:25.)

Marland: Old English, "land near the lake"

Marion, Marlin, Marlond, Marlondo

Marley: Old English, "meadow near the lake"

Marleigh, Marly

Marlin: Old English, "sea"

Mar, Mario, Marle, Marlis

Marlon: Old French, "wild hawk"

Marlen, Marlin, Marlinn, Marlonn

Marlow: Old English, "hill near the lake"

Marlo, Marloe, Marlowe

Marsden: Old English, "field near water"

Marden, Marsdon, Marston

Marsh: Old English, "swamp, marsh"

Marshall: Old French, "horse groomer"

Marchall, Marschal, Marsh, Marshal, Marshell

MARSHALL BROOMHALL
(1866–1937)

oversaw the literature ministry of China Inland Mission and wrote the classic biography of J. Hudson Taylor.

Marston: Old English, "town by the marsh"

Martin: Latin, "warlike one"
Mart, Marten, Marti (Spanish), Martie, Martine, Martino (Italian), Martinus, Marty, Martyn (Russian)

MARTIN LUTHER
(1483–1546)

was a successful Catholic priest who became a Protestant reformer. His mastery of the biblical languages enabled him to write an excellent German translation of the Bible.

Marvel: Latin, "a miracle"
Marvell, Marvelle

Marvin: Old English, "good or famous friend"

Marv, Marven, Mervin, Mervyn, Merwin, Merwyn, Murvin

MARTYN LLOYD-JONES
(1899–1981)

was initially a medical doctor but then became a Protestant minister noted for his exceptional, verse-by-verse style of preaching through the Bible. He taught at Westminster Chapel in London.

Masato: Japanese, "justice"

Mason: Old French, "stonecutter"
Maison, Masen, Sonnie, Sonny

Mataio: Hawaiian, a variation of Matthew, "gift of the Lord"

Mateo: Spanish, a variation of Matthew, "gift of the Lord"

Mather: Old English, "conqueror, powerful army"
Maither, Matther

***Mathusala:** See Methuselah

***Mattaniah:** Hebrew, "gift of

Jehovah"

There are nine Mattaniahs in the Old Testament, all of them minor characters.

*Matthan: Hebrew, "a gift"

There are two Matthans in the New Testament. (See Matthew 1:15; Luke 3:29.)

*Matthew: Hebrew, "gift of the Lord"

Mat, Mateo (Spanish), Matheu (German), Mathew, Mathias, Matias, Matt, Mattaus, Matteo (Italian), Matthaus, Mattheus, Matthias, Matthieu (French) Mattias, Mattie, Matty— additional variations are possible

Matthew was also known as Levi. He was a tax collector who gave up everything to become a disciple of Jesus. (See Luke 5:27, 29.)

MATTHEW HENRY (1662–1714)

was an English nonconformist minister and popular Bible commentator.

*Matthias: Hebrew, "gift of God"

Mathias, Mattias

Matthias was the disciple chosen to replace Judas. (See Acts 1:23–26.)

Maurice: Latin, "dark-skinned"

Maurey, Maurie, Maurise, Maury, Morey, Morice, Moris, Morrice, Morrie, Morris

Mawuli: Ewe (Ghana), "there is a God"

Max: A diminutive of Maxwell, "Mack's stream," or Maximilian, "greatest, distinguished one"

Maks, Maxence, Maxson

Maximilian: Latin, "greatest, distinguished one"

Mac, Mack, Maks, Max, Maxey, Maxemillan, Maxie, Maxim, Maximillian, Maximo (Spanish), Maximos (Greek), Maxy—additional variations are possible

Maxwell: Old English, "Mack's stream"

Maxwelle

Mayer: Latin, "he who is greater"

Maier, Meir, Meyer

Mayfield: Old English, "strong one's field"

Mayhew: Hebrew, "gift of the

Lord"—an Old French variation of Matthew

Mayhue

Maynard: Old German, "powerful"

May, Mayne, Maynhard, Menard

Mead: Old English, "from the meadow"

Meade, Meed, Meid

Medwin: Old German, "strong friend"

Medvin, Medwyn

*Mehida: Hebrew, "famous"

(See Ezra 2:52.)

*Mehir: Hebrew, "a reward"

(See 1 Chronicles 4:11.)

Meir: Hebrew, "radiant"

Mayer, Meier, Meiri, Meyer, Myer

Mel: A diminutive of Melvin

*Melatiah: Hebrew, "Jehovah has set free"

(See Nehemiah 3:7.)

Melbourne: Old English, "mill stream"

Mel, Melborn, Melburn, Milbourn, Milbourne, Milburn, Millburn

*Melchi: Hebrew, "Jehovah is my king"

Two Melchis are mentioned in the New Testament, both of whom are ancestors of Christ. (See Luke 3:24, 28.)

*Melchizedek: Hebrew, "king of righteousness"

Melchizedek was the king and priest of Salem; Abraham received a blessing from him. (See Genesis 14:17–24.)

Meldon: Old English, "mill hill"

Melden

Melville: Old English, "town with a mill"

Mel, Melburn, Meldon, Melford, Melton, Melwood

Melvin: Irish Gaelic, "chief"

Malvin, Malvyn, Mel, Mell, Melvyn, Melwin, Melwyn, Vin, Vinnie, Vinny

*Menahem: Hebrew, "comforter"

Menachem, Nachum, Nahum

(See 2 Kings 15:14–23.)

Mendel: Hebrew, "wisdom"

Mandel

Mercer: Middle English, "storekeeper"

Merce

Meredith: Welsh, "protector of the sea"

Meredyth, Merideth, Meridith, Merri, Merry

Merle: Latin, "thrush" (a bird)

Merlin: Middle English, "falcon, hawk"

Marion, Marlon, Merlyn

Merrick: Old English, "ruler of the sea"

Merrik, Meyrick

Merrill: Latin, "he who is a famous one"

Meril, Merill, Merrel, Merrell, Merril, Meryl

Merton: Old English, "town by the sea"

Merwyn, Murton

Mervin: Old Welsh, "famous friend"

Merv, Merven, Mervyn, Merwin, Merwyn

*Mesha: Hebrew, "freedom"

There are three Meshas in the Old Testament, all of whom are minor characters.

*Meshach: Hebrew, "that draws with force"

Meshach was one of the friends of Daniel who refused to worship an idol and was protected while in a fiery furnace. (See Daniel 3.)

*Meshech: Hebrew, "drawing out"

Mesech

(See 1 Chronicles 1:5, 17.)

*Methuselah: Hebrew, "it shall be sent"

Mathusala

Methuselah lived longer than anyone else in history—969 years. (See Genesis 5:21–27.) God sent the flood upon the earth after Methuselah died.

Meyer: German, "farmer"

Mayer, Mayor, Meier, Meir, Myer

Mhina: Swahili, "he who is delightful"

*Micah: Hebrew, "Who is like God?"—a variation of Michael

Micaiah, Mikal, Mike, Mikey, Mycah

There are seven Micahs in the Old Testament, the most significant of whom is the prophet who wrote the book of the Bible that bears his name.

*Michael: Hebrew, "Who is like God?"

Maguel, Micael, Mical, Michail, Michal, Micheal, Michel (French), Michele (Italian), Mick, Mickey, Mickie, Micky, Miguel (Spanish), Mikael, Mike, Mikel, Mikey, Mikhail (Russian), Mikkel, Miky, Mitch, Mitchell, Mychal— additional variations are possible

There are ten men named Michael in Scripture, and there is also the archangel Michael. (See Daniel 10:13, 21; Jude 9; Revelation 12:7.)

MICHAEL W. SMITH
(1957–)

is a Christian singer and songwriter who has had numerous hit songs and has won both Dove and Grammy awards.

*Midian: Hebrew, "contention"

Midian was a son of Abraham and his wife Keturah. (See Genesis 25:2.)

Miguel: Spanish, a variation of Michael, "Who is like God?"

Mikala: Hawaiian variation of Michael, "Who is like God?"

Miles: Old German, "beloved, gentle"

Milan, Mills, Milo, Myles

MILES COVERDALE
(1488–1569)

was an English Bible translator who produced the first complete English Bible.

Millard: Old English, "caretaker of the mill"

Millerd, Millward, Milward

Miller: Old English, "one who works in a mill"

Millar, Myller

Mills: Old English, "near the mills"

Milo: German variation of Miles, "beloved, gentle"

Mylo

Milton: Old English, "village mill"

Milt, Milten, Miltin, Milty, Mylton

Minkah: Akan (Ghana), "justice"

*Mishael: Hebrew, "Who is what God is?"

There are three Mishaels in the Old Testament, the most significant of whom is the friend of Daniel. (See Daniel 1:6–7.)

Mitchell: A variation of Michael, "Who is like God?"

Mitch, Mitchel, Mitchill, Mytch

Moises: Spanish, a variation of Moses, "saved" or "the one drawn out"

Monroe: Irish Gaelic, "mouth of the Roe River"

Monro, Munro, Munroe

Montague: French, "steep mountain"

Montagew, Montagu, Monte, Monty

Montgomery: Old English, "wealthy one" or "mountain hunter"

Monte, Montgomerie, Montie, Monty

Monty: A diminutive of names beginning with *Mont-*, such as Montgomery

Moore: Old English, "the moors"

More

*Mordecai: Hebrew, possibly "a little man" or "worshipper of Marduk"

Mordechai, Mordy, Mort, Mortie, Morty

Mordecai raised his cousin Esther, adopting her after her parents died. Esther later became the queen of Persia and, with Mordecai's encouragement, helped save the Jewish people from annihilation. This story is told in the book of Esther.

Morgan: Welsh, "dweller by the sea"

Morgen, Morgun

Morley: Old English, "meadow by the moor"

Moorley, Moorly, Morlee, Morleigh, Morly

Morris: Old English, "uncultivated marshland"

Mo, Morey, Morice, Moris, Morrey, Morrie, Morrison, Morry

Morse: Old English, "son of Maurice"

Morrison

Mortimer: Latin, "quiet water"

Mort, Morty, Mortymer

Morton: Old English, "town on

the moor"

Morten

*Moses: Hebrew, possibly "saved" or "the one drawn out (from the water)"

Mioshe, Mioshye, Mo, Moe, Moise (French/Italian), Moises (Spanish), Mose, Moshe, Mozes

Moses was chosen by God to lead the people of Israel out of slavery from Egypt and into the Promised Land. The biblical account of his life spans the books of Exodus through Deuteronomy.

Muir: Scottish Gaelic, "moor"

Murdock: Irish Gaelic, "sailor"

Murdo, Murdoch, Murtagh, Murtaugh

Murphy: Irish Gaelic, "from the sea"

Murfee, Murfey, Murfie, Murphee, Murphey, Murphie

Murray: Scottish Gaelic, possibly "seaman, sailor"

Murrey, Murry

Myles: A variation of Miles, "beloved, gentle"

Myron: Greek, "fragrant oil"

Marion, Marino, Marwin, Merwin

N

*Naaman: Hebrew, "pleasant"

There are four Naamans in Scripture, the most notable of whom is the Syrian army captain who was cured of leprosy through the prophet Elisha. (See 2 Kings 5.)

Nachman: Hebrew, "comforter"

Menachem, Menahem, Nacham, Nachmann, Nahum

*Naham: Hebrew, "consolation" (See 1 Chronicles 4:19.)

*Nahum: Hebrew, "full of comfort"

Nehemiah, Nemiah

Nahum was a prophet who warned the city of Nineveh of God's judgment. You can read about what happened in the book of the Bible that bears his name.

Naoko: Japanese, "honest"

Napana: Hawaiian, a variation of Nathan, "give" or "gift of God"

Napoleon: Italian, "from Naples"

Leon, Leone, Nap, Napoleone

Nassor: Swahili, "he who is victorious"

Nat: A diminutive of Nathan
Nathaniel

Nathan: Hebrew, "giver" or "gift of God"

Nat, Natan, Nataniel (Spanish), Nate, Nathen

There are ten Nathans in the Bible. Two of the key ones are the third child of David (see 2 Samuel 5:14) and the prophet who confronted King David about his sin with Bathsheba (see 2 Samuel 7:2–17).

> **NATHANIEL WILLIAM TAYLOR (1786–1858)**
>
> was a graduate of Yale who, in 1822, was appointed the first professor of theology at the school.

Nathaniel: Hebrew, "given by God"

Nat, Natanael, Nataniel, Nate, Nathan, Nathaneal, Nathanial, Natty, Neal, Nethanel, Nethaniel, Niel, Thaniel

Nathaniel was the disciple whom Jesus said was *"a true Israelite, in whom there is nothing false"* (John 1:47).

Neal: Irish, a variation of Neil, "champion"

Neale, Neall, Nealle, Niles

Nebai: Hebrew, "fruit of the Lord"

(See Nehemiah 10:19.)

Ned: A diminutive of names such as Edward and Edmund

> **NED BERNARD STONEHOUSE (1902–1962)**
>
> was a New Testament scholar at Westminster Theological Seminary who was influenced by the great theologian J. Gresham Machen.

Nehemiah: Hebrew, "God's compassion"

Nechemia, Nechemiah, Nechemya

There are three Nehemiahs in the Old Testament. One, along with Ezra, helped a large group of Israelites to return to Jerusalem at the end of their Babylonian captivity and begin to rebuild the wall of Jerusalem. (See Ezra 2:2; Nehemiah 7:7.) Another coordinated the completion of

the rebuilding of the wall.
(See the book of Nehemiah.)
The third helped in the
completion of the wall.
(See Nehemiah 3:16.)

*Nehum: Hebrew, "consolation"
(See Nehemiah 7:7.)

Neil: Gaelic, "champion"

Neal, Neale, Neall, Nealle,
Neel, Neile, Neill, Neille,
Niel—additional variations
are possible

Nelson: English, "son of Neil" or
"champion"

Nealson, Neils, Neilson, Nels,
Nelsen, Nilson

L. NELSON BELL
(1894–1973)

was a longtime missionary
in China and the father of
Ruth Bell Graham, the wife
of evangelist Billy Graham.

Nemesio: Spanish, "justice"

*Nemuel: Hebrew, "God is
spreading"
(See Numbers 26:9, 12.)

*Neriah: Hebrew, "lamp of
Jehovah"
Neriah was the scribe

and messenger of the
prophet Jeremiah.
(See Jeremiah 32:12.)

Nestor: Greek, "traveler" or "aged
wisdom"

Nester, Nesterio, Nestore,
Nestorio

Neville: Latin, "new estate"

Nev, Nevil, Nevile, Nevyle

Nevin: Old English, "middle"

Nev, Nevan, Neven, Nevins

Newell: Old English, "new hall"

Newall, Newel, Newhall

Newman: Old English,
"newcomer"

Neuman, Neumann,
Newmann

Newton: Middle English, "new
town"

Ngoli: Ibo (Nigeria), "happiness"

Ngozi: Ibo (Nigeria), "blessing"

Niall: Irish Gaelic, "champion"
Neil, Nial

Niamke: Yoruba (Nigeria), "he
who is God's gift"

*Nicodemus: Greek, "the people's
conqueror"

Nicodemus was a Pharisee,

a Jewish religious leader during the time of Jesus. (See John 3:1–9.)

NICHOLAS OF HEREFORD (d. 1420)

had a role in helping to produce John Wycliffe's early version of the Bible by translating text from the Latin Vulgate into English.

NICKY CRUZ (1938–)

is a former gang member turned evangelist who reaches out to troubled teens through Teen Challenge and Nicky Cruz Outreach. His story is told in his best-selling autobiography, *Run, Baby, Run* (1968).

*Nicolas: Greek, "victorious people"

Claus, Cole, Klaas, Klaus, Niccolo (Italian), Nichol, Nicholas, Nichole, Nicholl, Nichols, Nick, Nickey, Nickie, Nicklas, Nickolas, Nicky, Nicol, Nicola, Nicolas, Nicolaus, Nicole (French), Niki, Nikki, Nikkolas, Nikky,

Niklas, Nikolai (Russian), Nikolas, Nikolaus—additional variations are possible; some of the spelling variations above are used for both boys and girls. (See Acts 6:5.)

Nigel: Latin, "dark one"

Nig, Nye

Nikolao: Hawaiian, a variation of Nicolas, "victorious people"

*Noah: Hebrew, "peace, comforter, rest"

Noa, Noach, Noak, Noë

Noah built the ark and warned people of God's coming judgment upon the earth. The account of the great flood is given in Genesis 6–8.

Noel: French, "Christmas"—a name for both boys and girls

Natal, Natale, Nowel, Nowell

Noelani: Hawaiian, "heavenly mist"

Nolan: Irish Gaelic, "famous, noble"

Noland, Nolen, Nolin, Nollan

Norbert: Old German, "brilliant hero"

Bert, Bertie, Berty, Norb, Norberto

Norman: Old English, "man from

the north"

Norm, Normand, Normando (Spanish), Normen, Normie

NORMAN GEISLER
(1932–)

is a theologian, philosopher, and prolific author who has written extensively on defending the Christian faith.

Norris: Latin, "northerner"

Northrop: Old English, "from the north farm"

Northrup

Norton: Old English, "from the northern town"

Norval: Old German, "he who is of the north"

Norville: Old French, "northern town"

Norval, Norvel, Norvell, Norvil, Norvill

Norvin: Old English, "northern friend"

Norvyn, Norwin, Norwyn

Norwell: Old English, "woods in

the north"

Norwood: Old English, "north forest"

Nuncio: Italian, "messenger"

Nunzio

Nyamekye: Akan (Ghana), "God's gift"

Nye: Middle English, "islander, island dweller"

Nyle

O

*Obadiah: Hebrew, "servant of God"

Obadias, Obadya, Obe, Obed, Obediah

There are several Obadiahs in the Bible, the most prominent of whom is the prophet of Judah who wrote the Old Testament book that bears his name.

*Obed: Hebrew, "servant"

There are five Obeds in the Bible, the most notable of whom is the son of Boaz and Ruth, who was an ancestor of Jesus Christ. (See Ruth 4:17–22.)

Octavius: Latin, "eighth child"

Octave, Octavian, Octavio, Octavo, Octavus

Ogden: Old English, "oak valley"

Ogdan, Ogdon

Okechuku: Ibo (Nigeria), "gift of God"

Olaf: Scandinavian, "ancestor"

Olaff, Olav, Olave, Ole, Olen, Olie, Olif, Olin

Oliver: Latin, "olive tree," or Old Norse, "kind one"

Oliverio (Spanish), Olivero, Olivier (French), Oliviero (Italian), Olivio, Olley, Ollie, Olliver

OLE KRISTIAN HALLESBY
(1879–1961)

was a Norwegian theologian and writer who also supported foreign missions. He resisted the Nazi movement in World War II and spent time in a concentration camp. His best-known book is titled *Prayer*.

Olubayo: Yoruba (Nigeria), "highest joy"

OLIVER HOLDEN
(1765–1844)

was an American minister and hymn writer who also served in the Massachusetts House of Representatives.

Olujimi: Yoruba (Nigeria), "God gave this to me"

Olushola: Yoruba (Nigeria), "God has blessed"

Oluyemi: Yoruba (Nigeria), "fulfillment from God"

*Onesimus: Greek, "profitable"

Onesimus was a slave who ran away from his master, Philemon. After Onesimus became a Christian, the apostle Paul urged him to return, and the apostle sent a letter to Philemon, appealing to him on Onesimus's behalf. Read about Onesimus's story in the New Testament book of Philemon.

Oran: A variation of Oren, "pine tree" or "pale-skinned"

Oren, Orin, Orran, Orren, Orrin

Orel: Latin, "golden"

    Oral, Oriel, Orrel

**OREL HERSHISER
(1958–)**

was a pitcher for the Los Angeles Dodgers baseball team who won both the Cy Young Award and the World Series MVP award in 1988. Orel shares about his faith in his book *Out of the Blue.*

Oren: Hebrew, "pine tree" or Irish Gaelic, "pale-skinned"

    Oran, Orin, Orren, Orrin

Orlando: Spanish, a variation of Roland, "fame of the land"

    Arlando, Lanny, Orlan, Orland, Roland, Rolando

Orman: Old German, "he who is a mariner"

    Ormand

Ormond: Old English, "from the bear mountain"

    Ormand, Ormonde

Orson: Latin, "bear"

    Orsen, Orsin, Orsis, Orsonio, Urson

Orville: Latin, "from the golden village"

    Orv, Orval, Orvell, Orvil

Orvin: Old English, "spear friend"

    Arvin, Arvyn, Ervin, Ervyn, Irvin, Irvyn, Orwin, Orwyn

Osahar: Fon (Benin), "God hears"

Osakwe: Fon (Benin), "God agrees"

Osayaba: Fon (Benin), "God forgives"

Osaze: Fon (Benin), "whom God likes"

Osborn: Old English, "divine warrior"

    Osborne, Osbourn, Osbourne, Osburn, Osburne, Ozzie

Oscar: Old Norse, "divine spear, spear of God"

    Oskar, Osker, Ossie, Ozzy

Osten: A variation of Austin, "majestic"

    Austen, Austin, Ostin, Ostyn

Oswald: Old English, "god of the forest"

    Ossie, Osvald, Oswall, Oswell, Ozzie, Ozzy, Waldo (German)

J. OSWALD SANDERS
(1902–1992)

was an active missions spokesman and statesman, as well as a Bible teacher in New Zealand and Southeast Asia. He wrote thirty-two books, including the classics *Spiritual Leadership* and *Spiritual Maturity*.

OSWALD CHAMBERS
(1874–1917)

was a lecturer, preacher, and writer who became a Christian under the ministry of Charles Spurgeon. He is best known for writing the classic devotional book *My Utmost for His Highest*.

*Othni: Hebrew, "lion of God" (See 1 Chronicles 26:7.)

*Othniel: Hebrew, "lion of God" Othniel was the younger brother of Caleb and the first of Israel's judges. (See Joshua 15:17; Judges 3:7–11.)

Otis: Greek, "acute hearing" Oates, Otes

Otto: Old German, "he who is prosperous" Odo, Othello, Otho, Ottmar

Owen: Welsh, "young warrior" Ewan, Ewen, Ovin, Owain, Owin

OWEN THOMAS
(1812–1891)

was a Welsh preacher, theologian, and writer who translated some key Christian works into Welsh.

Oz: Hebrew, "strength" Ozzie, Ozzy

P

Pablo: Spanish, a variation of Paul, "small" Pablos

Page: French, "young attendant" Padget, Padgett, Paget, Pagett, Paige

Pakelika: Hawaiian, a variation of Patrick, "member of nobility"

Pakiana: Hawaiian, a variation of Sebastian, "honorable, respected"

Palani: Hawaiian, a variation of Frank, sometimes a diminutive of Franklin or Francis but often a proper name in its own right

Palmer: Old English, "peaceful pilgrim"
Pallmer, Palmar

Parker: Old English, "guardian of the park"
Parke, Parkes, Parkman, Parks

Parkin: Old English, "little Peter"
Parken

Parnell: Old French, "little Peter"
Parrnell, Pernell

PATRICK HAMILTON (1503–1528)

was influenced by the writings of Martin Luther, and he was the first martyr of the Scottish Reformation.

Parrish: Middle English, "from the churchyard"
Parrie, Parrisch, Parry

Pascal: Italian, "pertaining to Easter or Passover"
Pascale, Pasquale

Patrick: Latin, "member of nobility"
Pat, Patric, Patrice, Patricio, Patryk

Patton: Old English, "from the warrior's estate"
Pat, Paten, Paton, Patten

***Paul:** Latin, "small"
Pablo (Spanish), Paolo (Italian), Paulin, Paulinus, Paulos, Paulus, Pavel (Russian)—additional variations are possible
Paul (first known as Saul) was a zealous Jewish religious leader who persecuted the early Christians. His miraculous conversion to Christ is told in Acts 9. He wrote many of the New Testament epistles.

Paulo: Spanish and Hawaiian, a variations of Paul, "small"

Paxton: Latin, "town of peace"
Paxon, Payton

Payne: Latin, "countryman"
Paine

Payton: Old English, "warrior's estate"
Paton, Patton, Paxton, Peyton

***Pedaiah:** Hebrew, "redemption of

the Lord"

There are six Pedaiahs in the Bible, all of whom are minor characters.

Pedro: Spanish, a variation of Peter

Pedrio, Pepe, Petrolino, Piero (Italian)

Pekelo: Hawaiian, a variation of Peter, "rock"

Peleke: Hawaiian, a variation of Fred, from Frederick, ""peaceful ruler"

Peleki: Hawaiian, a variation of Percy, "the perceptive"

Pell: Middle English, "parchment"

Pembroke: Celtic, "from the headland"

Pembrook

Penley: Old English, "enclosed meadow"

Penleigh, Penly, Pennleigh, Pennley

Penn: Old English, "enclosure"

Pen

Percival: Old French, "pierce the veil"

Perce, Perceval, Percey, Perci, Percivall, Percy, Purcell

Percy: French, "the perceptive"

Pearcy, Percey, Perci, Percie

*Perez: Hebrew, "bursting through"

Phares, Pharez

(See Genesis 38:29.)

Perkin: Old English, "little Peter"

Perkins, Perkyn, Perrin

Perry: Middle English, "pear tree"

Parry, Perrie

*Peter: Greek, "rock"

Peder, Pedro (Spanish), Pete, Petey, Petr, Pierce, Piero (Italian), Pierre (French), Pierson (Peter's son), Pieter, Pietr—additional variations are possible

Peter was a leader among the twelve apostles of Jesus (see Matthew 10:2) and wrote the New Testament books of 1 and 2 Peter.

PEDER PALLADIUS (1503–1560)

was a key leader in the Danish church, a Reformer, and a Bible translator.

---

*Pethuel: Hebrew, "God delivers"

Pethuel was the father of the

prophet Joel. (See Joel 1:1.)

PETER MARSHALL
(1902–1949)

was born in Scotland and became a popular preacher who also served as chaplain to the U.S. Senate from 1947 to 1949. His story is told in the best-selling book (and popular movie) *A Man Called Peter* (1951).

Peyton: Old English, "fighting man's estate"

Payton

*Phanuel: Hebrew, "face of God"

Phanuel was the father of Anna the prophetess, who gave thanks to God when she saw the baby Jesus. (See Luke 2:36–38.)

Phelan: Gaelic, "little wolf"

Phelps: Old English, "son of Philip"

*Philemon: Greek, "loving"

Philemon was a well-to-do Christian whom the apostle Paul remembered for his love and kindness. Paul encouraged Philemon to be forgiving when his runaway slave, Onesimus, returned. His words to Philemon are found in the New Testament book that bears his name.

Philip: Greek, "lover of horses"

Felip, Felipe (Spanish), Felippo (Italian), Filip, Filippo, Fillip, Phil, Philippe (French), Phillip, Phillipe, Phillips

Philip was one of the twelve apostles and an evangelist. One of his amazing witnessing encounters is recorded in Acts 8:26–40.

PoPo (PHILIP PAUL)
BLISS
(1838–1876)

was an American hymn writer and gospel singer. He wrote "Hallelujah! What a Savior!" and "It Is Well with My Soul."

PHILLIPS BROOKS
(1835–1893)

was a minister in the Episcopal Church. He wrote the words to "O Little Town of Bethlehem."

Philmore: A variation of Fillmore, "well known"

Pickford: Old English, "from the ford at the peak"

Pierce: A variation of Peter, "rock"
Pearce, Pearson, Peerce, Peirce, Pierson

Pierre: French, a variation of Peter, "rock"

PIERRE ROBERT OLIVÉTAN (c. 1506–1540)

was a cousin of John Calvin. His translation of the Bible into French was used by the French Reformers.

Pila: Hawaiian, a variation of Bill, from William, "resolute protector"

Pilipo: Hawaiian variation of Philip, "lover of horses"

Pitney: Old English, "island of the stubborn one"
Pittney

Pitt: Old English, "pit"

Placido: Spanish, "he who is serene"
Placedo, Placidus, Placijo

Plato: Greek, "broad shouldered"
Platon

Pollard: Middle English, "cropped hair"
Poll, Pollerd

Pomeroy: Old French, "apple orchard"
Pommeray, Pommeroy

Ponce: Spanish, "fifth"

Porter: Latin, "gatekeeper"
Port

Powell: Old English, a surname related to Paul, "small"
Powel

Prentice: Middle English, "apprentice, a learner"
Prentis, Prentiss

Prescott: Old English, "priest's dwelling"
Prescot, Scott, Scottie, Scotty

Presley: Old English, "priest's meadow"
Presly, Pressley, Prestley, Priestley, Priestly

Preston: Old English, "priest's estate"

Preye: Ibo (Nigeria), "God's gift, God's blessing"

Proctor: Latin, "official"
Prockter, Procter

Puluke: Hawaiianized variation of Bruce, "from the woods"

Q

Quentin: Latin, "the fifth"
Quent, Quenten, Quenton, Quint, Quintin, Quinton, Quintus

Quigley: Irish Gaelic, possibly "messy hair"

Quillan: Irish Gaelic, "cub, endearing"
Quill, Quillen

Quimby: Old Norse, "dweller at the woman's estate"

Quincy: Latin, "estate of the fifth son"
Quin, Quincey, Quinsy

Quinlan: Irish Gaelic, "he who is strong"
Quin

Quinn: Irish Gaelic, "he who is wise"

Quinto: Spanish, a variation of Quintus, Latin, "fifth"

Quinton: A variation of Quinten, Latin, "fifth"

Quon: Chinese, "bright"
Kwan

R

Radbert: Old English, "bright counselor"
Rad, Bert

Radburn: Old English, "red stream"
Rad, Radborn, Radborne, Radbourn, Radbourne, Radburne

Radcliff: Old English, "red cliff"
Radcliffe, Radclyffe, Raddy

Radford: Old English, "red ford"

Radley: Old English, "red meadow"
Radlee, Radleigh, Radly

Radnor: Old English, "red shore"

Rafael: Spanish, a variation of Raphael, "God has healed"

Rafferty: Irish Gaelic, "prosperous"
Rafe, Raferty, Raff, Rafferty

*Raguel: Hebrew, "shepherd" or "friend of God"
Raguel—also known as Jethro and Reuel—was the father-in-

law of Moses. (See Numbers 10:29.)

*Raham: Hebrew, "friend, affection"
(See 1 Chronicles 2:44.)

Rainart: German, "mighty judgment"
Rainhard, Rainhardt, Reinart, Reinhard, Reinhardt, Reinhart

Rainier: Old German, "deciding warrior"
Rainer, Rayner, Raynier

Raleigh: Old English, "dweller of the roe-deer meadow"
Ralegh, Rawleigh, Rawley, Rawly

Ralph: Old English, "advisor, counselor"
Rafe, Raff, Ralf, Ralston, Raul, Rawley, Rolf, Rolph

Ralston: Old English, "Ralph's settlement"

Ramiro: Portuguese, "he who is a great judge"

Ramón: Spanish, a variation of Raymond, "wise guardian"

Ramsay: Old English, "strong island"
Ram, Ramsey

Rand: A diminutive of Randolph

Randall: Old English, "strong shield"
Rand, Randal, Randel, Randell, Randey, Randi, Randie, Randl, Randle, Randy

Randolph: Old English, "shield-wolf"
Rand, Randal, Randall, Randell, Randolf, Randy

Randy: A diminutive of Randall or Randolph
Randey, Randi, Randie

Ranger: Old French, "guardian of the forest"
Rainger, Range

Ransom: Latin, "redemption"—or Old English, "Ronald's son"
Ransome

Raoul: French, a variation of Ralph, "advisor, counselor"
Raúl (Spanish), Roul, Rowl

*Rapha: Hebrew, "he has healed"
Raphah
(See 1 Chronicles 8:2, 37.)

Raphael: Hebrew, "God has healed"
Rafal, Rafael (Spanish),

Rafaele (Italian), Rafaelo, Rafe, Rafel, Raffael, Rafi, Ravel

Jewish tradition teaches that Raphael is one of the four angels that stand next to God's throne (the others are Gabriel, Michael, and Uriel).

Raúl: Spanish, a variation of Ralph, "advisor, counselor"

Ravi: Hindi, "sun"
Ravid, Raviv

> ### RAVI ZACHARIAS
> ### (1946–)
>
> a descendant of a line of Hindu priests, is a Christian apologist who speaks internationally and has written several books, including *Can Man Live Without God?*

Rawlin: Old French, a diminutive of Roland
Rawlinson, Rawson

Ray: A diminutive of Raymond
Rae, Rai, Raye, Reigh, Rey

Rayburn: Old English, "a stream where deer go"
Raeborn, Raeborne, Raeburn, Ray, Rayborn, Raybourne, Rayburne

Rayford: A variation of Ray, from Raymond, "wise guardian"

Raymond: Old English, "wise guardian"
Raemond, Raimond, Raimundo, Ramón, Ramond, Ramonde, Ramone, Ray, Raymon, Raymundo (Portuguese/Spanish), Raynold

Raynor: Scandinavian, "mighty army"
Ragnar, Rainer, Rainier, Rainor, Raynar, Rayner

Read: Old English, "red-haired"
Reade, Red, Redd, Reed, Reid, Reide

Redford: Old English, "river crossing with red stones"
Ford, Red, Redd

Redley: Old English, "red meadow"
Radley, Redleigh, Redly

Redmond: Irish variation of Raymond, "wise guardian"
Radmond, Radmund, Redmund

Reece: Welsh, "fiery, enthusiastic"

Rees, Reese, Rhys, Ries

Reed: Old English, "red-haired"
Read, Reade, Reid

Reese: A variation of Reece, "fiery, enthusiastic"

Regan: Irish Gaelic, "little king"
Reagan, Reagen, Regen

Reginald: Old English, "powerful"
Naldo, Rainault, Rainhold, Raynald, Reg, Reggie, Regin, Reginaldo (Spanish), Reginalt, Reginauld (French), Reginault (French), Reinald, Reinhold, Renaud, Renault, Rene, Reynold, Reynolds

**REGINALD HEBER
(1783–1826)**

was a missionary and songwriter who served in India and wrote more than fifty hymns, including "Holy, Holy, Holy."

Reinhart: Old German, "brave counsel"

Remington: Old English, "raven-family settlement"

Renatus: Latin, "to be born again"
Rene

René: French, "reborn"—also a name for girls

Renfred: Old English, "powerful peace"

Renny: Irish Gaelic, "small and mighty"

Renshaw: Old English, "raven woods"
Renishaw

Renzo: A diminutive of Lorenzo

*****Reuben:** Hebrew, "behold, a son"
Reubin, Reuven, Rube, Rubén (Spanish), Rubens, Rubin, Ruby
Reuben was the firstborn son of Jacob and Leah and the head of one of the twelve tribes of Israel. (See Genesis 49:1–3.)

**R. A. (REUBEN ARCHER)
TORREY
(1856–1928)**

was an evangelist who was appointed by D. L. Moody as the first superintendent of what is now Moody Bible Institute. He also served as dean of what is now Biola University and wrote more than forty books.

*Reuel: Hebrew, "God is a friend"
There are four Reuels in the
Old Testament. (See
Genesis 36:4–17;
Exodus 2:18;
Numbers 2:14; 1
Chronicles 9:8.)

Rex: Latin, "king"
Rei, Rexer, Rexford

Rexford: Old English, "king's
ford"

Rey: Spanish, "king"
Reyes

Reynard: Old German, "mighty,
brave"
Rainard, Ray, Raynard,
Reinhard, Reinhardt, Renard,
Renardo (Spanish), Renaud,
Renauld, Rey, Reynaud,
Reynauld

Reynold: A variation of Reginald,
"powerful"
Reinaldo, Reinold (Dutch),
Renaldo, Renauld, Renault
(French), Reynaldo (Spanish),
Reynolds, Rinaldo

Rhett: Welsh variation of Reece,
"fiery, enthusiastic"

Rhodes: Greek, "roses"
Rhoads, Rhodas, Rodas

Rhys: Welsh, "he who is fiery,
zealous"
Rase, Ray, Reece, Reese, Rey,
Royce

Richard: Old German, "strong
ruler"
Dick, Dickie, Dicky, Ric,
Ricardo (Spanish), Riccardo
(Italian), Rich, Richardo,
Richart (Dutch), Richie,
Rick, Rickard (Swedish),
Rickey, Ricki, Rickie, Ricky,
Rikard, Riki, Rikki, Ritchard,
Ritchie—additional variations
are possible

RICHARD BAXTER (1615–1691)

was an English Puritan
minister and prolific author
known for his book *The
Saints' Everlasting Rest*.
He was also a noted
hymn writer.

Richmond: Old German,
"powerful protector"

Rick: A diminutive of Richard
Frederick, Ric, Rickey, Rickie,
Ricky, Rik, Rikki, Rikky

Rico: Italian, a diminutive of
names such as Enrico and
Ricardo

Rider: Old English, "horseman"
Red, Ridder, Ridley, Ryder, Ryerson

Ridge: A modern name meaning "a narrow range of hills or mountains"

Ridley: Old English, "red meadow"
Riddley, Ridly

Riley: Irish Gaelic, "valiant"
Reilly, Ryley

Ripley: Old English, "from the shouter's meadow"
Rip, Ripleigh, Riply

Roald: Old German, "famous ruler"

Roarke: Irish Gaelic, "famous ruler"
Rorke, Rourke

Rob: A diminutive of Robert

Robert: Old English, "bright, famous"
Bert, Bertie, Bob, Bobbie, Bobby, Rob, Robb, Robby, Robers (French), Roberto (Spanish), Robertson, Robi, Robson, Robyn, Robynson, Rubert, Ruberto (Italian), Rupert, Ruperto—additional variations are possible

ROBERT MURRAY M'CHEYNE (1813–1843)

a minister in the Church of Scotland, was a much-loved preacher, pastor, poet, and prayer warrior who died of typhus at the age of twenty-nine. His story is told in Andrew Bonar's classic *Memoir and Remains of the Rev. Robert Murray M'Cheyne*.

R. C. (ROBERT CHARLES) SPROUL (1939–)

is an American pastor and theologian and the founder of Ligonier Ministries. He is a prolific author whose works include *Faith Alone* and *Scripture Alone*.

Robin: A diminutive of Robert—a name for both boys and girls
Roban, Robben, Robbyn, Robyn

Robinson: Old English, "son of

Robert" or"shining with fame"
Robeson, Robyn, Robynson

ROBERT MORRISON
(1782–1834)

was a London Missionary
Society worker in China
from 1807 to 1834. He
helped translate the Bible
into Chinese.

Rocco: German/Italian, "rock,
rest"
Roch, Roche, Rochus, Rock,
Rocko, Rocky

Rochester: Old English, "stone
fortress"
Chester, Chet, Rock, Rocky

Rock: A variation of Rocco, "rock,
rest"
Rocky

Rockley: Old English, "rock
meadow"
Rocklee, Rockleigh, Rockly

Rockwell: Old English, "rocky
spring, a well in the rocks"
Rock, Rockne, Rocky

Rocky: A variation of Rocco,
"rock, rest"

Rod: A diminutive of Roderick
Rodd, Roddie, Roddy

Roderick: Old German, "famous
ruler"
Broderick, Brodrick,
Rhoderick, Rod, Rodd,
Roddie, Roddrick, Roddy,
Roderic, Rodrick, Rodrik,
Rodrigo (Spanish), Rodrigue
(French), Rodrigues,
Rodriguez, Rodrique (French),
Rodriquez—additional
variations are possible

Rodney: Old English, "island
clearing"
Rod, Rodd, Roddy, Rodnee,
Rodnie

Rodrigo: Spanish, a variation of
Roderick, "famous ruler"

Roe: Middle English, "roe deer"
Row, Rowe

Rogan: Irish Gaelic, "redhead"
Roan

Roger: Old German, "famous
spearman"
Rodge, Rodger, Rodgers, Rog,
Rogers, Rogiero (Italian), Roj,
Ruggiero (Italian)

Roland: Old German, "fame of
the land"

Orlando (Italian), Roeland, Rolan, Rolando (Portuguese, Spanish), Roley, Rollan, Rolland, Rollie, Rollin, Rollins, Rollo, Rolly, Rowe, Rowland

Rolf: A variation of Rudolph, "famous for courage, famous wolf"

Rolfe, Rolle, Rollo, Rolph, Rowland

Ronald: Old Norse, "mighty power"

Ranald, Renaldo, Ron, Ronaldo (Portuguese), Ronel, Roneld, Ronell, Roni, Ronnie, Ronny

Ronson: Old English, "son of Ronald"

Roper: Old English, "he who is a rope maker"

Rory: Irish Gaelic, "red king"

Roric, Rurik

Rosario: Italian, "rosary, crown"

Roscoe: Old Norse, "from the deer forest"

Rosco, Ross, Rossie, Rossy

Ross: Scottish Gaelic, "from the peninsula"

Roscoe, Rossie, Rossy,

Roswald, Royce

Rowan: Irish Gaelic, "red-haired"—or Old English, "rugged"

ROWLAND HILL (1744–1833)

was a prominent evangelical minister and the first chairman of the Religious Tract Society in the United Kingdom.

Roan, Rohan, Rowe, Rowen, Rowney

Rowe: A variation of Roland, "fame of the land"

Rowland: A variation of Roland, "fame of the land"

Roy: Gaelic, "red"—or Old French, "king"

Roi, Roye, Royle, Royston

Royce: Old English, "royalty, son of the king"

Roice, Roy

Royden: Old English, "rye hill"

Roy, Roydan, Roydon

Royston: Old English, "Royce's town"

Rudolph: Old German, "famous for courage, famous wolf"— use with care, in light of the well-known children's story character Rudolph the red-nosed reindeer

Raoul (French), Raúl (Spanish), Rolf, Rolfe, Rolph, Rolphe, Roul, Rudey, Rudi, Rudie, Rudolf, Rudolfo (Spanish and Italian), Rudy

Rudy: A diminutive of names beginning with *Rud-*

Rudee, Rudey, Rudi, Rudie

Rudyard: Old English, "red paddock"

Rudd, Ruddie, Ruddy, Rudel, Rudy

Ruford: Old English, "red ford, rough ford"

Rufford

*Rufus: Latin, "red-haired, fair countenance"

Rufe, Ruffus, Rufous, Ruskin, Russ, Rusty

Rufus was the son of Simon the Cyrenian, who was told to carry Jesus' cross. (See Mark 15:21.) Some believe the Rufus mentioned in Mark is the same one mentioned in Romans 16:13 by the apostle Paul.

Rupert: Italian/Spanish, a variation of Robert, "bright, famous"

Ruprecht (German)

Rushford: Old English, "ford with rushes"

Ruskin: Old French, "red-haired"

Rush, Russ

Russell: French, "red-haired, red-skinned"

Russ, Russel

> **RUSSELL HERMAN CONWELL (1843–1925)**
>
> was an atheist who, after being seriously wounded during the Civil War, became a Christian. He was an author and biographer, best known for his classic *Acres of Diamonds*.

Rusty: French, "red-haired"

Rustin

Rutherford: Old English, "from the cattle crossing"

Ryan: Irish Gaelic, "king"

Rhyan, Rian, Rien, Ry, Ryane, Rye, Ryen, Ryuan, Ryun

Ryder: English, "one who rides"

Ryland: Old English, "land where rye is grown"
Ryeland, Rylan

Ryle: Old English, "rye hill"
Ryal, Ryel

S

Sadiki: Swahili, "a man of truth"

Salehe: Swahili, "he who is righteous"

Salem: Hebrew, "peace"
Salim, Shalom, Shelomi, Shlomi, Sholom

Salim: Swahili, "peaceful"

***Salmon**: Hebrew, "peace"
Salma, Salmah, Zalman
(See Ruth 4:20.)

Salvador: Latin, "preserved" or "savior"
Sal, Salvadore, Salvator, Salvatore, Salvidor, Xavier, Xaviero, Zavier, Zaviero

Sam: A diminutive of Samuel or Samson

***Samson**: Hebrew, "strong, child of the sun"
Sam, Sammie, Sammy, Sampson, Sams, Sansom, Sanson, Sansone

Samson was one of Israel's most famous judges. He led Israel for twenty years and was of legendary strength. Yet he repeatedly disobeyed God, which led to his downfall. For this reason, the name is rarely used by parents. His life story is told in Judges 13–16.

SAMSON OCCOM (1723–1792)

was a Native American (Mohican) who became a Christian during the Great Awakening. He became one of the best-known missionary preachers to the American Indians.

***Samuel**: Hebrew, "heard by God, appointed by God"
Sam, Sammey, Sammie, Sammy, Samuele (Italian), Samuelle, Samwell, Samy

Samuel was a prophet, a priest, and one of Israel's last judges. He was Israel's spiritual leader in the transition from God as King to the human kings

Saul and David. He is among the key characters in the Old Testament books of 1 and 2 Samuel.

SAMUEL MARSDEN (1764–1838)

was an Englishman who worked and served in a convict settlement in New South Wales, Australia. He also pioneered missionary work in New Zealand.

SAMUEL POLLARD (1864–1915)

was an evangelist and philanthropist in China for nearly twenty years. Many people became Christians under his ministry.

SAMUEL RUTHERFORD (1600–1661)

was a Scottish minister who was persecuted and sent into exile. During that exile, he wrote much of his classic *Letters*.

Sanborn: Old English, "from the sandy brook"
Sandy

Sancho: Latin and Spanish, "sacred"
Sanche, Sanchez, Sancos

Sanders: Middle English, "son of Alexander"
Sander, Sanderson, Saunders, Saunderson, Zanders

Sandy: A diminutive of Alexander—a name for both boys and girls
Sandey, Sandie

Sanford: Old English, "sandy river crossing"
Sandford, Sandy

Santiago: Spanish, "St. James"
Sandiago, Sandiego, Santeago, Santigo

Santo: Italian and Spanish, "holy"
Santos

Sargent: Old French, "officer"
Sarge, Sargeant, Sergent

*Saul: Hebrew, "the one who asks"
Saulo, Shaul, Sol, Sollie, Solly
In the Old Testament, Saul was the first king of Israel. However, he misused God's blessings and was disobedient, so God took the kingdom

away from him and appointed David as king. (See 1 Samuel.) In the New Testament, Saul was the original name of the apostle Paul, whose conversion to Christianity is described in Acts 9.

Sawyer: Middle English, "he who saws"

Saw, Sawyere

Sayer: Old German, "victorious people"

Saer, Say, Sayers, Sayre, Sayres

Schuyler: Dutch, "shield, scholar"

Schuylar, Skuyler, Skylar, Skyler, Skylor

Scott: Old English, "from Scotland"

Scot, Scoti, Scotti, Scottie, Scotty

Sean: Irish, a variation of John, "God is gracious"—a name for both boys and girls

Shane, Shannon, Shanon, Shaughn, Shaun, Shawn

Sebastian: Greek, "honorable, respected"

Bastian, Bastien, Seb, Sebastiano (Italian), Sebastien (French), Sebestian, Sebo

Sedgwick: Old English, "sword place"

Sedgewick, Sedgewyck, Sedgwyck

SEBASTIAN
(d. c. 303)

was a martyr who was killed during the persecution under the Roman emperor Diocletian.

SEBASTIAN CASTELLIO
(1515–1563)

was a Protestant theologian who translated the Bible into classical Latin and colloquial French.

Seeley: Old French, "he who is blessed"

Sealey, Seely, Seelye

Segel: Hebrew, "treasure"

Segev: Hebrew, "majestic"

Sekou: West Africa, "great warrior, leader"

Seldon: Old English, "willow valley"

Selden, Shelden, Sheldon

Selwyn: Old English, "friend of the family"

Selwin, Win, Winnie, Winny, Wyn, Wynn

Sergio: Latin, "he who is a servant"

Sergei, Sergey, Sergi, Sergio, Sergios

*Seth: Hebrew, "the appointed of God"

Seth was the third son born to Adam and Eve. (See Genesis 4:25–26.)

Seton: Old English, "seaside town"

Seward: Old English, "sea guardian"

Sewerd, Siward

Sewell: Old English, "victory and strength"

Sewald, Sewall

Seymour: Old French, "from St. Maur"

Seamor, Seamore, Seamour, Seymore

Shad: A diminutive of Shadrach

*Shadrach: Babylonian, "command of Aku" (the Babylonian moon god)

The name given to Hananiah, one of Daniel's three friends. (See Daniel 1:7.) Together with Abednego and Meshach, he was protected from harm in the fiery furnace. (See Daniel 3:12–20.)

Shalom: Hebrew, "peace," a common greeting in Hebrew

Sholom, Solomon

*Shamgar: Hebrew, "sword"

Shamgar was the third judge of Israel. He helped to deliver the people from the Philistines. (See Judges 3:31.)

*Shammua: Hebrew, "famous"

Shammuah

There are four Shammuas in Scripture, the two most notable of whom are a man sent into the Promised Land as a spy by Moses (see Numbers 13:4) and the son of King David and Bathsheba (see 2 Samuel 5:14).

Shanahan: Irish Gaelic, "clever"

Shanan, Shannan

Shane: A variation of Sean, from John, "God is gracious"

Shaine, Shayne

Shannon: Hebrew, "peaceful"—or Irish Gaelic, "wise one"

Shanan, Shanen, Shannan,
Shannen, Shanon

*Shaul: Hebrew, "asked"

There are three Shauls in the
Old Testament, all of whom
are minor characters.

Shaun: A variation of Sean, from
John, "God is gracious"

**SHAUN ALEXANDER
(1977–)**

is a former running back
for the Seattle Seahawks
football team and the winner
of the NFL's Most Valuable
Player award in 2005. The
story of God's work in
his life is told in the book
Touchdown Alexander.

Shaw: Old English, "from the
grove"

Shawn: A variation of Sean, from
John, "God is gracious"
Shawne, Shawnel, Shawnell,
Shawon

Shay: A variation of Shea,
"admirable"

Shea: Gaelic, "admirable"— a
name for both boys and girls

Shae, Shay, Shaye, Shaylon,
Shays

Sheffield: Old English, "crooked
meadow"
Sheff, Sheffie, Sheffy

Shelby: Old English, "from the
ledge estate" or "place where
willows grow"
Selbey, Shelbey, Shelbi,
Shelbie

Sheldon: Old English, "from the
ledge hill"—also a variation of
Seldon, "willow valley"
Shelden, Sheldin

**SHELDON JACKSON
(1834–1909)**

was a Presbyterian minister
who served for many years as
a missionary in the western
frontier of the United States
and Alaska. He helped to
establish schools for
Eskimo children.

Shelton: Old English, "lives on the
edge of town"

*Shem: Hebrew, "renown"
Sem
Shem was one of Noah's
sons and an ancestor of Jesus

Christ. (See Genesis 5:32.)

*Shemaiah: Hebrew, "God is fame" or "Jehovah has heard"

Shemaiah is one of the more common names in the Bible. Among those given this name were a number of priests and Levites. (See 1 Chronicles 9:14, 16; 2 Chronicles 17:8; 2 Chronicles 31:15; 35:9; Ezra 10:21.)

*Shemuel: Hebrew, "heard of God"

There are three Shemuels in Scripture, all of whom are minor characters.

Shepherd: Old English, "shepherd"

Shep, Shepard, Shephard, Shepp, Sheppard, Shepperd

Shepley: Old English, "sheep meadow"

Shapley, Shepleigh, Shepply, Ship, Shipley

Sherborn: Old English, "bright stream"

Sherborne, Sherbourn, Sherburn, Sherburne

Sheridan: Irish Gaelic, "seeker, wild one"

Sheredan, Sheridon, Sherridan

Sherlock: Old English, "he who has bright hair"

Sherlocke, Shurlock, Shurlocke

Sherman: Old English, "woodcutter" or "cloth cutter"

Scherman, Schermann, Shearman, Shermann

Sherwin: Middle English, "swift runner"

Sherwind, Sherwinn, Sherwyn, Sherwynne

Sherwood: Old English, "from the forest"

Sherwin, Sherwoode, Shurwood, Wood, Woodie, Woody

*Shiloh: Hebrew, possibly, "God's gift"

A place name in the Bible. (See Joshua 18:1; 1 Samuel 1:3; 3:21.)

*Shimei: Hebrew, "Jehovah is famous"

Shimhi, Shimi

The name Shimei appears numerous times in Scripture. (See 1 Kings 4:18; 1 Chronicles 3:19; 8:21; 25:3; 2 Chronicles 31:12–13; Zechariah 12:13.)

Shimron: Hebrew, "a guard"
(See Genesis 46:13.)

Shing: Chinese, "victory"

Shlomo: A variation of Solomon,
"peaceful, man of peace"
Shelomi, Shelomo, Shlomi

Sidney: Old French, "from St.
Denis"—also a contraction of
St. Denis
Sid, Syd, Sydney

Siegfried: Old German,
"victorious peace"
Sig, Sigfrid, Sigvard

*Silas: A variation of Silvanus, "of
the forest"
Silas was one of the apostle
Paul's key companions in
ministry. (See Acts 15:40;
16:19, 25, 29.)

Silvanus: Latin, "of the forest"
Silvain (French), Silvana,
Silvano (Italian), Silvio, Sylas,
Sylvan, Sylvanus, Sylvio

Silvester: Latin, "from the forest"
Silvestre, Silvestro, Sylvester

*Simeon: See Simon

*Simon: Greek, a variation of the
Hebrew name Shimeon,
"one who hears"
Shimon, Shimone, Si, Sim,
Simeon, Simion (Slavic),
Simmonds, Simmons, Simms,
Simone, Sims, Sy, Symms,
Symon
The variation Simeon appears
several times in the Bible. The
two most notable men named
Simeon are the son of Jacob
and Leah (see Genesis 29:33)
and a devout man awaiting the
coming of the Christ
(see Luke 2:25–34).

Sinclair: Old French, "from St.
Clair"
Sinclare, Synclair

Siyolo: Zulu (South Africa), "this
is joy"

Skerry: Old Norse, "stony isle"

Skip: Middle Dutch, "ship's boss"
Skipp, Skipper, Skippie,
Skippy

Skyler: Dutch, "scholar"
Schuyler, Schyler, Skylar,
Skylor

Slade: Old English, "child of the
valley"
Slaide, Slayde

Slater: Old English, "hewer of
slates"

Sloan: Irish Gaelic, "he who is a warrior"

Sloane

Smith: Old English, "blacksmith"

Smithson, Smitty, Smyth, Smythe, Smythson

Snowden: Old English, "snow" or "sheltered place"

Snowdon

Sol: Latin/Spanish, "sun, sunshine"

SOLOMON STODDARD (1643–1729)

was a key leader in the Protestant church in America who had a strong interest in revival. He was the grandfather of Jonathan Edwards.

*Solomon: Hebrew, "peaceful, man of peace"

Salamón (Spanish), Salman, Salmon, Salmone, Salomon, Salomone, Shalmon, Sheloma (Yiddish), Solaman, Solmon, Solomon, Zalman (Yiddish)

Solomon was the son of King David and Bathsheba. After David's death, Solomon ascended the throne and ruled for forty years. His life story is recorded in 1 Kings 1–11.

Somerset: Old English, "summer settlement"

Soren: Scandinavian, a variation of Severus, an old Latin name

Spark: Middle English, "happy"

Sparke, Sparkie, Sparky

Spencer: Middle English, "dispenser of provisions"

Spence, Spens, Spense, Spenser

Spike: Latin, "point, spike"

Ssanyu: Uganda, "he brings happiness"

Stacy: Old English, "stable, prosperous"

Stace, Stacee, Stacey

Stafford: Old English, "shallow river crossing"

Staffard, Staford

Stancliff: Old English, "stony cliff"

Standish: Old English, "stony parkland"

Stanfield: Old English, "stony field"

Stansfield

Stanford: Old English, "stony ford"

Stan, Stamford, Standford

Stanislaus: Latin, "stand of glory"

Stanislas (French), Stanislus, Stanislao (Spanish)

Stanley: Old English, "rocky meadow"

Stan, Stanfield, Stanlee, Stanleigh, Stanly

Stanton: Old English, "stone settlement"

Stan, Stanton, Staunton

Stanwood: Old English, "stone woods"

Steadman: Old English, "farmstead occupant"

Steadmann, Stedman

Stein: German, "stone"

Steen, Sten, Steno, Stensen, Stenssen

*Stephen: Greek, "crowned one"

Esteban (Spanish), Estefan, Estevan, Stafan, Staffan, Steban, Steben, Stefan (German), Stefano (Italian), Steffen, Stephan, Stephens, Stephenson, Stevan, Steve, Steven, Stevie, Stevy— additional variations are possible

Stephen was the first Christian martyr in the New Testament. The accounts of his selection for ministry service and his martyrdom are found in Acts 6–7.

STEPHEN CHARNOCK (1628–1680)

was an English Puritan theologian and writer. His classic *Discourses Upon the Existence and Attributes of God* is considered one of the best studies on God.

Sterling: Old English, "high quality, genuine"

Stirling

Steve: A diminutive of Stephen

Stewart: Old English, "steward"

Steward, Stuart

Stoddard: Old English, "he who is a horse herder"

Stoddart

Storm: Old English, "storm, turbulent"

Stratford: Old English, "shallow river crossing"

Strafford

Struthers: Irish Gaelic, "near the brook"
Struther

Stuart: Old English, "a steward"
Steward, Stewart, Stu

Suhuba: Swahili, "a good friend"

Sullivan: Irish Gaelic, "dark eyes"
Sullavan, Sullevan, Sully

Sumner: Old French, "summoner"

Sutcliff: Old English, "south cliff"
Sutcliffe

Sutton: Old English, "from the southern town"

Suubi: Uganda, "he who brings hope"

Sven: Scandinavian, "youthful"
Svein, Sveinn, Svend, Swain, Swen, Swensen, Swenson

Sydney: A variation of Sidney, "from St. Denis"—also a contraction of St. Denis

Sylvester: Latin, "of the forest"
Silvester, Sly

T

Tabor: English, "drum beater"

Tab, Tabb, Tabby, Taber

Tad: A diminutive of Thaddeus
Tadd, Thad

Taggart: Irish Gaelic, "son of the priest"
Taggert

Talbot: Old French, "valley-bright" or "reward"
Talbert, Talbott

Tanner: Old English, "leatherworker"
Tan, Tanier, Tann, Tannen, Tanney, Tannis, Tannon, Tanny

Tate: Middle English, "cheerful, happy"
Tait, Taitt, Tayte

Taylor: Middle English, "tailor"
Tailer, Tailor, Tayler

Teague: Irish Gaelic, "poet"
Taig, Teagan, Tegan, Teger, Teigan, Teige, Teigen, Teigue

Ted: A diminutive of Theodore
Tedd, Teddey, Teddie, Teddy

Telford: Old French, "iron piercer"
Telfer, Telfor, Telfour, Tellfer, Tellfour

Tennant: Old English, "tenant, one who rents"
Tenant, Tennent

Tennessee: Cherokee (Native American), the name of a state in the United States
Tenn, Tenny

Tennyson: Middle English, "son of Dennis"
Tenny

Teodoro: Spanish, a variation of Theodore, "gift of God"

*Terah: Hebrew, "turning, duration"
(See Genesis 11:26; 20:12.)

Terrance: Latin, "smooth, polished one"
Tarrance, Terence, Terrence, Terrey, Terri, Terris, Terry, Torrance, Torrence, Torrey

Terrell: Old German, "belonging to Thor" (the god of thunder in Norse mythology)
Tarrall, Terrall, Terrel, Terrill, Terryl, Terryll, Tirrell, Tyrrell

Terry: A diminutive of Terence—a name for both boys and girls
Terrey, Terri, Terrie

Tex: A modern name, from an abbreviation of the state of Texas

*Thaddeus: Greek, "courageous" or "tender"
Tad, Tadd, Thad, Thaddaos, Taddeo (Italian), Tadeo (Spanish), Thaddaeus, Thaddaus, Thadeus
Thaddeus was one of the twelve disciples. He is also called Judas, son of James. (See Matthew 10:3; Luke 1:16; Acts 1:13.)

Thane: Old English, "warrior" or "landowner"
Thain, Thaine, Thayne

Thatcher: Old English, "he who is a roof thatcher"
Thacher, Thatch, Thaxter

Thayer: Old English, meaning uncertain

Theo: A diminutive of Theodore

Theodore: Greek, "gift of God"
Fedor, Feodor (Russian), Fyodor (Russian), Tadd, Taddeus, Ted, Tedd, Teddie, Teddy, Teodoro (Spanish), Thaddeus, Theo, Theodor, Tod, Todd—additional variations are possible

> ### THEODORE JACOBUS FRELINGHUYSEN (1691–1748)
>
> a Dutch Reformed minister who moved to America, was among the early forerunners of the religious revival known as the Great Awakening.

Theophilus: Greek, "loved by God"

Theophilus was the recipient of the books of Luke and Acts. (See Luke 1:3; Acts 1:1.)

*Thomas: Aramaic, "twin"

Thom, Thoma, Thomason, Thompson, Thomson, Tom, Tomas (German), Tommey, Tommie, Tommy—additional variations are possible

Thomas was one of the twelve disciples. (See Matthew 10:3; Mark 3:16–19; Luke 6:13; Acts 1:13.)

Thor: Old Norse, "thunder"

Tor, Tore, Torre, Tyrell, Tyrus

Thornton: Old English, "town near thornbushes"

Thorn, Thorndike

Thorpe: Old English, "village"

Thorp

Thurman: Old English, "servant of Thor"

Thurmon

Thurston: Scandinavian, "Thor's stone"

Thorstan, Thorsten, Thorston, Thurstain, Thurstan, Thursten

Till: German, "people's ruler"

Thilo, Tillman, Tilmann

Timoteo: Spanish, a variation of Timotheos (Greek)

*Timothy: Greek, "honored of God"

Tim, Timmie, Timmy, Timoteo (Spanish), Timothe, Timotheus (German), Timothey, Tymothy

Timothy grew up in a Christian home and was the apostle Paul's *"true son in the faith"* (1 Timothy 1:1). He was an evangelist and church leader. Paul's exhortations to him are found in the New Testament books of 1 and 2 Timothy.

Tino: Spanish, a diminutive of Agostino and other *-tino* names

Teeno, Teino, Tyno

Tito: Spanish variation of Titos (Greek)

Tim LaHaye
(1926–)

is the author of more than
fifty books and the coauthor
(with Jerry Jenkins) of the
megaselling *Left Behind*
series of novels. A former
pastor, he is also the
cofounder of the Pre-Trib
Research Center, a Bible
prophecy study group.

Timothy Richard
(1845–1919)

was considered one of the
great missionaries to China.
He was involved in both
ministry and education and
had a key role in establishing
the first modern university
in Shansi province.

*Titus: Greek, "honor"

Tito, Titos, Tytus

Titus was a Greek who
became a Christian under the
apostle Paul's ministry. He
proved to be a faithful servant.
(See 2 Corinthians 7:6, 13.)
Paul's letter to him constitutes
the New Testament book
of Titus.

Titus Coan
(1801–1882)

was a pastor and Bible
teacher in Hawaii for nearly
fifty years. He helped
establish several churches,
most of which were led by
native Hawaiian pastors.

*Tobiah: Hebrew, "God is good"

Tobe, Tobee, Tobey, Tobi,
Tobias, Tobie, Tobijah, Tobin,
Toby, Tobye, Tobyn

(See 2 Chronicles 17:8;
Zechariah 6:10, 14.)

Toby: A diminutive of Tobiah

Tavi, Tobe, Tobee, Tobey, Tobi,
Tobie, Tobin

TobyMac (Toby McKeehan)
(1964–)

is a Christian recording
artist and singer-songwriter
who started with the group
DCTalk and now
performs solo.

Todd: Middle English, "fox"

Tod, Toddie, Toddy

Tom: A diminutive of Thomas

Thom, Tomm, Tommy

Tomás: Spanish, a variation of Thomas, "twin"

Tommy: A diminutive of Thomas
Tommey, Tommie

Tony: A diminutive of Anthony
Toney, Toni, Tonie, Tonio
(Portuguese)

**TONY (ANTHONY) EVANS
(1949–)**

was the first African American to receive a Ph.D. from Dallas Theological Seminary. He is the senior pastor of a multicultural church and the founder of Urban Alternative, an organization committed to bringing both spiritual and community growth to urban areas.

Tor: Hebrew, "turtledove," or Norwegian, "thunder"
Thor

Torrance: Irish Gaelic, "from the hills"
Tore, Torey, Torin, Torr, Torrence, Torrens, Torrey, Torry

Townsend: Old English, "from the end of town"
Town, Towney, Towny

Tracy: Latin, "bold, courageous"— a name for both boys and girls
Trace, Tracey, Treacy

Travis: Old French, "at the crossroads"
Traver, Travers, Travus, Travys

Trent: Latin, "rapid stream"
Trenten, Trentin, Trenton

Trevor: Welsh, "large homestead"
Trefor, Trev, Trevar, Trever

Trey: Middle English, "three"
Trai, Traye, Tre

Tristan: Welsh, "sorrowful"
Tris, Tristam

Troy: Irish Gaelic, "foot soldier"
Troi, Troye

Truman: Old English, "faithful one"
Trueman, Truett, Trumaine, Trumann

Tucker: Middle English, "a tucker of cloth"
Tuck, Tuckerman

Tudor: Welsh variation of Theodore, "gift of God"

Tumaini: Nwera (Kenya), "hope"

Tumwebaze: Uganda, "Let us remember God"

Turner: Middle English, "lathe worker, woodworker"

Tusabomu: Uganda, "We pray thanks to God"

Ty: Short form of names that begin with *Ty-*

*Tychicus: Greek, "he who is fortunate"

Tychicus was a helper to the apostle Paul, sometimes accompaning him on his journeys. (See Acts 20:4.) Paul spoke highly of him. (See Colossians 4:7.)

Tyler: Middle English, "maker of tiles"—a name for both boys and girls

Tilar, Ty, Tylar, Tyller, Tylor

Tyrone: Greek, "sovereign"

Tirone, Tirown, Ty, Tye, Tyron

Tyson: Old French, "high-spirited, firebrand"

Thyssen, Ty, Tye, Tyssen

U

Udell: Old English, "yew-tree valley"

Del, Dell, Udale, Udall

Udolf: Old English, "wolf wealth"

Udolfo, Udolph

Ugo: Italian, a variation of Hugh, "wise one, mentally sharp"

Uleki: Hawaiian, a variation of Ulysses, "one who dislikes injustice, wrathful"

Ulf: Old German, "wolf"

Ulmer: Old English, "fame of the wolf"

Ullmar, Ulmar

Ulrich: Old German, "power of the wolf"

Uli, Ullric, Ulrick, Ulrik

ULRICH VON HUTTEN (1488–1523)

was a German Reformer who came under the influence of Martin Luther.

Ulysses: Latin/Greek, "one who dislikes injustice, wrathful"

Ulises, Ulisses, Ulysse

ULRICH ZWINGLI
(1484–1531)

was a key leader of the Swiss Reformation and the founder of the Swiss Reformed Churches. He had a major influence in bringing about positive changes in civil and state matters in Zurich, Switzerland.

Umberto: Italian, "umber" (earth-colored)

Umi: Yao (Malawi), "life"

Upton: Old English, "upper settlement"

*Uriah: Hebrew, "Jehovah is my light"

Uri, Yuri, Yuria, Yuriah

The name Uriah appears several times in the Bible. Most notably, it was name of Bathsheba's husband. (See 2 Samuel 11.)

*Uriel: Hebrew, "flame of God"

Uri, Yuri

(See 1 Chronicles 6:24; 2 Chronicles 13:2.)

*Uzziel: Hebrew, "God is strong, power"

Uziel, Uzziah

Six different men bear the name Uzziel in Scripture, including a man who, during King Hezekiah's reign, carried out a successful military campaign against the Amalekites. (See 1 Chronicles 4:42–43.)

V

Vail: Old English, "valley"

Vaile, Vaill, Val, Vale

Val: A diminutive of Valentine

Valdemar: Old German, "famous ruler"

Waldemar

Valentine: Latin, "strong, brave"

Val, Valentin (French/ Spanish), Valentino (Italian), Valentinus, Valentyn

Valerian: Latin, "strong"

Valerio, Valerius, Valery, Valeryan, Valory

Van: Dutch, "of noble descent"— also a short form of some Dutch surnames

Vann, Von, Vonn

Vance: Old English, "marshland"

Varick: Old German, "leader who defends"

Varrick, Warick, Warrick

Vaughn: Welsh, "small"

Vaughan, Von

Venturo: Spanish, a variation of Valerius (Latin)

Vern: A diminutive of the names Verne and Vernon

Verne: Latin, "springlike"

Vern

Vernon: Latin, "belonging to spring"

Lavern, Laverne, Vern, Vernal, Verne, Vernen, Verney

Verrill: Old French, "he who is loyal"

Verill, Verrall, Verrell, Veryl

Veston: Latin, "town of churches"

Victor: Latin, "conqueror"

Vic, Vick, Victer, Victoir, Victoriano, Victorio (Spanish), Viktor, Vittorio (Italian)

Vincent: Latin, "conqueror"

Vicente (Spanish), Vin, Vince, Vincene, Vincento, Vincenzo (Italian), Vinnie, Vinny

Vincento: Spanish, a variation of Vincent, "conqueror"

Virgil: Latin, "staff bearer"

Verge, Vergil, Virge

Vladimir: Slavic, "world prince"

Ladimir, Vladmir

J. (JOHN) VERNON McGEE (1904–1988)

was a longtime Presbyterian pastor at Church of the Open Door in Pasedena, California. He was also a popular teacher on his *Thru the Bible* radio program, a five-year broadcast in which he took his listeners through studies of each book of the Bible. The program continues to air on radio stations around the world.

W

Wade: Old English, "river crossing"

Waddell, Wadell, Wayde

Wagner: Old German, "wagon builder" or "wagon driver"

Waggoner, Wagoner

Waite: Middle English, "guard, watchman"

Waite, Wayte

Walaka: Hawaiian, a variation of Walter, "powerful warrior"

Walcott: Old English, "cottage by the wall"
Wallcot, Wallcott, Wolcott

Waldemar: Old German, "famous ruler"
Valdemar

Walden: Old English, "from the forest valley"
Waldon

Waldo: A diminutive of Waldemar
Wald, Wallie, Wally

Walena: Hawaiianized variation of Warren, "he who is a protector, watchman"

Walford: Old English, "brook ford"

Walfred: Old German, "ruler of peace"
Walfried

Walker: Old English, "thickener of cloth"

Wallace: Gaelic, "from Wales"
Wal, Wall, Wallach, Wallas,
Wallie, Wallis, Wally, Walsh,
Welch, Welsh

Wally: A diminutive of names such as Walter and Wallace
Wallie

W. A. (WALLIE AMOS) CRISWELL (1909–2002)

was an outstanding Baptist preacher and a prolific author. He was the senior pastor of First Baptist Church of Dallas, Texas, for nearly fifty years.

Walter: Old German, "powerful warrior"
Wally, Walt, Walterio (Spanish), Walther

Walton: Old English, "fortified town"
Walt

Walwyn: Old English, "Welsh friend"
Walwin, Walwinn, Walwynn, Welwyn

Ward: Old English, "defender, guard"
Warde, Warden, Worden

Wardell: Old English, "watchman's hill"

Wardley: Old English, "watchman's meadow"
Wardleigh

Warner: Old German, "army guard"
Werner, Wernher

Warren: Old English, "he who is a protector, watchman"
Varner, Ware, Warrin, Warriner

WARREN WIERSBE
(1929–)

is a Bible teacher who taught on the popular *Back to the Bible* radio program. He is also the author of more than eighty books.

Washington: Old English, possibly a village name
Wash, Washburn

Watson: Old English, "son of Walter"

Wayland: Old English, "land by the path"
Walen, Way, Waylan, Waylen, Waylin, Waylon, Weyland, Weylin

Wayne: Old English, "wagon maker"
Duane, Dwaine, Dwayne, Wain, Waine, Wayne

Webb: A diminutive of Webster

Webster: Old English, "a weaver"
Web, Webb

Welby: Old German, "well-farm"
Welbey, Welbie, Wellbey, Wellby

Weldon: Old English, "well-hill"
Welden

Wells: Old English, "from the springs"

Wendell: Old German, "wanderer"
Wendall, Wendel, Wyndell, Wynn

Werner: Old German, "protecting warrior"
Warner, Wernhar, Wernher

Wes: Short form of names that begin with *Wes-*

Wesley: Old English, "from the west meadow"

Lee, Leigh, Wes, Wesly, Wessley, West, Westley

Westby: Old English, "western farmstead"
Westbey, Westbie

Westcott: Old English, "western cottage"
Wescot, Wescott, Westcot

Weston: Old English, "west farm"
Westen, Westin

Wheatley: Old English, "wheat field"
Wheatly

Whitby: Old English, "white farm"
Whitbey, Whitbie

Whitcomb: Old English, "white valley"
Whitcombe

Whitfield: Old English, "white field"

Whitley: Old English, "white meadow"

Whitney: Old English, "from the white island"
Whit

Wikoli: Hawaiianized variation of Victor, "conqueror"

Wilbert: Old German, "he who is bright"
Wilburt

Wilbur: Old German, "brilliant"
Wilber, Wilbert, Wilburt, Willbur

WILFRED THOMASON GRENFELL (1865–1940)

a British medical missionary, served for more than forty years with the fishermen and the native Eskimos and Indians in Labrador and Newfoundland, Canada.

Wiley: Old English, "crafty"
Willey, Wylie

Wilford: Old English, "willow-ford"

WILLIAM FOXWELL ALBRIGHT (1891–1971)

was a prominent American archaeologist and scholar of the Bible lands.

Wilfred: Old English, "resolute and peaceful"

WILLIAM BOOTH
(1829–1912)

was an evangelist and the founder of the Salvation Army.

WILLIAM CAREY
(1761–1834)

is often called the "father of modern missions." He was a pioneer missionary to India, and he started the Baptist Missionary Society.

WILLIAM TYNDALE
(1494–1536)

was an English Reformer and martyr who translated the Bible from its original languages into English.

WILSON CARLILE
(1847–1942)

was an Anglican minister in England who founded the Church Army, which reached out to those who lived in urban slums.

Wilfrid, Wilfried, Wilfryd, Will, Willfred, Willfrid, Willfried, Willfryd

Will: Short form of names beginning with *Will-*

Willard: Old German, "he who is brave"
Will, Willerd, Willie, Willy

William: Old German, "resolute protector"
Bill, Billie, Billy, Vilhelm, Villiam, Wil, Wilem, Wilhelm, Will, Willem, Willi, Willie, Willis, Wills, Willson, Willy—additional variations are possible

Wilson: Old English, "son of William"
Willson

Winfred: English, "peaceful friend"

Winslow: Old English, "friend's hill"

Winston: Old English, "friendly town"
Win, Winnie, Winny, Winsten, Winstonn, Winton, Wynston, Wystan

Winthrop: English, "friend's village"

Wolcott: English, "wolf's cottage"

Wolfgang: Old German, "traveling wolf"

WOLFGANG FABRICIUS CAPITO (1478–1541)

was a Protestant Reformer and theologian who had contact with Martin Luther and Huldrych (Ulrich) Zwingli.

Woodrow: Old English, "row by the woods"
Wood, Woodie, Woody

Woodward: Old English, "forest warden"
Woodard

Woody: A diminutive of Woodrow

Wyatt: Old French, "small fighter"
Wiatt, Wyatte, Wye, Wyeth

Wycliff: Old English, "white cliff"
Wycliffe

Wylie: Old English, "he who is clever"
Wiley, Wye

Wyndham: Old English, "village near a winding way"
Windham, Wynndham

Wynn: Welsh, "fair one"
Win, Winn, Winnie, Winny, Wynne

X

Xan: A diminutive of Alexander

Xanthus: Latin, "golden-haired"

Xavier: Basque, "new house"
Javier, Saviero, Xaver (German), Xever, Zavier

Xenos: Greek, "hospitality"
Zeno, Zenos

Xerxes: Persian, "monarch"

Ximenes: Spanish, a variation of Simon, from the Hebrew name Shimeon, "one who hears"
Ximenez

Y

Note: Some names beginning with Y can be altered to begin with I or J.

Yagil: Hebrew, "rejoice"
Yagel

Yahya: Swahili, "God's gift"

Yale: Old English, "heights, upland"
Yael

Yancy: possibly a Native American word that means "Englishman"
Yance, Yancey, Yantsey

Yankov: Hebrew, a variation of Jacob, "one who supplants another"
Yachov, Yacov, Yakob, Yakov, Yancob

Yannis: Greek, a variation of John, "God is gracious"
Yannakis, Yanni

Yardley: Old English, "fenced meadow"
Yardlee, Yardleigh, Yardly, Yarley

Yasuo: Japanese, "calm"

Yavin: Hebrew, "God will understand"
Jabin, Jehoram, Joram, Yadin, Yadon, Yavniel, Yediel, Yehoram

Yehudi: Hebrew, "praise"—related to the masculine Jude and the feminine Judith

Judah, Yechaudi, Yehuda, Yehudah

Yigal: Hebrew, "God will redeem"
Yagel, Yigael, Yigdal

Yitzhak: Hebrew, "laughter"
Itzak, Izaak, Yitzchak

Yochanan: Hebrew, "the Lord is gracious"
Johanan, Yohannan

Yohance: Hausa (Nigeria), "God's gift"

Yora: Hebrew, "to teach"
Jorah, Yorah

York: Celtic, "boar settlement" or "yew-tree settlement"

Yves: French, a variation of Ivo (German)
Ives

Z

*Zacchaeus: Hebrew, "God remembers"

Zacchaeus was a Jew whom his fellow Jews despised because he worked as a tax collector for the Roman government. His encounter with Jesus and subsequent conversion is described in Luke 19:1–10.

*Zachariah: Hebrew, "the Lord has remembered"

Zacarias (Spanish), Zacary, Zach, Zachari (German), Zacharias, Zachary, Zack, Zackariah, Zackerias, Zackery, Zak, Zakarias, Zecheriah, Zekariah, Zeke—additional variations are possible

In the Old Testament, Zechariah was the son of Jeroboam II who succeeded him as king of Israel. (See 2 Kings 14:29.) Zechariah was also the grandfather of King Hezekiah. (See 2 Chronicles 29:1.)

In the New Testament, Zechariah was the father of John the Baptist. The fascinating account of the angelic visitor who announced John the Baptist's birth and of Zechariah not being unable to speak until the baby was born is given in Luke 1.

*Zacharias: See Zachariah

Zachary: Hebrew, "the Lord has remembered"—a popular form of Zachariah

Zaccary, Zaccery, Zachery, Zackarey, Zackary, Zackery

> **ZACHARIAS URSINUS (1534–1583)**
>
> was a German Reformer who helped to craft the Heidelberg Catechism, a key document expressing the beliefs of Christians.

> **ZACHARY MACAULAY (1768–1838)**
>
> was a longtime advocate in the fight to end the slave trade.

Zack: A diminutive of Zachary

*Zadok: Hebrew, "fair, righteous" Zadoc, Zaydok

There are several Zadoks in the Bible, one of the more notable of whom is a man who was chosen by King Solomon to serve as priest because he was loyal. (See 1 Kings 1:8.)

Zakkai: Hebrew, "pure, innocent"

Zale: Greek, "sea-strength" Zayle

*Zalmon: Hebrew, "his shade, shady" Salmon (See 2 Samuel 23:28.)

Zane: English, possibly, a variation of John, "God is gracious"

Zain, Zaine, Zayne

Zared: Hebrew, "trap"

*Zebadiah: Hebrew, "gift of Jehovah"

Zeb, Zebediah

This name appears several times in the Bible. (See 1 Chronicles 12:7; 26:2; 27:7.)

*Zebedee: Hebrew, "the gift of God"

Zebedee was the father of James and John, two of the twelve apostles. (See Matthew 10:2.)

*Zebulun: Hebrew, "dwelling of honor"

Zebulen, Zebulon, Zevulon, Zevulun

Zebulun was the tenth son of Jacob, born to Jacob's wife Leah. (See Genesis 30:20.)

*Zechariah: Hebrew, "God has remembered"

Zecher

The name Zechariah appears many times in Scripture, but the most notable Zechariah is the "minor" prophet who prophesied about the nation of Israel's eventual restoration and redemption. His prophecies are recorded in the Old Testament book that bears his name.

*Zedekiah: Hebrew, "righteousness of the Lord"

Zed, Zedechiah, Zedekias

Zedekiah was the last king of the southern kingdom of Judah before it was conquered by King Nebuchadnezzar of Babylon. (See 2 Kings 24:17–25:7.)

Zeke: A diminutive of Ezekiel

*Zenas: Greek, "hospitable"

Zenios, Zenon

(See Titus 3:13.)

*Zephaniah: Hebrew, "hidden by God"

Zeph, Zephan, Zevadia

There are a few Zephaniahs in the Bible, the most notable of whom is the "minor" prophet Zephaniah, who wrote the book of the Old Testament that bears his name.

*Zerah: Hebrew, "morning brightness"

The name Zerah appears frequently in Scripture. (See Numbers 26:13; Joshua 7:1,

24; 1 Chronicles 1:37, 44; 6:21.)

*Zereth: Hebrew, "brightness" (See 1 Chronicles 4:7.)

*Zeri: Hebrew, "balm" (See 1 Chronicles 25:3.)

Zev: Hebrew, "wolf"
Seff, Sif, Zeeb, Zeev

*Zichri: Hebrew, "famous" or "remembers"
Zichri is a popular name that appears several times in the Bible. (See Exodus 6:21; 1 Chronicles 8:19, 23, 27; 2 Chronicles 17:16; Nehemiah 11:9; 12:17.)

Zindel: Yiddish, a variation of Alexander, "he who defends"
Zindil

Ziolo: Spanish, derived from the Greek name Zoë, "life"

Ziv: Hebrew, "brilliance, light of God"
Ziven, Zivon

Zuberi: Swahili, "he who is strong"

*Zuriel: Hebrew, "the Lord my rock"
(See Numbers 3:35.)

Selected Sources for Bible Names

Christianson, Laura. *The Adoption Decision: 15 Things You Want to Know Before Adopting*. Eugene, OR: Harvest House, 2007.

Douglas, J. D., gen. ed. *Twentienth-Century Dictionary of Christian Biography*. Grand Rapids, MI: Baker Books, 1995.

Douglas, J. D., and Philip Comfort. *Who's Who in Christian History*. Wheaton, IL: Tyndale House, 1992.

Lockyer, Herbert. *All the Men of the Bible*. Grand Rapids, MI: Zondervan, 1988.

———. *All the Women of the Bible*. Grand Rapids, MI: Zondervan, 1988.

Reid, Daniel G., Robert D. Linder, Bruce L. Shelley, Harry S. Stout, and Craig A. Noll, eds. *Concise Dictionary of Christianity in America*. Downers Grove, IL: InterVarsity Press, 1995.

Tucker, Ruth A. *Guardians of the Great Commission: The Story of Women in Modern Missions*. Grand Rapids, MI: Academie Books, 1988.

Willmington, Harold L. *Willmington's Complete Guide to Bible Knowledge*. Vol. 1, *Old Testament People*. Wheaton, IL: Tyndale House, 1990.

———. *Willmington's Complete Guide to Bible Knowledge*. Vol. 2, *New Testament People*. Wheaton, IL: Tyndale House, 1990.

Woodbridge, John. *Ambassadors for Christ*. Chicago: Moody Press, 1994.

———. *More than Conquerors*. Chicago: Moody Press, 1992.

Baby Name Worksheet

_____   _____

_____   _____

_____   _____

_____   _____

_____   _____

_____   _____

_____   _____

_____   _____

_____   _____

_____   _____

_____   _____

_____   _____

_____   _____

_____   _____

Baby Name Worksheet

_____   _____

_____   _____

_____   _____

_____   _____

_____   _____

_____   _____

_____   _____

_____   _____

_____   _____

_____   _____

_____   _____

_____   _____

_____   _____

Baby Name Worksheet

_____   _____

_____   _____

_____   _____

_____   _____

_____   _____

_____   _____

_____   _____

_____   _____

_____   _____

_____   _____

_____   _____

_____   _____

_____   _____

Baby Name Worksheet

_____   _____

_____   _____

_____   _____

_____   _____

_____   _____

_____   _____

_____   _____

_____   _____

_____   _____

_____   _____

_____   _____

_____   _____

_____   _____

About the Authors

Nick Harrison is the author of several books, including *Magnificent Prayer, Promises to Keep,* and *365 WWJD.* He and his wife, Beverly, have three grown daughters and four grandchildren. They live in Eugene, Oregon.

Steve Miller is the author of *One-Minute Promises* and *One-Minute Praises.* He and his wife, Becky, coauthored *A Child's Garden of Prayer.* They have three sons and reside in Oregon's Willamette Valley.